Artificial Intelligence and Machine Learning Fundamentals

Develop real-world applications powered by the latest AI advances

Zsolt Nagy

Artificial Intelligence and Machine Learning Fundamentals

Author: Zsolt Nagy

Reviewer: Richard Ackon

Managing Editor: Steffi Monteiro

Acquisitions Editor: Koushik Sen

Production Editor: Nitesh Thakur

Editorial Board: David Barnes, Ewan Buckingham, Simon Cox, Manasa Kumar, Alex Mazonowicz, Douglas Paterson, Dominic Pereira, Shiny Poojary, Saman Siddiqui, Erol Staveley, Ankita Thakur, and Mohita Vyas.

First published: December 2018

Production reference: 1071218

Published by Packt Publishing Ltd.

Livery Place, 35 Livery Street

Birmingham B3 2PB, UK

ISBN 978-1-78980-165-1

Table of Contents

AI with Search Techniques and Games 29

Classification   137

Preface

About

This section briefly introduces the author, what the book covers, the technical skills you'll need to get started, and the hardware and software requirements required to complete all of the included activities and exercises.

About the Book

Machine learning and neural networks are fast becoming pillars on which you can build intelligent applications. The book begins by introducing you to Python and discussing the use of AI search algorithms. You will learn math-heavy topics, such as regression and classification, illustrated by Python examples.

You will then progress on to advanced AI techniques and concepts, and work on real-life datasets to form decision trees and clusters. You will be introduced to neural networks, which are a powerful tool benefiting from Moore's law being applied to 21st-century computing power. By the end of this book, you will feel confident and will look forward to building your own AI applications with your newly-acquired skills!

About the Author

Zsolt Nagy is an engineering manager in an ad tech company heavy on data science. After acquiring his Master's in inference on ontologies, he mainly used AI to analyze online poker strategies to aid professional poker players in decision-making. After the poker boom ended, he put his efforts into building a T-shaped profile in leadership and software engineering.

Objectives

- Understand the importance, principles, and fields of AI
- Learn how to use Python to implement basic artificial intelligence for pathfinding and beating games
- Implement regression and classification exercises in Python applied to real-world problems
- Perform predictive analysis in Python using decision trees and random forests
- Perform clustering in Python using the k-means and mean shift algorithms
- Understand the fundamentals of deep learning via practical examples

Audience

Software developers who think that their future is more lucrative as a data scientist or who want to use machine learning to enrich their current personal or professional projects. Prior experience of AI is not needed, however, knowledge of at least one programming language (preferably Python) and high school-level math is required. Although this is a beginner-level book on AI, intermediate students will benefit from improving their Python by implementing practical applications, using and refreshing their fundamental AI knowledge.

Approach

This book takes a hands-on approach to teaching you about artificial intelligence and machine learning with Python. It contains multiple activities that use real-life scenarios for you to practice and apply your new skills in a highly relevant context.

Minimum Hardware Requirements

For the optimal student experience, we recommend the following hardware configuration:

- Processor: Intel Core i5 or equivalent
- Memory: 8 GB RAM
- Storage: 35 GB available space

Software Requirements

You'll also need the following software installed in advance:

- OS: Windows 7 SP1 64-bit, Windows 8.1 64-bit or Windows 10 64-bit, Ubuntu Linux, or the latest version of macOS
- Browser: Google Chrome (latest version)
- Anaconda (latest version)
- IPython (latest version)

Conventions

Code words in text, database table names, folder names, filenames, file extensions, pathnames, dummy URLs, user input, and Twitter handles are shown as follows: "The most common activation functions are **sigmoid** and **tanh** (the hyperbolic tangent function)"

A block of code is set as follows:

```
from sklearn.metrics.pairwise import euclidean_distances
points = [[2,3], [3,7], [1,6]]
euclidean_distances([[4,4]], points)
```

New terms and important words are shown in bold. Words that you see on the screen, for example, in menus or dialog boxes, appear in the text like this: "The optimal separator found by the support vector machines is called the **best separating hyperplane**."

Installation and Setup

Before you start this book, you will need to have Python 3.6 and Anaconda installed. You will find the steps to install them here:

Installing Python

Install Python 3.6 following the instructions at this link: https://realpython.com/installing-python/.

Installing a Virtual Environment

Install the Anaconda version from the following link. Anaconda is essential to avoid conflicting packages, saving you time/energy by avoiding frustrating errors.

To install Anaconda, click on the following link: https://www.anaconda.com/download/.

Choose your operating system and select the latest version of Python. Once your package is downloaded, run it.

After clicking **Next**, you will see a license agreement. Upon clicking **I Agree**, you can choose whether you want to install Anaconda for yourself or for all users of the computer. The latter requires administrator rights. Select **Just Me**.

Then, you must select the folder where you would like to install Anaconda. Make sure there are no spaces or long Unicode characters in the folder name. Make sure you have at least 3 GB of space on your computer, and that you have an internet connection fast enough to download the file.

On the next screen, you can select whether you want to add Anaconda to the **PATH** environment variable. Don't select this option, as you will be able to launch Anaconda from the **Start** menu.

Click **Install**. It will take a few minutes to install Anaconda on your computer. After the installation is complete, you can choose to learn more about Anaconda Cloud and Anaconda Support, or you can untick those boxes and finish the installation.

Starting Anaconda

You can find the installed Anaconda in the **Start** menu. If you have already installed Anaconda before starting this book, you may choose to upgrade it to Python 3. The cleanest way to do this is to uninstall and reinstall it.

The Anaconda Navigator gives you access to most of the tools you need for this book. Launch **IPython** by selecting the top-right option.

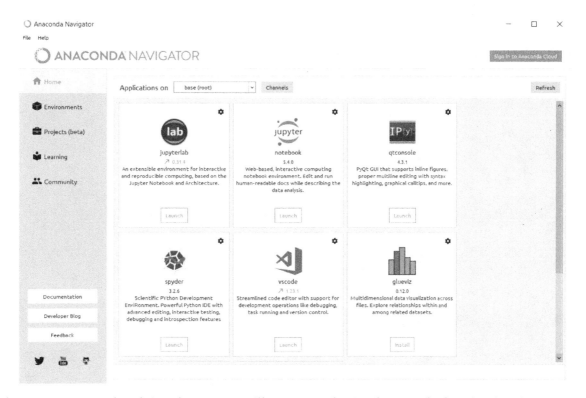

The Jupyter Notebook is where you will execute the Python code for this book.

Additional Resources

The code bundle for this book is also hosted on GitHub at: https://github.com/TrainingByPackt/Artificial-Intelligence-and-Machine-Learning-Fundamentals.

We also have other code bundles from our rich catalog of books and videos available at https://github.com/PacktPublishing/. Check them out!

Principles of Artificial Intelligence

Learning Objectives

By the end of this chapter, you will be able to:

- Describe the various fields of AI
- Explain the main learning models used in AI
- Explain why Python is a popular language for AI projects
- Model the state space in AI for a given game

In this chapter, you will learn about the purpose, fields, and applications of AI, coupled with a short summary of the features we'll use in Python.

Introduction

Before discussing different AI techniques and algorithms, we will look at the fundamentals of artificial intelligence and machine learning and go over a few basic definitions. Then, using engaging examples, we will move forward in the book. Real-world examples will be used to present the basic concepts of artificial intelligence in an easy-to-digest way.

If you want to be an expert at something, you need to be very good at the fundamentals. So, let's begin by understanding what artificial intelligence is:

Definition: Artificial Intelligence (AI) is a science that's used to construct intelligence using hardware and software solutions.

It is inspired by reverse engineering, for example, in the way that neurons work in the human brain. Our brain consists of small units called neurons, and networks of neurons called neural networks. Beyond neural networks, there are many other models in neuroscience that can be used to solve real-world problems in artificial intelligence.

Machine learning is a term that is often confused with artificial intelligence. It originates from the 1950s, and it was first defined by Arthur Lee Samuel in 1959.

Definition: Machine learning is a field of study concerned with giving computers the ability to learn without being explicitly programmed.

Tom Mitchell proposed a more mathematically precise definition of machine learning.

Definition: A computer program is said to learn from experience, E, with respect to a task, T, and a performance measure, P, if its performance on T, as measured by P, improves with experience E.

From these two definitions, we can conclude that machine learning is one way to achieve artificial intelligence. However, you can have artificial intelligence without machine learning. For instance, if you hardcode rules and decision trees, or you apply search techniques, you create an artificial intelligence agent, even though your approach has little to do with machine learning.

How does AI Solve Real World Problems?

Artificial intelligence automates human intelligence based on the way human brain processes information.

Whenever we solve a problem or interact with people, we go through a process. Whenever we limit the scope of a problem or interaction, this process can often be modeled and automated.

AI makes computers appear to think like humans.

Sometimes, it feels like AI knows what we need. Just think about the personalized coupons you receive after shopping online. By the end of this book, you will understand that to choose the most successful products, you need to be shown how to maximize your purchases – this is a relatively simple task. However, it is also so efficient, that we often think that computers "know" what we need.

AI is performed by computers that are executing low-level instructions.

Even though a solution may appear to be intelligent, we write code, just like with any other software solutions. Even if we are simulating neurons, simple machine code and computer hardware executes the "thinking" process.

Most AI applications have one primary objective. When we interact with an AI application, it seems human-like because it can restrict a problem domain to a primary objective. Therefore, we get a chance to break down complex processes and simulate intelligence with the help of low-level computer instructions.

AI may stimulate human senses and thinking processes for specialized fields.

We must simulate human senses and thoughts, and sometimes trick AI into believing that we are interacting with another human. In special cases, we can even enhance our own senses.

Similarly, when we interact with a chatbot, we expect the bot to understand us. We expect the chatbot or even a voice recognition system to provide a computer-human interface that fulfills our expectations. In order to meet these expectations, computers need to emulate the human thought processes.

Diversity of Disciplines

A self-driving car that couldn't sense that other cars were driving on the same highway would be incredibly dangerous. The AI agent needs to process and sense what is around it in order to drive the car. But that is itself is not enough. Without understanding the physics of moving objects, driving the car in a normal environment would be an almost impossible, not to mention deadly, task.

In order to create a usable AI solution, different disciplines are involved. For example:

- **Robotics:** To move objects in space
- **Algorithm Theory:** To construct efficient algorithms
- **Statistics:** To derive useful results, predict the future, and analyze the past

- **Psychology:** To model how the human brain works

- **Software Engineering:** To create maintainable solutions that endure the test of time

- **Computer Science or Computer Programming:** To implement our software solutions in practice

- **Mathematics:** To perform complex mathematical operations

- **Control Theory:** To create feed-forward and feedback systems

- **Information Theory:** To represent, encode, decode, and compress information

- **Graph Theory:** To model and optimize different points in space and to represent hierarchies

- **Physics:** To model the real world

- **Computer Graphics and Image Processing** to display and process images and movies

In this book, we will cover a few of these disciplines. Remember, focus is power, and we are now focusing on a high-level understanding of artificial intelligence.

Fields and Applications of Artificial Intelligence

Now that we know what Artificial Intelligence is, let's move on and investigate different fields in which AI is applied.

Simulation of Human Behavior

Humans have five basic senses simply divided into visual, auditory, kinesthetic, olfactory, and gustatory. However, for the purposes of understanding how to create intelligent machines, we can separate disciplines as follows:

- Listening and speaking

- Understanding language

- Remembering things

- Thinking

- Seeing

- Moving

A few of these are out of scope for us, because the purpose of this book is to understand the fundamentals. In order to move a robot arm, for instance, we would have to study complex university-level math to understand what's going on.

Listening and Speaking

Using speech recognition system, AI can collect the information. Using speech synthesis, it can turn internal data into understandable sounds. Speech recognition and **speech synthesis** techniques deal with the recognition and construction of sounds humans emit or that humans can understand.

Imagine you are on a trip to a country where you don't speak the local language. You can speak into the microphone of your phone, expect it to "understand" what you say, and then translate it into the other language. The same can happen in reverse with the locals speaking and AI translating the sounds into a language you understand. Speech recognition and speech synthesis make this possible.

> **Note**
>
> An example of speech synthesis is Google Translate. You can navigate to https://translate.google.com/ and make the translator speak words in a non-English language by clicking the loudspeaker button below the translated word.

Understanding Language

We can understand natural language by processing it. This field is called **natural language processing**, or NLP for short.

When it comes to natural language processing, we tend to learn languages based on **statistical learning**.

Remembering Things

We need to represent things we know about the world. This is where creating **knowledge bases** and hierarchical representations called **ontologies** comes into play. Ontologies categorize things and ideas in our world and contain relations between these categories.

Thinking

Our AI system has to be an expert in a certain domain by using an expert system. An **expert system** can be based on mathematical logic in a deterministic way, as well as in a fuzzy, non-deterministic way.

The knowledge base of an expert system is represented using different techniques. As the problem domain grows, we create hierarchical ontologies.

We can replicate this structure by modeling the network on the building blocks of the brain. These building blocks are called neurons, and the network itself is called a **neural network**.

There is another key term you need to connect to neural networks: **deep learning**. Deep learning is deep because it goes beyond pattern recognition and categorization. Learning is imprinted into the neural structure of the network. One special deep learning task, for instance, is **object recognition** using **computer vision**.

Seeing

We have to interact with the real world through our senses. We have only touched upon auditory senses so far, in regard to speech recognition and synthesis. What if we had to see things? Then, we would have to create **computer vision** techniques to learn about our environment. After all, recognizing faces is useful, and most humans are experts at that.

Computer vision depends on **image processing**. Although image processing is not directly an AI discipline, it is a required discipline for AI.

Moving

Moving and touching are natural to us humans, but they are very complex tasks for computers. Moving is handled by **robotics**. This is a very math-heavy topic.

Robotics is based on **control theory**, where you create a feedback loop and control the movement of your object based on the feedback gathered. Interestingly enough, control theory has applications in other fields that have absolutely nothing to do with moving objects in space. This is because the feedback loops required are similar to those modeled in economics.

Simulating Intelligence – The Turing Test

Alan Turing, the inventor of the Turing machine, an abstract concept that's used in algorithm theory, suggested a way to test intelligence. This test is referred to as the **Turing test** in AI literature.

Using a text interface, an interrogator chats to a human and a chatbot. The job of the chatbot is to mislead the interrogator to the extent that they cannot tell whether the computer is human or not.

What disciplines do we need to pass the Turing test?

First of all, we need to understand a spoken language to know what the interrogator is saying. We do this by using **Natural Language Processing (NLP)**. We also have to respond.

We need to be an expert on things that the human mind tends to be interested in. We need to build an **Expert System** of humanity, involving the taxonomy of objects and abstract thoughts in our world, as well as historical events and even emotions.

Passing the Turing test is very hard. Current predictions suggest we won't be able to create a system good enough to pass the Turing test until the late 2020's. Pushing this even further, if this is not enough, we can advance to the Total Turing Test, which also includes movement and vision.

AI Tools and Learning Models

In the previous sections, we discovered the fundamentals of artificial intelligence. One of the core tasks for artificial intelligence is learning.

Intelligent Agents

When solving AI problems, we create an actor in the environment that can gather data from its surroundings and influence its surroundings. This actor is called an intelligent agent.

An intelligent agent:

- Is autonomous
- Observes its surroundings through sensors
- Acts in its environment using actuators
- Directs its activities toward achieving goals

Agents may also learn and have access to a knowledge base.

We can think of an agent as a function that maps perceptions to actions. If the agent has an internal knowledge base, perceptions, actions, and reactions may alter the knowledge base as well.

Actions may be rewarded or punished. Setting up a correct goal and implementing a carrot and stick situation helps the agent learn. If goals are set up correctly, agents have a chance of beating the often more complex human brain. This is because the number one goal of the human brain is survival, regardless of the game we are playing. An agent's number one motive is reaching the goal itself. Therefore, intelligent agents do not get embarrassed when making a random move without any knowledge.

Classification and Prediction

Different goals require different processes. Let's explore the two most popular types of AI reasoning: **classification** and **prediction**.

Classification is a process for figuring out how an object can be defined in terms of another object. For instance, a father is a male who has one or more children. If Jane is a parent of a child and Jane is female, then Jane is a mother. Also, Jane is a human, a mammal, and a living organism. We know that Jane has a nationality as well as a date of birth.

Prediction is the process of predicting things, based on patterns and probabilities. For instance, if a customer in a standard supermarket buys organic milk, the same customer is more likely to buy organic yoghurt than the average customer.

Learning Models

The process of AI learning can be done in a supervised or unsupervised way. Supervised learning is based on labeled data and inferring functions from training data. Linear regression is one example. Unsupervised learning is based on unlabeled data and often works on cluster analysis.

The Role of Python in Artificial Intelligence

In order to put the basic AI concepts into practice, we need a programming language that supports artificial intelligence. In this book, we have chosen Python. There are a few reasons why Python is such a good choice for AI:

- Python is a **high-level programming language**. This means that you don't have to worry about memory allocation, pointers, or machine code in general. You can write code in a convenient fashion and rely on Python's robustness. Python is also **cross-platform compatible**.

- The strong emphasis on **developer experience** makes Python a very popular choice among software developers. In fact, according to a 2018 developer survey by https://www.hackerrank.com, across all ages, Python ranks as the number one preferred language of software developers. This is because Python is easily readable and simple. Therefore, Python is great for **rapid application development**.

- Despite being an interpreted language, Python is comparable to other languages used in data science such as R. Its main advantage is **memory efficiency**, as Python can handle large, in-memory databases.

> **Note**
>
> Python is a multi-purpose language. It can be used to create desktop applications, database applications, mobile applications, as well as games. The network programming features of Python are also worth mentioning. Furthermore, Python is an excellent prototyping tool.

Why is Python Dominant in Machine Learning, Data Science, and AI?

To understand the dominant nature of Python in machine learning, data science, and AI, we have to compare Python to other languages also used in these fields.

One of the main alternatives is R. The advantage of Python compared to R is that Python is more general purpose and more practical.

Compared to Java and C++, writing programs in Python is significantly faster. Python also provides a high degree of flexibility.

There are some languages that are similar in nature when it comes to flexibility and convenience: Ruby and JavaScript. Python has an advantage over these languages because of the AI ecosystem available for Python. In any field, open source, third-party library support vastly determines the success of that language. Python's third-party AI library support is excellent.

Anaconda in Python

We already installed Anaconda in the preface. Anaconda will be our number one tool when it comes to experimenting with artificial intelligence.

This list is by far incomplete, as there are more than 700 libraries available in Anaconda. However, if you know these libraries, then you're off to a good start because you will be able to implement fundamental AI algorithms in Python.

Anaconda comes with packages, IDEs, data visualization libraries, and high-performance tools for parallel computing in one place. Anaconda hides configuration problems and the complexity of maintaining a stack for data science, machine learning, and artificial intelligence. This feature is especially useful in Windows, where version mismatches and configuration problems tend to arise the most.

Anaconda comes with the IPython console, where you can write code and comments in documentation style. When you experiment with AI features, the flow of your ideas resembles an interactive tutorial where you run each step of your code.

Note

IDE stands for Integrated Development Environment. While a text editor provides some functionalities to highlight and format code, an IDE goes beyond the features of text editors by providing tools to automatically refactor, test, debug, package, run, and deploy code.

Python Libraries for Artificial Intelligence

The list of libraries presented here is not complete as there are more than 700 available in Anaconda. However, these specific ones will get you off to a good start, because they will give you a good foundation to be able to implement fundamental AI algorithms in Python:

- **NumPy**: NumPy is a computing library for Python. As Python does not come with a built-in array data structure, we have to use a library to model vectors and matrices efficiently. In data science, we need these data structures to perform simple mathematical operations. We will extensively use NumPy in future modules.

- **SciPy**: SciPy is an advanced library containing algorithms that are used for data science. It is a great complementary library to NumPy, because it gives you all the advanced algorithms you need, whether it be a linear algebra algorithm, image processing tool, or a matrix operation.

- **pandas**: pandas provides fast, flexible, and expressive data structures such as one-dimensional series and two-dimensional DataFrames. It efficiently loads, formats, and handles complex tables of different types.

- **scikit-learn**: scikit-learn is Python's main machine learning library. It is based on the NumPy and SciPy libraries. scikit-learn provides you with the functionality required to perform both classification and regression, data preprocessing, as well as supervised and unsupervised learning.

- **NLTK**: We will not deal with natural language processing in this book but NLTK is still worth mentioning, because this library is the main natural language toolkit of Python. You can perform classification, tokenization, stemming, tagging, parsing, semantic reasoning, and many other services using this library.

- **TensorFlow**: TensorFlow is Google's neural network library, and it is perfect for implementing deep learning artificial intelligence. The flexible core of TensorFlow can be used to solve a vast variety of numerical computation problems. Some real-world applications of TensorFlow include Google voice recognition and object identification.

A Brief Introduction to the NumPy Library

The NumPy library will play a major role in this book, so it is worth exploring it further.

After launching your IPython console, you can simply import NumPy as follows:

```
import numpy as np
```

Once NumPy has been imported, you can access it using its alias, **np**. NumPy contains the efficient implementation of some data structures such as vectors and matrices. Python does not come with a built-in array structure, so NumPy's array comes in handy. Let's see how we can define vectors and matrices:

```
np.array([1,3,5,7])
```

The output is as follows:

```
array([1, 3, 5, 7])
```

We can declare a matrix using the following syntax:

```
A = np.mat([[1,2],[3,3]])
A
```

The output is as follows:

```
matrix([[1, 2],
        [3, 3]])
```

The array method creates an array data structure, while **mat** creates a matrix.

We can perform many operations with matrices. These include addition, subtraction, and multiplication:

Addition in matrices:

```
A + A
```

The output is as follows:

```
matrix([[2, 4],
        [6, 6]])
```

Subtraction in matrices:

```
A - A
```

The output is as follows:

```
matrix([[0, 0],
        [0, 0]])
```

Multiplication in matrices:

```
A * A
```

The output is as follows:

```
matrix([[ 7,  8],
        [12, 15]])
```

Matrix addition and subtraction works cell by cell.

Matrix multiplication works according to linear algebra rules. To calculate matrix multiplication manually, you have to align the two matrices, as follows:

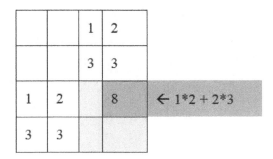

Figure 1.1: Multiplication calculation with two matrices

To get the (i,j)th element of the matrix, you compute the dot (scalar) product on the ith row of the matrix with the jth column. The scalar product of two vectors is the sum of the product of their corresponding coordinates.

Another frequent matrix operation is the determinant of the matrix. The determinant is a number associated with square matrices. Calculating the determinant using NumPy is easy:

```
np.linalg.det( A )
```

The output is **-3.0000000000000004**.

Technically, the determinant can be calculated as **1*3 - 2*3 = -3**. Notice that NumPy calculates the determinant using floating-point arithmetic, and therefore, the accuracy of the result is not perfect. The error is due to the way floating-points are represented in most programming languages.

We can also transpose a matrix, like so:

```
np.matrix.transpose(A)
```

The output is as follows:

```
matrix([[1, 3],
        [2, 3]])
```

When calculating the transpose of a matrix, we flip its values over its main diagonal.

NumPy has many other important features, and therefore, we will use it in most of the chapters in this book.

Exercise 1: Matrix Operations Using NumPy

We will be using IPython and the following matrix to solve this exercise. We will start by understanding the NumPy syntax:

$$A = \begin{bmatrix} 1 & 2 & 3 \\ 4 & 5 & 6 \\ 7 & 8 & 9 \end{bmatrix}$$

Figure 1.2: Simple Matrix

Using NumPy, calculate the following:

- The square of the matrix
- The determinant of the matrix
- The transpose of the matrix

Let's begin with NumPy matrix operations:

1. Import the NumPy library.

```
import numpy as np
```

2. Create a two-dimensional array storing the matrix:

```
A = np.mat([[1,2,3],[4,5,6],[7,8,9]])
```

Notice the **np.mat** construct. If you have created an **np.array** instead of **np.mat**, the solution for the array multiplication will be incorrect.

3. NumPy supports matrix multiplication by using the asterisk:

```
A * A
```

The output is as follows:

```
matrix([[ 30,  36,  42],
        [ 66,  81,  96],
        [102, 126, 150]])
```

As you can see from the following code, the square of A has been calculated by performing matrix multiplication. For instance, the top-left element of the matrix is calculated as follows:

```
1 * 1 + 2 * 4 + 3 * 7
```

The output is **30**.

4. Use **np.linalg.det** to calculate the determinant of the matrix:

```
np.linalg.det( A )
```

The output **is** **-9.51619735392994e-16**.

The determinant is almost zero according to the preceding calculations. This inefficiency is due to floating-point arithmetic. The actual determinant is zero.

You can conclude this by calculating the determinant manually:

```
1*5*9 + 2*6*7 + 3*4*8 - 1*6*8 - 2*4*9 - 3*5*7
```

The output is **0**.

Whenever you work with NumPy, make sure that you factor in the possibility of floating-point arithmetic rounding errors, even if you appear to be working with integers.

5. Use **np.matrix.transpose** to get the transpose of the matrix:

```
np.matrix.transpose(A)
```

The output is as follows:

```
matrix([[1, 4, 7],
        [2, 5, 8],
        [3, 6, 9]])
```

If **T** is the transpose of matrix A, then **T[j][i]** is equal to **A[i][j]**.

NumPy comes with many useful features for vectors, matrices, and other mathematical structures.

Python for Game AI

An **AI game player** is nothing but an **intelligent agent** with a clear goal: to win the game and defeat all other players. Artificial Intelligence experiments have achieved surprising results when it comes to games. Today, no human can defeat an AI in the game of chess.

The game Go was the last game where human grandmasters could consistently defeat a computer player. However, in 2017, Google's game-playing AI defeated the Go grandmaster.

Intelligent Agents in Games

An intelligent agent plays according to the rules of the game. The agent can sense the **current state** of the game through its **sensors** and can evaluate the **utility** of potential steps. Once the agent finds the **best possible step**, it performs the action using its actuators. The agent finds the best possible action to **reach the goal** based on the information it has. Actions are either **rewarded** or **punished**. The carrot and stick are excellent examples of rewards and punishment. Imagine a donkey in front of your cart. You put a carrot in front of the eyes of the donkey, so the poor animal starts walking toward it. As soon as the donkey stops, the rider may apply punishment with a stick. This is not a human way of moving, but rewards and punishment control living organisms to some extent. The same happens to humans at school, at work, and in everyday life as well. Instead of carrots and sticks, we have income and legal punishment to shape our behavior.

In most games and gamified applications, a good sequence of actions results in a reward. When a human player feels rewarded, a hormone called dopamine is released. Dopamine is also referred to as the chemical of reward. When a human achieves a goal or completes a task, dopamine is released. This hormone makes you feel happy. Humans tend to act in a way that maximizes their happiness. This sequence of actions is called a **compulsion loop**. Intelligent agents, on the other hand, are only interested in their goal, which is to maximize their reward and minimize their punishment.

When modeling games, we must determine their **state space**. An action causes a **state transition**. When we explore the consequences of all possible actions, we get a **decision tree**. This tree goes deeper as we start exploring the possible future actions of all players until the game ends.

The strength of AI is the execution of millions of possible steps each second. Therefore, game AI often boils down to a **search exercise**. When exploring all of the possible sequences of moves in a game, we get the **state tree** of a game.

Consider a chess AI. What is the problem with evaluating all possible moves by building a state tree consisting of all of the possible sequences of moves?

Chess is an EXPTIME game complexity-wise. The number of possible moves explodes combinatorially.

White starts with 20 possible moves: the 8 pawns may move either one or two steps, and the two knights may move either up-up-left, or up-up-right. Then, black can make any of these twenty moves. There are already 20*20 = 400 possible combinations after just one move per player.

After the second move, we get 8,902 possible board constellations, and this number just keeps on growing. Just take seven moves, and you have to search through 10,921,506 possible constellations.

The average length of a chess game is approximately 40 moves. Some exceptional games take more than 200 moves to finish.

As a consequence, the computer player simply does not have time to explore the whole state space. Therefore, the search activity has to be guided with proper rewards, punishment, and simplifications of the rules.

Breadth First Search and Depth First Search

Creating a game AI is often a search exercise. Therefore, we need to be familiar with the two primary search techniques: Breadth First Search (BFS) and Depth First Search (DFS).

These search techniques are applied on a **directed rooted tree**. A tree is a data structure that has nodes, and edges connecting these nodes in such a way that any two nodes of the tree are connected by exactly one path:

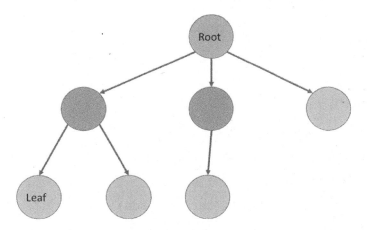

Figure 1.3: A directed rooted tree

When the tree is rooted, there is a special node in the tree called the root, where we begin our traversal. A directed tree is a tree where the edges may only be traversed in one direction. Nodes may be internal nodes or leaves. **Internal nodes** have at least one edge through which we can leave the node. A **leaf** has no edges pointing out from the node.

In AI search, the root of the tree is the starting state. We traverse from this state by generating successor nodes of the search tree. Search techniques differ regarding which order we visit these successor nodes in.

Suppose we have a tree defined by its root, and a function that generates all the successor nodes from the root. In this example, each node has a value and a depth. We start from 1 and may either increase the value by 1 or 2. Our goal is to reach the value 5.

```python
root = {'value': 1, 'depth': 1}

def succ(node):
    if node['value'] == 5:
        return []
    elif node['value'] == 4:
        return [{'value': 5,'depth': node['depth']+1}]
    else:
        return [
            {'value': node['value']+1, 'depth':node['depth']+1},
            {'value': node['value']+2, 'depth':node['depth']+1}
        ]
```

We will first perform DFS on this example:

```python
def bfs_tree(node):
    nodes_to_visit = [node]
    visited_nodes = []
    while len(nodes_to_visit) > 0:
        current_node = nodes_to_visit.pop(0)
        visited_bodes.append(current_node)
        nodes_to_visit.extend(succ(current_node))
    return visited_nodes


bfs_tree(root)
```

The output is as follows:

```
[{'depth': 1, 'value': 1},
{'depth': 2, 'value': 2},
{'depth': 2, 'value': 3},
{'depth': 3, 'value': 3},
{'depth': 3, 'value': 4},
{'depth': 3, 'value': 4},
{'depth': 3, 'value': 5},
{'depth': 4, 'value': 4},
{'depth': 4, 'value': 5},
{'depth': 4, 'value': 5},
{'depth': 4, 'value': 5},
{'depth': 5, 'value': 5}]
```

Notice that breadth first search finds the shortest path to a leaf first, because it enumerates all nodes in the order of increasing depth.

If we had to traverse a graph instead of a directed rooted tree, breadth first search would look different: whenever we visit a node, we would have to check whether the node had been visited before. If the node had been visited before, we would simply ignore it.

In this chapter, we only use **Breadth First Traversal** on trees. Depth First Search is surprisingly similar to Breadth First Search. The difference between **Depth First Traversals** and BFS is the sequence in which you access the nodes. While BFS visits all the children of a node before visiting any other nodes, DFS digs deep in the tree first:

```python
def dfs_tree(node):
    nodes_to_visit = [node]
    visited_nodes = []
    while len(nodes_to_visit) > 0:
        current_node = nodes_to_visit.pop()
        visited_nodes.append(current_node)
        nodes_to_visit.extend(succ(current_node))
    return visited_nodes


dfs_tree(root)
```

The output is as follows:

```
[{'depth': 1, 'value': 1},
 {'depth': 2, 'value': 3},
 {'depth': 3, 'value': 5},
 {'depth': 3, 'value': 4},
 {'depth': 4, 'value': 5},
 {'depth': 2, 'value': 2},
 {'depth': 3, 'value': 4},
 {'depth': 4, 'value': 5},
 {'depth': 3, 'value': 3},
 {'depth': 4, 'value': 5},
 {'depth': 4, 'value': 4},
 {'depth': 5, 'value': 5}]
```

As you can see, the DFS algorithm digs deep fast. It does not necessarily find the shortest path first, but it is guaranteed to find a leaf before exploring a second path.

In game AI, the BFS algorithm is often better for the evaluation of game states, because DFS may get lost. Imagine starting a chess game, where a DFS algorithm may easily get lost in searching.

Exploring the State Space of a Game

Let's explore the state space of a simple game: Tic-Tac-Toe.

In Tic-Tac-Toe, a 3x3 game board is given. Two players play this game. One plays with the sign X, and the other plays with the sign O. X starts the game, and each player makes a move after the other. The goal of the game is to get three of your own signs horizontally, vertically, or diagonally.

Let's denote the cells of the Tic-Tac-Toe board as follows:

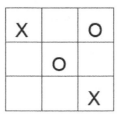

Figure 1.4: Tic-Tac-Toe Board

In the following example, X started at position 1. O retaliated at position 5, X made a move at position 9, and then O moved to position 3:

Figure 1.5: Tic-Tac-Toe Board with noughts and crosses

This was a mistake by the second player, because now X is forced to place a sign on cell 7, creating two future scenarios for winning the game. It does not matter whether O defends by moving to cell 4 or 8 – X will win the game by selecting the other unoccupied cell.

Note

You can try out the game at http://www.half-real.net/tictactoe/.

For simplicity, we will only explore the state space belonging to the cases when the AI player starts. We will start with an AI player that plays randomly, placing a sign in an empty cell. After playing with this AI player, we will create a complete decision tree. Once we generate all possible game states, you will experience their combinatoric explosion. As our goal is to make these complexities simple, we will use several different techniques to make the AI player smarter, and to reduce the size of the decision tree. By the end of this experiment, we will have a decision tree that has less than 200 different game endings, and as a bonus, the AI player will never lose a single game.

To make a random move, you will have to know how to choose a random element from a list using Python. We will use the **choice** function of the random library:

```
from random import choice

choice([2, 4, 6, 8])
```

The output is **6**.

The output of the choice function is a random element of the list.

> **Note**
>
> We will use the factorial notation in the following exercise. Factorial is denoted by the "!" exclamation mark. By definition, $0! = 1$, and $n! = n*(n-1)!$. In our example, $9! = 9* 8! = 9*8*7! = ... = 9*8*7*6*5*4*3*2*1$.

Exercise 2: Estimating the Number of Possible States in Tic-Tac-Toe Game

Make a rough estimate of the number of possible states on each level of the state space of the Tic-Tac-Toe game:

- In our estimation, we will not stop until all of the cells of the board have been filled. A player might win before the game ends, but for the sake of uniformity, we will continue the game.

- The first player will choose one of the nine cells. The second player will choose one out of the eight remaining cells. The first player can then choose one out of the seven remaining cells. This goes on until either player wins the game, or the first player is forced to make the ninth and last move.

- The number of possible decision sequences are therefore $9! = 362880$. A few of these sequences are invalid, because a player may win the game in less than nine moves. It takes at least five moves to win a game, because the first player needs to move three times.

- To calculate the exact size of the state space, we would have to calculate the number of games that are won in five, six, seven, and eight steps. This calculation is simple, but due to its exhaustive nature, it is out of scope for us. We will therefore settle for the magnitude of the state space.

> **Note**
>
> After generating all possible Tic-Tac-Toe games, researchers counted 255,168 possible games. Out of those games, 131,184 were won by the first player, 77,904 were won by the second player, and 46,080 games ended with a draw. Visit http://www.half-real.net/tictactoe/allgamesoftictactoe.zip to download all possible Tic-Tac-Toe games.

Even a simple game like Tic-Tac-Toe has a lot of states. Just imagine how hard it would be to start exploring all possible chess games. Therefore, we can conclude that brute-force search is rarely ideal.

Exercise 3: Creating an AI Randomly

In this section, we'll create a framework for the Tic-Tac-Toe game for experimentation. We will be modelling the game on the assumption that the AI player always starts the game. Create a function that prints your internal representation and allow your opponent to enter a move randomly. Determine whether a player has won. To ensure that this happens correctly, you will need to have completed the previous exercises:

1. We will import the choice function from the **random** library:

```
from random import choice
```

2. We will model the nine cells in a simple string for simplicity. A nine-character long Python string stores these cells in the following order: "123456789". Let's determine the index triples that must contain matching signs so that a player wins the game:

```
combo_indices = [
    [0, 1, 2],
    [3, 4, 5],
    [6, 7, 8],
    [0, 3, 6],
    [1, 4, 7],
    [2, 5, 8],
    [0, 4, 8],
    [2, 4, 6]
]
```

3. Let's define the *sign* constants for empty cells, the AI, and the opponent player:

```
EMPTY_SIGN = '.'
AI_SIGN = 'X'
OPPONENT_SIGN = 'O'
```

4. Let's create a function that prints a board. We will add an empty row before and after the board so that we can easily read the game state:

```
def print_board(board):
    print(" ")
    print(' '.join(board[:3]))
    print(' '.join(board[3:6]))
    print(' '.join(board[6:]))
    print(" ")
```

5. We will describe a move of the human player. The input arguments are the boards, the row numbers from 1 to 3, and the column numbers from 1 to 3. The return value of this function is a board containing the new move:

```
def opponent_move(board, row, column):
    index = 3 * (row - 1) + (column - 1)
    if board[index] == EMPTY_SIGN:
        return board[:index] + OPPONENT_SIGN + board[index+1:]
    return board
```

6. It is time to define a random move of the AI player. We will generate all possible moves with the **all_moves_from_board** function, and then we will select a random move from the list of possible moves:

```
def all_moves_from_board_list(board, sign):
    move_list = []
    for i, v in enumerate(board):
        if v == EMPTY_SIGN:
            move_list.append(board[:i] + sign + board[i+1:])
    return move_list


def ai_move(board):
    return choice(all_moves_from_board(board, AI_SIGN))
```

7. After defining the moves, we have to determine whether a player has won the game:

```python
def game_won_by(board):
    for index in combo_indices:
        if board[index[0]] == board[index[1]] == board[index[2]] != EMPTY_
SIGN:
            return board[index[0]]
    return EMPTY_SIGN
```

8. Last, but not least, we will create a game loop so that we can test the interaction between the computer player and the human player. Although we will carry out an exhaustive search in the following examples:

```python
def game_loop():
    board = EMPTY_SIGN * 9
    empty_cell_count = 9
    is_game_ended = False
    while empty_cell_count > 0 and not is_game_ended:
        if empty_cell_count % 2 == 1:
            board = ai_move(board)
        else:
            row = int(input('Enter row: '))
            col = int(input('Enter column: '))
            board = opponent_move(board,      row, col)
        print_board(board)
        is_game_ended = game_won_by(board) != EMPTY_SIGN
        empty_cell_count = sum(
            1 for cell in board if cell == EMPTY_SIGN
        )
    print('Game has been ended.')
```

9. Use the **game_loop** function to run the game:

```python
game_loop()
```

As you can see, even an opponent who's playing randomly may win from time to time if their opponent makes a mistake.

Activity 1: Generating All Possible Sequences of Steps in a Tic-Tac-Toe Game

This activity will explore the combinatoric explosion that is possible when two players play randomly. We will be using a program, building on the previous results, that generates all possible sequences of moves between a computer player and a human player. Assume that the human player may make any possible move. In this example, given that the computer player is playing randomly, we will examine the wins, losses, and draws belonging to two randomly playing players:

1. Create a function that maps the **all_moves_from_board** function on each element of a list of board spaces/squares. This way, we will have all of the nodes of a decision tree.

2. The decision tree starts with [**EMPTY_SIGN * 9**], and expands after each move. Let's create a **filter_wins** function that takes finished games out of the list of moves and appends them in an array containing the board states won by the AI player and the opponent player:

3. Then, with a **count_possibilities** function that prints the number of decision tree leaves that ended with a draw, were won by the first player, and were won by the second player.

4. We have up to 9 steps in each state. In the 0th, 2nd, 4th, 6th, and 8th iteration, the AI player moves. In all other iterations, the opponent moves. We create all possible moves in all steps and take out finished games from the move list.

5. Then, execute the number of possibilities to experience the combinatoric explosion.

As you can see, the tree of board states consists of 266,073 leaves. The **count_possibilities** function essentially implements a BFS algorithm to traverse all the possible states of the game. Notice that we count these states multiple times because placing an X in the top-right corner on step 1 and placing an X in the top-left corner on step 3 leads to similar possible states as starting with the top-left corner and then placing an X in the top-right corner. If we implemented the detection of duplicate states, we would have to check fewer nodes. However, at this stage, due to the limited depth of the game, we'll omit this step.

A **decision tree** is very similar to the data structure examined by `count_possibilities`. In a decision tree, we explore the utility of each move by investigating all possible future steps up to a certain extent. In our example, we could calculate the utility of the first moves by observing the number of wins and losses after fixing the first few moves.

> **Note**
>
> The root of the tree is the initial state. An internal state of the tree is a state in which a game has not been ended and moves are possible. A leaf of the tree contains a state where a game has ended.
>
> The solution for this activity can be found on page 258.

Summary

In this chapter, we have learned what Artificial Intelligence is, as well as its multiple disciplines.

We have seen how AI can be used to enhance or substitute human brainpower, to listen, speak, understand language, store and retrieve information, think, see, and move. Then, we moved on to learn about intelligent agents that act in their environment, solving a problem in a seemingly intelligent way to pursue a previously determined goal. When agents learn, they can learn in a supervised or an unsupervised way. We can use intelligent agents to classify things or make predictions about the future.

We then introduced Python and learned about its role in the field of Artificial Intelligence. We looked at a few important Python libraries for developing intelligent agents and preparing data for agents. As a warm-up, we concluded this chapter with an example, where we used the NumPy library to perform some matrix operations in Python. We also learned how to create a search space for a Tic Tac Toe game. In the next chapter, we will learn how intelligence can be imparted with the help of search space.

AI with Search Techniques and Games

In this chapter, we will be looking at creating intelligent agents.

Introduction

In the previous chapter, we understood the significance of an intelligent agent. We also examined the game states for a game AI. In this chapter, we will focus on how to create and introduce intelligence into an agent.

We will look at reducing the number of states in the state space and analyze the stages that a game board can undergo and make the environment work in such a way that we win. By the end of this chapter, we will have a Tic-Tac-Toe player who never loses a match.

Exercise 4: Teaching the Agent to Win

In this exercise, we will see how the steps needed to win can be reduced. We will be making the agent that we developed in the previous chapter detect situations where it can win a game. Compare the number of possible states to the random play as an example.

1. We will be defining two functions, **ai_move** and **all_moves_from_board**. We will create **ai_move** so that it returns a move that will consider its own previous moves. If the game can be won in that move, **ai_move** will select that move.

    ```
    def ai_move(board):
        new_boards = all_moves_from_board(board, AI_SIGN)
        for new_board in new_boards:
            if game_won_by(new_board) == AI_SIGN:
                return new_board
        return choice(new_boards)
    ```

2. Let's test the application with a game loop. Whenever the AI has the opportunity to win the game, it will always place the X in the right cell:

    ```
    game_loop()
    ```

3. The output is as follows:

    ```
    . X .
    . . .
    . . .

    Enter row: 3
    Enter column: 1

    . X .
    . . .
    0 . .
    ```

```
. X X

. . .

O . .


Enter row: 2
Enter column: 1

. X X

O . .

O . .



X X X

O . .

O . .


Game has been ended.
```

4. To count all the possible moves, we have to change the **all_moves_from_board** function to include this improvement. We must do this so that, if the game is won by **AI_SIGN**, it will return that value:

```
def all_moves_from_board(board, sign):
    move_list = []
    for i, v in enumerate(board):
        if v == EMPTY_SIGN:
            new_board = board[:i] + sign + board[i+1:]
            move_list.append(new_board)
            if game_won_by(new_board) == AI_SIGN:
                return [new_board]
    return move_list
```

5. We then generate all possible moves. As soon as we find a move that wins the game for the AI, we return it. We do not care whether the AI has multiple options to win the game in one move – we just return the first possibility. If the AI cannot win, we return all possible moves.

6. Let's see what this means in terms of counting all of the possibilities at each step:

```
count_possibilities()
```

7. The output is as follows:

```
step 0. Moves: 1
step 1. Moves: 9
step 2. Moves: 72
step 3. Moves: 504
step 4. Moves: 3024
step 5. Moves: 8525
step 6. Moves: 28612
step 7. Moves: 42187
step 8. Moves: 55888
First player wins: 32395
Second player wins: 23445
Draw 35544
Total 91344
```

Activity 2: Teaching the Agent to Realize Situations When It Defends Against Losses

In this section, we will discuss how to make the computer player play better so that we can reduce the state space and the number of losses. We will force the computer to defend against the player putting their third sign in a row, column, or diagonal line:

1. Create a function called **player_can_win** that takes all the moves from the board using the **all_moves_from_board** function and iterates over it using a variable called **next_move**. On each iteration, it checks whether the game can be won by the sign, and then it returns true or false.

2. Extend the AI's move so that it prefers making safe moves. A move is safe if the opponent cannot win the game in the next step.

3. Test the new application. You will find that the AI has made the correct move.

4. Place this logic in the state space generator and check how well the computer player is doing by generating all possible games.

We not only got rid of almost two thirds of the possible games again, but most of the time, the AI player either wins or settles for a draw. Despite our efforts to make the AI better, it can still lose in 962 ways. We will eliminate all of these losses in the next activity.

> **Note**
>
> The solution for this activity can be found on page 261.

Activity 3: Fixing the First and Second Moves of the AI to Make it Invincible

This section will discuss how an exhaustive search can be focused so that it can find moves that are more useful than others. We will be reducing the possible games by hardcoding the first and the second move:

1. Count the number of empty fields on the board and make a hardcoded move in case there are 9 or 7 empty fields. You can experiment with different hardcoded moves.

2. Occupying any corner, and then occupying the opposite corner, leads to no losses. If the opponent occupied the opposite corner, making a move in the middle results in no losses.

3. After fixing the first two steps, we only need to deal with 8 possibilities instead of 504. We also guided the AI into a state, where the hardcoded rules were enough to never lose a game.

> **Note**
>
> The solution for this activity can be found on page 263.

Let's summarize the important techniques that we applied to reduce the state space:

1. **Empirical simplification**: We accepted that the optimal first move is a corner move. We simply hardcoded a move instead of considering alternatives to focus on other aspects of the game. In more complex games, empirical moves are often misleading. The most famous chess AI victories often contain a violation of the common knowledge of chess grandmasters.

2. **Symmetry**: After we started with a corner move, we noticed that positions 1, 3, 7, and 9 are equivalent from the perspective of winning the game. Even though we didn't take this idea further, notice that we could even rotate the table to reduce the state space even further, and consider all four corner moves as the exact same move.

3. **Reduction of different permutations leading to the same state**: Suppose we can make the moves A or B and suppose our opponent makes move X, where X is not equal to either move A or B. If we explore the sequence A, X, B, and we start exploring the sequence B, X, then we don't have to consider the sequence B, X, A. This is because the two sequences lead to the exact same game state, and we have already explored a state containing these three moves before.

4. **Forced moves for the player**: When a player collects two signs horizontally, vertically, or diagonally, and the third cell in the row is empty, we are forced to occupy that empty cell either to win the game, or to prevent the opponent from winning the game. Forced moves may imply other forced moves, which reduces the state space even further.

5. **Forced moves for the opponent**: When a move from the opponent is clearly optimal, it does not make sense to consider scenarios when the opponent does not make the optimal move. When the opponent can win the game by occupying a cell, it does not matter whether we go on a long exploration of the cases when the opponent misses the optimal move. We save a lot less by not exploring cases when the opponent fails to prevent us from winning the game. This is because after the opponent makes a mistake, we will simply win the game.

6. **Random move**: When we can't decide and don't have the capacity to search, we move randomly. Random moves are almost always inferior to a search-based educated guess, but at times, we have no other choice.

Heuristics

In this topic, we will formalize informed search techniques by defining and applying heuristics to guide our search.

Uninformed and Informed Search

In the Tic-Tac-Toe example, we implemented a greedy algorithm that first focused on winning, and then focused on not losing. When it comes to winning the game immediately, the greedy algorithm is optimal, because there is never a better step than winning the game. When it comes to not losing, it matters how we avoid the loss. Our algorithm simply chose a random safe move without considering how many winning opportunities we have created.

Breadth First Search and Depth First Search are uniform, because they consider all possible states in the game. An informed search explores the space of available states intelligently.

Creating Heuristics

If we want to make better decisions, we apply heuristics to guide the search in the right direction by considering longer-term utility. This way, we can make a more informed decision in the present based on what could happen in the future. This can also help us solve problems faster. We can construct heuristics as follows:

- Educated guesses on the utility of making a move in the game
- Educated guesses on the utility of a given game state from the perspective of a player
- Educated guesses on the distance from our goal

Heuristics are functions that evaluate a game state or a transition to a new game state based on their utility. Heuristics are the cornerstones of making a search problem informed.

In this book, we will use utility and cost as negated terms. Maximizing utility and minimizing the cost of a move are considered synonyms.

A commonly used example for a heuristic evaluation function occurs in pathfinding problems. Suppose we are looking for a path in the tree of states that leads us to a goal state. Each step has an associated cost symbolizing travel distance. Our goal is to minimize the cost of reaching a goal state.

The following is an example heuristic for solving the pathfinding problem: take the coordinates of the current state and the goal. Regardless of the paths connecting these points, calculate the distance between these points. The distance of two points in a plane is the length of the straight line connecting the points. This heuristic is called the Euclidean distance.

Suppose we define a pathfinding problem in a maze, where we can only move up, down, left, or right. There are a few obstacles in the maze that block our moves. A heuristic we can use to evaluate how close we are from the goal state is called the Manhattan distance, which is defined as the sum of the horizontal and vertical distances between the corresponding coordinates of the current state and the end state.

Admissible and Non-Admissible Heuristics

The two heuristics we just defined on pathfinding problems are called admissible heuristics when used on their given problem domain. Admissible means that we may underestimate the cost of reaching the end state but that we never overestimate it. In the next topic, we will explore an algorithm that finds the shortest path between the current state and the goal state. The optimal nature of this algorithm depends on whether we can define an admissible heuristic function.

An example of a non-admissible heuristic is the Manhattan distance applied on a two-dimensional map. Imagine that there is a direct path between our current state and the goal state. The current state is at the coordinates (2, 5), and the goal state is at the coordinates (5, 1).

The Manhattan distance of the two nodes is as follows:

```
abs(5-2) + abs(1-5) = 3 + 4 = 7
```

As we overestimated the cost of traveling from the current node to the goal, the Manhattan distance is not admissible when we can move diagonally.

Heuristic Evaluation

Create a heuristic evaluation of a Tic-Tac-Toe game state from the perspective of the starting player.

We can define the utility of a game state or the utility of a move. Both work, because the utility of the game state can be defined as the utility of the move leading to it.

Heuristic 1: Simple Evaluation of the Endgame

Let's define a simple heuristic by evaluating a board: we can define the utility of a game state or the utility of a move. Both work, because the utility of the game state can be defined as the utility of the move leading to it. The utility for the game can be:

- +1, if the state implies that the AI player will win the game

- –1, if the state implies that the AI player will lose the game

- 0, if a draw has been reached or no clear winner can be identified from the current state

This heuristic is simple, because anyone can look at a board and analyze whether a player is about to win.

The utility of this heuristic depends on whether we can play many moves in advance. Notice that we cannot even win the game within five steps. We saw in topic A that by the time we reach step 5, we have 13,680 possible combinations leading to it. In most of these 13,680 cases, our heuristic returns zero.

If our algorithm does not look deeper than these five steps, we are completely clueless on how to start the game. Therefore, we could invent a better heuristic.

Heuristic 2: Utility of a Move

- Two AI signs in a row, column, or diagonal, and the third cell is empty: +1000 for the empty cell.

- Opponent has two in a row, column, or diagonally, and the third cell is empty: +100 for the empty cell.

- One AI signs in a row, column, or diagonal, and the other two cells are empty: +10 for the empty cells.

- No AI or opponent signs in a row, column, or diagonal: +1 for the empty cells.

- Occupied cells get a value of minus infinity. In practice, due to the nature of the rules, –1 will also do.

Why do we use a multiplicator factor of 10 for the four rules? Because there are eight possible ways of making three in a row, column, and diagonal. So, even by knowing nothing about the game, we are certain that a lower-level rule may not accumulate to override a higher-level rule. In other words, we will never defend against the opponent's moves if we can win the game.

> **Note**
>
> As the job of our opponent is also to win, we can compute this heuristic from the opponent's point of view. Our task is to maximize this value too so that we can defend against the optimal plays of our opponent. This is the idea behind the Minmax algorithm as well. If we wanted to convert this heuristic to a heuristic describing the current board, we could compute the heuristic value for all open cells and take the maximum of the values for the AI character so that we can maximize our utility.

For each board, we will create a utility matrix. For example, consider the following board:

Figure 2.1: Tic-Tac-Toe game state

From here, we can construct its utility matrix:

-1	-1	110
0	-1	10
-1	-1	-1

Figure 2.2: Tic-Tac-Toe game utility matrix

On the second row, the left cell is not very useful if we were to select it. Note that if we had a more optimal utility function, we would reward blocking the opponent.

The two cells of the third column both get a 10-point boost for two in a row.

The top-right cell also gets 100 points for defending against the diagonal of the opponent.

From this matrix, it is evident that we should choose the top-right move.

We can use this heuristic both to guide us toward an optimal next move, or to give a more educated score on the current board by taking the maximum of these values. We have technically used parts of this heuristic in Topic A in the form of hardcoded rules. Note, though, that the real utility of heuristics is not the static evaluation of a board, but the guidance it provides on limiting the search space.

Exercise 5: Tic-Tac-Toe Static Evaluation with a Heuristic Function

Perform static evaluation on the Tic–Tac–Toe game using heuristic function.

1. In this section, we will create a function that takes the Utility vector of possible moves, takes three indices inside the utility vector representing a triple, and returns a function. The returned function expects a points parameter and modifies the Utilities vector such that it adds points to each cell in the (i, j, k) triple, as long as the original value of that cell is non-negative. In other words, we increase the utility of empty cells only.

```python
def init_utility_matrix(board):
    return [0 if cell == EMPTY_SIGN else -1 for cell in board]


def generate_add_score(utilities, i, j, k):
    def add_score(points):
        if utilities[i] >= 0:
            utilities[i] += points
        if utilities[j] >= 0:
            utilities[j] += points
        if utilities[k] >= 0:
            utilities[k] += points
    return add_score
```

2. We now have everything to create the utility matrix belonging to any board constellation:

```
def utility_matrix(board):
    utilities = init_utility_matrix(board)
    for [i, j, k] in combo_indices:
        add_score = generate_add_score(utilities, i, j, k)
        triple = [board[i], board[j], board[k]]
        if triple.count(EMPTY_SIGN) == 1:
            if triple.count(AI_SIGN) == 2:
                add_score(1000)
            elif triple.count(OPPONENT_SIGN) == 2:
                add_score(100)
        elif triple.count(EMPTY_SIGN) == 2 and triple.count(AI_SIGN) == 1:
            add_score(10)
        elif triple.count(EMPTY_SIGN) == 3:
            add_score(1)
    return utilities
```

3. We will now create a function that strictly selects the move with the highest utility value. If multiple moves have thise same utility, the function returns both moves.

```
def best_moves_from_board(board, sign):
    move_list = []
    utilities = utility_matrix(board)
    max_utility = max(utilities)
    for i, v in enumerate(board):
        if utilities[i] == max_utility:
            move_list.append(board[:i] + sign + board[i+1:])
    return move_list


def all_moves_from_board_list(board_list, sign):
    move_list = []
    get_moves = best_moves_from_board if sign == AI_SIGN else all_moves_
from_board
    for board in board_list:
        move_list.extend(get_moves(board, sign))
    return move_list
```

4. Let's run the application.

    ```
    count_possibilities()
    ```

The output will be as follows:

```
step 0. Moves: 1
step 1. Moves: 1
step 2. Moves: 8
step 3. Moves: 24
step 4. Moves: 144
step 5. Moves: 83
step 6. Moves: 214
step 7. Moves: 148
step 8. Moves: 172
First player wins: 504
Second player wins: 12
Draw 91
Total 607
```

Using Heuristics for an Informed Search

We have not experienced the real power of heuristics yet, as we made moves without the knowledge of the effects of our future moves, thus effecting reasonable play from our opponents.

This is why a more accurate heuristic leads to more losses than simply hardcoding the first two moves in the game. Note that in previous topic, we selected these two moves based on statistics we generated based on running the game with fixed first moves. This approach is essentially what heuristic search should be all about. Static evaluation cannot compete with generating hundreds of thousands of future states and selecting a play that maximizes our rewards.

Types of Heuristics

Therefore, a more accurate heuristic leads to more losses than simply hardcoding the first two moves in the game. Note that in Topic A, we selected these two moves based on statistics I generated based on running the game with fixed first moves. This approach is essentially what a heuristic search should be all about. Static evaluation cannot compete with generating hundreds of thousands of future states and selecting a play that maximizes our rewards.

- This is because our heuristics are not exact, and most likely not admissible either.

We saw in the preceding exercise that heuristics are not always optimal: in the first topic, we came up with rules that allowed the AI to always win the game or finish with a draw. These heuristics allowed the AI to win very often, at the expense of losing in a few cases.

- A heuristic is said to be admissible if we may underestimate the utility of a game state, but we never overestimate it.

In the Tic-Tac-Toe example, we likely overestimated the utility in a few game states. Why? Because we ended up with a loss twelve times. A few of the game states that led to a loss had a maximum heuristic score. To prove that our heuristic is not admissible, all we need to do is find a potentially winning game state that we ignored while choosing a game state that led to a loss.

There are two more features that describe heuristics: Optimal and Complete:

- **Optimal heuristics** always find the best possible solution.
- **Complete heuristics** have two definitions, depending on how we define the problem domain. In a loose sense, a heuristic is said to be complete if it always finds a solution. In a strict sense, a heuristic is said to be complete if it finds all possible solutions. Our Tic-Tac-Toe heuristic is not complete, because we ignored many possible winning states on purpose, favoring a losing state.

Pathfinding with the A* Algorithm

In the first two topics, we learned how to define an intelligent agent, and how to create a heuristic that guides the agent toward a desired state. We learned that this was not perfect, because at times we ignored a few winning states in favor of a few losing states.

We will now learn a structured and optimal approach so that we can execute a search for finding the shortest path between the current state and the goal state: the **A*** (**"A star" instead of "A asterisk"**) algorithm:

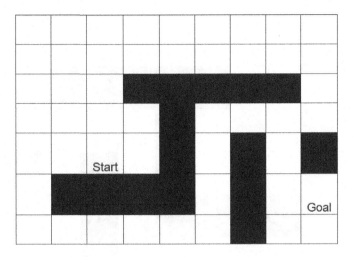

Figure 2.3: Finding the shortest path in a maze

For a human, it is simple to find the shortest path, by merely looking at the image. We can conclude that there are two potential candidates for the shortest path: route one starts upwards, and route two starts to the left. However, the AI does not know about these options. In fact, the most logical first step for a computer player would be moving to the square denoted by the number 3 in the following diagram:

Why? Because this is the only step that decreases the distance between the starting state and the goal state. All other steps initially move away from the goal state:

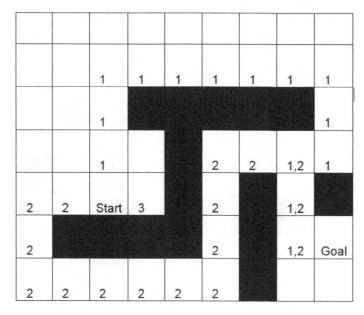

Figure 2.4: Shortest pathfinding game board with utilities

Exercise 6: Finding the Shortest Path to Reach a Goal

The steps to find the shortest path are as follows:

1. Describe the board, the initial state, and the final state using Python. Create a function that returns a list of possible successor states.

2. We will use tuples, where the first coordinate denotes the row number from 1 to 7, and the second coordinate denotes the column number from 1 to 9:

```
size = (7, 9)
start = (5, 3)
end = (6, 9)
obstacles = {
    (3, 4), (3, 5), (3, 6), (3, 7), (3, 8),
    (4, 5),
    (5, 5), (5, 7), (5, 9),
    (6, 2), (6, 3), (6, 4), (6, 5), (6, 7),
    (7, 7)
}
```

3. We will use array comprehension to generate the successor states in the following way. We move one left and one right from the current column, as long as we stay on the board. We move one up and one down from the current row, as long as we stay on the board. We take the new coordinates, generate all four possible tuples, and filter the results so that the new states can't be in the Obstacles list. It also makes sense to exclude moves that return to a field we had visited before to avoid infinite loops:

```
def successors(state, visited_nodes):
    (row, col) = state
    (max_row, max_col) = size
    succ_states = []
    if row > 1:
        succ_states += [(row-1, col)]
    if col > 1:
        succ_states += [(row, col-1)]
    if row < max_row:
        succ_states += [(row+1, col)]
    if col < max_col:
        succ_states += [(row, col+1)]
    return [s for s in succ_states if s not in visited_nodes if s not in
obstacles]
```

Exercise 7: Finding the Shortest Path Using BFS

To find the shortest path, follow these steps:

Find the shortest path by using the BFS algorithm.

Recall the basic BFS implementation.

1. We have to modify this implementation to include the cost. Let's measure the cost:

```
import math

def initialize_costs(size, start):
    (h, w) = size
    costs = [[math.inf] * w for i in range(h)]
    (x, y) = start
    costs[x-1][y-1] = 0
    return costs
```

```python
def update_costs(costs, current_node, successor_nodes):
    new_cost = costs[current_node[0]-1][current_node[1]-1] + 1
    for (x, y) in successor_nodes:
        costs[x-1][y-1] = min(costs[x-1][y-1], new_cost)


def bfs_tree(node):
    nodes_to_visit = [node]
    visited_nodes = []
    costs = initialize_costs(size, start)
    while len(nodes_to_visit) > 0:
        current_node = nodes_to_visit.pop(0)
        visited_nodes.append(current_node)
        successor_nodes = successors(current_node, visited_nodes)
        update_costs(costs, current_node, successor_nodes)
        nodes_to_visit.extend(successor_nodes)
    return costs
bfs_tree(start)
```

2. The output will be as follows:

```
[[6, 5, 4, 5, 6, 7, 8, 9, 10],
 [5, 4, 3, 4, 5, 6, 7, 8, 9],
 [4, 3, 2, inf, inf, inf, inf, inf, 10],
 [3, 2, 1, 2, inf, 12, 13, 12, 11],
 [2, 1, 0, 1, inf, 11, inf, 13, inf],
 [3, inf, inf, inf, inf, 10, inf, 14, 15],
 [4, 5, 6, 7, 8, 9, inf, 15, 16]]
```

3. You can see that a simple BFS algorithm successfully determines the cost from the start node to any nodes, including the target node. Let's measure the number of steps required to find the goal node:

```python
def bfs_tree_verbose(node):
    nodes_to_visit = [node]
    visited_nodes = []
    costs = initialize_costs(size, start)
    step_counter = 0
    while len(nodes_to_visit) > 0:
        step_counter += 1
        current_node = nodes_to_visit.pop(0)
        visited_nodes.append(current_node)
```

```
            successor_nodes = successors(current_node, visited_nodes)
            update_costs(costs, current_node, successor_nodes)
            nodes_to_visit.extend(successor_nodes)
            if current_node == end:
                print(
                    'End node has been reached in ',
                    step_counter, '
                    steps'
                )
                return costs
    return costs


    bfs_tree_verbose(start)
```

4. The end node has been reached in 110 steps:

```
[[6, 5, 4, 5, 6, 7, 8, 9, 10],
 [5, 4, 3, 4, 5, 6, 7, 8, 9],
 [4, 3, 2, inf, inf, inf, inf, inf, 10],
 [3, 2, 1, 2, inf, 12, 13, 12, 11],
 [2, 1, 0, 1, inf, 11, inf, 13, inf],
 [3, inf, inf, inf, inf, 10, inf, 14, 15],
 [4, 5, 6, 7, 8, 9, inf, 15, 16]]
```

We will now learn an algorithm that can find the shortest path from the start node to the goal node: the A* algorithm.

Introducing the A* Algorithm

A* is a complete and optimal heuristic search algorithm that finds the shortest possible path between the current game state and the winning state. The definition of complete and optimal in this state are as follows:

- Complete means that A* always finds a solution.

- Optimal means that A* will find the best solution.

To set up the A* algorithm, we need the following:

- An initial state

- A description of the goal states

- Admissible heuristics to measure progress toward the goal state

- A way to generate the next steps toward the goal

Once the setup is complete, we execute the A* algorithm using the following steps on the initial state:

1. We generate all possible next steps.

2. We store these children in the order of their distance from the goal.

3. We select the child with the best score first and repeat these three steps on the child with the best score as the initial state. This is the shortest path to get to a node from the starting node.

    `distance_from_end( node )` is an admissible heuristic estimation showing how far we are from the goal node.

In pathfinding, a good heuristic can be the Euclidean distance. If the current node is (x, y) and the goal node is (u, v), then:

distance_from_end(node) = *sqrt(abs(x − u) ** 2 + abs(y − v) ** 2)*

Where:

- **sqrt** is the square root function. Don't forget to import it from the math library.

- **abs** is the absolute value function. `abs( -2 ) = abs( 2 ) = 2`.

- `x ** 2` is *x* raised to the second power.

We will use the **distance_from_start** matrix to store the distances from the start node. In the algorithm, we will refer to this costs matrix as `distance_from_start( n1 )`. For any node, **n1**, that has coordinates **(x1, y1)**, this distance is equivalent to `distance_from_start[x1][y1]`.

We will use the **succ(n)** notation to generate a list of successor nodes from **n**.

Let's see the pseudo-code of the algorithm:

```
frontier = [start], internal = {}
# Initialize the costs matrix with each cell set to infinity.
# Set the value of distance_from_start(start) to 0.
while frontier is not empty:
    # notice n has the lowest estimated total
    # distance between start and end.
    n = frontier.pop()
    # We'll learn later how to reconstruct the shortest path
    if n == end:
        return the shortest path.
    internal.add(n)
    for successor s in succ(n):
        if s in internal:
            continue # The node was already examined
        new_distance = distance_from_start(n) + distance(n, s)
        if new_distance >= distance_from_start(s):
            # This path is not better than the path we have
            # already examined.
            continue
        if s is a member of frontier:
            update the priority of s
        else:
            Add s to frontier.
```

Regarding the retrieval of the shortest path, we can make use of the costs matrix. This matrix contains the distance of each node on the path from the start node. As cost always decreases when walking backward, all we need to do is start with the end node and walk backward greedily toward decreasing costs:

```
path = [end_node], distance = get_distance_from_start( end_node )

while the distance of the last element in the path is not 0:

    for each neighbor of the last node in path:

        new_distance = get_distance_from_start( neighbor )

        if new_distance < distance:

            add neighbor to path, and break out from the for loop

return path
```

A* shines when we have one Start state and one Goal state. The complexity of the A* algorithm is O(E), where E stands for all possible edges in the field. In our example, we have up to four edges leaving any node: up, down, left, and right.

> **Note**
>
> To sort the frontier list in the proper order, we must use a special Python data structure: a priority queue.

```
# Import heapq to access the priority queue
import heapq
# Create a list to store the data
data = []
# Use heapq.heappush to push (priorityInt, value) pairs to the queue
heapq.heappush(data, (2, 'first item'))
heapq.heappush(data, (1, 'second item'))
# The tuples are stored in data in the order of ascending priority
[(1, 'second item'), (2, 'first item')]
# heapq.heappop pops the item with the lowest score from the queue
heapq.heappop(data)
```

The output is as follows:

```
(1, 'second item')
# data still contains the second item
data
```

The output is as follows:

```
[(2, 'first item')]
```

Why is it important that the heuristic used by the algorithm is admissible?

Because this is how we guarantee the optimal nature of the algorithm. For any node **x**, we are measuring the sum of the following: The distances from the start node to **x** The estimated distance from **x** to the end node. If the estimation never overestimates the distance from **x** to the end node, we will never overestimate the total distance. Once we are at the goal node, our estimation is zero, and the total distance from the start to the end becomes an exact number.

We can be sure that our solution is optimal because there are no other items in the priority queue that have a lower estimated cost. Given that we never overestimate our costs, we can be sure that all of the nodes in the frontier of the algorithm have either similar total costs or higher total costs than the path we found.

Implement the A* algorithm to find the path with the lowest cost in the following game field:

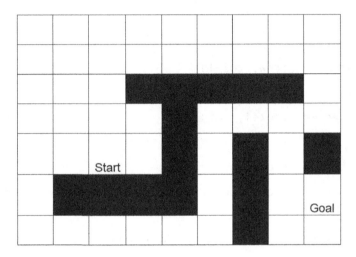

Figure 2.5: Shortest pathfinding game board

We'll reuse the initialization code from the game-modeling exercise:

```
import math
import heapq


size = (7, 9)
start = (5, 3)
end = (6, 9)
obstacles = {
    (3, 4), (3, 5), (3, 6), (3, 7), (3, 8),
    (4, 5),
    (5, 5), (5, 7), (5, 9),
    (6, 2), (6, 3), (6, 4), (6, 5), (6, 7),
    (7, 7)
}
```

```
# Returns the successor nodes of State, excluding nodes in VisitedNodes
def successors(state, visited_nodes):
    (row, col) = state
    (max_row, max_col) = size
    succ_states = []
    if row > 1:
        succ_states += [(row-1, col)]
    if col > 1:
        succ_states += [(row, col-1)]
    if row < max_row:
        succ_states += [(row+1, col)]
    if col < max_col:
        succ_states += [(row, col+1)]
    return [s for s in succ_states if s not in visited_nodes if s not in
obstacles]
```

We have also written code to initialize the cost matrix:

```
import math

def initialize_costs(size, start):
    costs = [[math.inf] * 9 for i in range(7)]
    (x, y) = start
    costs[x-1][y-1] = 0
    return costs
```

We will omit the function to update costs because we will do so inside the A* algorithm:

Let's initialize the A* algorithm's frontier and internal lists. For frontier, we will use a Python PriorityQueue. Do not directly execute this code, because we will use these four lines inside the A* search function:

```
frontier = []
internal = set()
heapq.heappush(frontier, (0, start))
costs = initialize_costs(size, start)
```

Now it is time to implement a heuristic function that measures the distance between the current node and the goal node using the algorithm we saw in the theory section:

```
def distance_heuristic(node, goal):
    (x, y) = node
    (u, v) = goal
    return math.sqrt(abs(x - u) ** 2 + abs(y - v) ** 2)
```

The last step is the translation of the A* algorithm into the functioning code:

```
def astar(start, end):
    frontier = []
    internal = set()
    heapq.heappush(frontier, (0, start))
    costs = initialize_costs(size, start)

    def get_distance_from_start(node):
        return costs[node[0] - 1][node[1] - 1]

    def set_distance_from_start(node, new_distance):
        costs[node[0] - 1][node[1] - 1] = new_distance

    while len(frontier) > 0:
        (priority, node) = heapq.heappop(frontier)
```

```
        if node == end:
            return priority
        internal.add(node)
        successor_nodes = successors(node, internal)
        for s in successor_nodes:
            new_distance = get_distance_from_start(node) + 1
            if new_distance < get_distance_from_start(s):
                set_distance_from_start(s, new_distance)
                # Filter previous entries of s
                frontier = [n for n in frontier if s != n[1]]
                heapq.heappush(frontier, (
                    new_distance + distance_heuristic(s, end), s
                )
                )


    astar(start, end)
    15.0
```

There are a few differences between our implementation and the original algorithm:

We defined a **distance_from_start** function to make it easier and more semantic to access the **costs** matrix. Note that we number the node indices starting with 1, while in the matrix, indices start with zero. Therefore, we subtract 1 from the node values to get the indices.

When generating the successor nodes, we automatically ruled out nodes that are in the Internal set. **successors = succ(node, internal)** makes sure that we only get the neighbors whose examination is not yet closed, meaning that their score is not necessarily optimal.

As a consequence, we may skip the step check, as internal nodes will never end up in **succ(n)**.

As we are using a priority queue, we have to determine the estimated priority of node s before inserting it. We will only insert the node to frontier, though, if we know that this node does not have an entry with a lower score.

It may happen that node s is already in the frontier queue with a higher score. In this case, we remove this entry before inserting it to the right place in the priority queue. When we find the end node, we simply return the length of the shortest path instead of the path itself.

To get a bit more information on the execution, let's print this information to the console. To follow what the A* algorithm does, execute this code and study the logs:

```python
def astar_verbose(start, end):
    frontier = []
    internal = set()
    heapq.heappush(frontier, (0, start))
    costs = initialize_costs(size, start)

    def get_distance_from_start(node):
        return costs[node[0] - 1][node[1] - 1]

    def set_distance_from_start(node, new_distance):
        costs[node[0] - 1][node[1] - 1] = new_distance

    steps = 0
    while len(frontier) > 0:
        steps += 1
        print('step ', steps, '. frontier: ', frontier)
        (priority, node) = heapq.heappop(frontier)
        print(
            'node ',
            node,
            'has been popped from frontier with priority',
            priority
        )
        if node == end:
            print('Optimal path found. Steps: ', steps)
            print('Costs matrix: ', costs)
            return priority
```

```
        internal.add(node)
        successor_nodes = successors(node, internal)
        print('successor_nodes', successor_nodes)
        for s in successor_nodes:
            new_distance = get_distance_from_start(node) + 1
            print(
                's:',
                s,
                'new distance:',
                new_distance,
                ' old distance:',
                get_distance_from_start(s)
            )
            if new_distance < get_distance_from_start(s):
                set_distance_from_start(s, new_distance)
                # Filter previous entries of s
                frontier = [n for n in frontier if s != n[1]]
                new_priority = new_distance + distance_heuristic(s, end)
                heapq.heappush(frontier, (new_priority, s))
                print(
        'Node',
        s,
        'has been pushed to frontier with priority',
        new_priority
    )
    print('Frontier', frontier)
    print('Internal', internal)
    print(costs)
astar_verbose(start, end)
```

The output is as follows:

```
step  1 . Frontier:  [(0, (5, 3))]
Node  (5, 3) has been popped from Frontier with priority 0
successors [(4, 3), (5, 2), (5, 4)]
s: (4, 3) new distance: 1  old distance: inf
Node (4, 3) has been pushed to Frontier with priority 7.324555320336759
s: (5, 2) new distance: 1  old distance: inf
Node (5, 2) has been pushed to Frontier with priority 8.071067811865476
s: (5, 4) new distance: 1  old distance: inf
Node (5, 4) has been pushed to Frontier with priority 6.0990195135927845
step  2 . Frontier:  [(6.0990195135927845, (5, 4)), (8.071067811865476, (5,
2)), (7.324555320336759, (4, 3))]
Node  (5, 4) has been popped from Frontier with priority 6.0990195135927845
successors [(4, 4)]
s: (4, 4) new distance: 2  old distance: inf
Node (4, 4) has been pushed to Frontier with priority 7.385164807134504
...
step  42 . Frontier:  [(15.0, (6, 8)), (15.60555127546399, (4, 6)),
(15.433981132056603, (1, 1)), (15.82842712474619, (4, 7))]
Node  (6, 8) has been popped from Frontier with priority 15.0
successors [(7, 8), (6, 9)]
s: (7, 8) new distance: 15  old distance: inf
Node (7, 8) has been pushed to Frontier with priority 16.414213562373096
s: (6, 9) new distance: 15  old distance: inf
Node (6, 9) has been pushed to Frontier with priority 15.0
step  43 . Frontier:  [(15.0, (6, 9)), (15.433981132056603, (1,
1)), (15.82842712474619, (4, 7)), (16.414213562373096, (7, 8)),
(15.60555127546399, (4, 6))]
Node  (6, 9) has been popped from Frontier with priority 15.0
Optimal path found. Steps:  43
```

```
Costs matrix:  [[6, 5, 4, 5, 6, 7, 8, 9, 10], [5, 4, 3, 4, 5, 6, 7, 8, 9],
[4, 3, 2, inf, inf, inf, inf, inf, 10], [3, 2, 1, 2, inf, 12, 13, 12, 11],
[2, 1, 0, 1, inf, 11, inf, 13, inf], [3, inf, inf, inf, inf, 10, inf, 14,
15], [4, 5, 6, 7, 8, 9, inf, 15, inf]]
```

We have seen that the A * search returns the right values. The question is, how can we reconstruct the whole path?

Remove the print statements from the code for clarity and continue with the A* algorithm that we implemented in step 4. Instead of returning the length of the shortest path, we have to return the path itself. We will write a function that extracts this path by walking backward from the end node, analyzing the costs matrix. Do not define this function globally yet. We will define it as a local function in the A* algorithm that we created previously:

```python
def get_shortest_path(end_node):
    path = [end_node]
    distance = get_distance_from_start(end_node)
    while distance > 0:
        for neighbor in successors(path[-1], []):
            new_distance = get_distance_from_start(neighbor)
            if new_distance < distance:
                path += [neighbor]
                distance = new_distance
                break  # for
    return path
```

Now that we know how to deconstruct the path, let's return it inside the A* algorithm:

```python
def astar_with_path(start, end):
    frontier = []
    internal = set()
    heapq.heappush(frontier, (0, start))
    costs = initialize_costs(size, start)

    def get_distance_from_start(node):
        return costs[node[0] - 1][node[1] - 1]

    def set_distance_from_start(node, new_distance):
```

```python
            costs[node[0] - 1][node[1] - 1] = new_distance


    def get_shortest_path(end_node):
        path = [end_node]
        distance = get_distance_from_start(end_node)
        while distance > 0:
            for neighbor in successors(path[-1], []):
                new_distance = get_distance_from_start(neighbor)
                if new_distance < distance:
                    path += [neighbor]
                    distance = new_distance
                    break   # for
        return path


    while len(frontier) > 0:
        (priority, node) = heapq.heappop(frontier)
        if node == end:
            return get_shortest_path(end)
        internal.add(node)
        successor_nodes = successors(node, internal)
        for s in successor_nodes:
            new_distance = get_distance_from_start(node) + 1
            if new_distance < get_distance_from_start(s):
                set_distance_from_start(s, new_distance)
                # Filter previous entries of s
                frontier = [n for n in frontier if s != n[1]]
                heapq.heappush(frontier, (
                    new_distance + distance_heuristic(s, end), s
                )
                )


astar_with_path( start, end )
```

The output is as follows:

```
[(6, 9),
 (6, 8),
 (5, 8),
 (4, 8),
 (4, 9),
 (3, 9),
 (2, 9),
 (2, 8),
 (2, 7),
 (2, 6),
 (2, 5),
 (2, 4),
 (2, 3),
 (3, 3),
 (4, 3),
 (5, 3)]
```

Technically, we do not need to reconstruct the path from the costs matrix. We could record the parent node of each node in a matrix, and simply retrieve the coordinates to save a bit of searching.

A* Search in Practice Using the simpleai Library

The **simpleai** library is available on GitHub, and contains many popular AI tools and techniques.

> **Note**
>
> You can access the library at https://github.com/simpleai-team/simpleai. The documentation of the Simple AI library can be accessed here: http://simpleai. readthedocs.io/en/latest/.To access the **simpleai** library, first you have to install it:

```
pip install simpleai
```

Once simpleai has been installed, you can import classes and functions from the simpleai library in the Jupyter QtConsole of Python:

```
from simpleai.search import SearchProblem, astar
```

Search Problem gives you a frame for defining any search problems. The **astar** import is responsible for executing the A* algorithm inside the search problem.

For simplicity, we have not used classes in the previous code examples to focus on the algorithms in a plain old style without any clutter. The **simpleai** library will force us to use classes, though.

To describe a search problem, you need to provide the following:

- **constructor**: This initializes the state space, thus describing the problem. We will make the Size, Start, End, and Obstacles values available in the object by adding it to these as properties. At the end of the constructor, don't forget to call the super constructor, and don't forget to supply the initial state.

- **actions(state)**: This returns a list of actions that we can perform from a given state. We will use this function to generate the new states. Semantically, it would make more sense to create action constants such as UP, DOWN, LEFT, and RIGHT, and then interpret these action constants as a result. However, in this implementation, we will simply interpret an action as "move to **(x, y)**", and represent this command as **(x, y)**. This function contains more-or-less the logic that we implemented in the **succ** function before, except that we won't filter the result based on a set of visited nodes.

- **result(state0, action)**: This returns the new state of action applied on the state0.

- **is_goal(state)**: This returns true if the state is a goal state. In our implementation, we will have to compare the state to the end state coordinates.

- **cost(self, state, action, newState)**: This is the cost of moving from state to **newState** via action. In our example, the cost of a move is uniformly 1:

```
import math
from simpleai.search import SearchProblem, astar

class ShortestPath(SearchProblem):
    def __init__(self, size, start, end, obstacles):
        self.size = size
        self.start = start
        self.end = end
```

```
            self.obstacles = obstacles
            super(ShortestPath, self).__init__(initial_state=self.start)

        def actions(self, state):
            (row, col) = state
            (max_row, max_col) = self.size
            succ_states = []
            if row > 1:
                succ_states += [(row-1, col)]
            if col > 1:
                succ_states += [(row, col-1)]
            if row < max_row:
                succ_states += [(row+1, col)]
            if col < max_col:
                succ_states += [(row, col+1)]
            return [s for s in succ_states if s not in self._obstacles]

        def result(self, state, action):
            return action

        def is_goal(self, state):
            return state == end

        def cost(self, state, action, new_state):
            return 1
        def heuristic(self, state):
            (x, y) = state
            (u, v) = self.end
            return math.sqrt(abs(x-u) ** 2 + abs(y-v) ** 2)

size = (7, 9)
start = (5, 3)
end = (6, 9)
obstacles = {
    (3, 4), (3, 5), (3, 6), (3, 7), (3, 8),
    (4, 5),
    (5, 5), (5, 7), (5, 9),
    (6, 2), (6, 3), (6, 4), (6, 5), (6, 7),
    (7, 7)
}

searchProblem = ShortestPath(Size, Start, End, Obstacles)
```

```
result = astar( searchProblem, graph_search=True )

result
Node <(6, 9)>
result.path()
[(None, (5, 3)),
 ((4, 3), (4, 3)),
 ((3, 3), (3, 3)),
 ((2, 3), (2, 3)),
 ((2, 4), (2, 4)),
 ((2, 5), (2, 5)),
 ((2, 6), (2, 6)),
 ((2, 7), (2, 7)),
 ((2, 8), (2, 8)),
 ((2, 9), (2, 9)),
 ((3, 9), (3, 9)),
 ((4, 9), (4, 9)),
 ((4, 8), (4, 8)),
 ((5, 8), (5, 8)),
 ((6, 8), (6, 8)),
 ((6, 9), (6, 9))]
```

The **simpleai** library made the search description a lot easier than the manual implementation. All we need to do is define a few basic methods, and then we have access to an effective search implementation.

Game AI with the Minmax Algorithm and Alpha-Beta Pruning

In the first two topics, we saw how hard it was to create a winning strategy for a simple game such as Tic-Tac-Toe. The last topic introduced a few structures for solving search problems with the A* algorithm. We also saw that tools such as the **simpleai** library help us reduce the effort we put in to describe a task with code.

We will use all of this knowledge to supercharge our game AI skills and solve more complex problems.

Search Algorithms for Turn-Based Multiplayer Games

Turn-based multiplayer games such as Tic-Tac-Toe are similar to pathfinding problems. We have an initial state, and we have a set of end states, where we win the game.

The challenge with turn-based multiplayer games is the combinatoric explosion of the opponent's possible moves. This difference justifies treating turn-based games differently than a regular pathfinding problem.

For instance, in the Tic-Tac-Toe game, from an empty board, we can select one of the nine cells and place our sign there, assuming we start the game. Let's denote this algorithm with the function **succ**, symbolizing the creation of successor states. Consider we have the initial state denoted by **Si**.

`succ(Si) returns [ S1, S2, ..., Sn ]`, where `S1, S2, ..., Sn` are successor states:

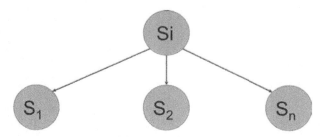

Figure 2.6: Tree diagram denoting the successor states of the function

Then, the opponent also makes a move, meaning that from each possible state, we have to examine even more states:

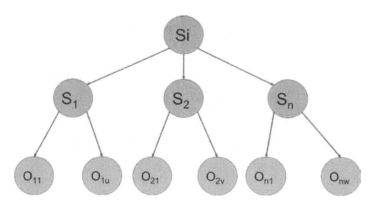

Figure 2.7: Tree diagram denoting parent-successor relationships

The expansion of possible future states stops in one of two cases:

- The game ends

- Due to resource limitations, it is not worth explaining any more moves beyond a certain depth for a state with a certain utility

Once we stop expanding, we have to make a static heuristic evaluation of the state. This is exactly what we did in the first two topics, when choosing the best move; however, we never considered future states.

Therefore, even though our algorithm became more and more complex, without using the knowledge of possible future states, we had a hard time detecting whether our current move would likely be a winner or a loser. The only way for us to take control of the future was to change our heuristic knowing how many games we would win, lose, or tie in the future. We could either maximize our wins or minimize our losses. We still didn't dig deeply enough to see whether our losses could have been avoided through smarter play on the AI's end.

All of these problems can be avoided by digging deeper into future states and recursively evaluating the utility of the branches. To consider future states, we will learn the Minmax algorithm and its variant, the Negamax algorithm.

The Minmax Algorithm

Suppose there's a game where a heuristic function can evaluate a game state from the perspective of the AI player. For instance, we used a specific evaluation for the Tic-Tac-Toe exercise:

- +1,000 points for a move that won the game

- +100 points for a move preventing the opponent from winning the game

- +10 points for a move creating two in a row, column, or diagonal

- +1 point for a move creating one in a row, column, or diagonal

This static evaluation is very easy to implement on any node. The problem is, as we go deep into the tree of all possible future states, we don't know what to do with these scores yet. This is where the Minmax algorithm comes into play.

Suppose we construct a tree with each possible move that could be performed by each player up to a certain depth. At the bottom of the tree, we evaluate each option. For the sake of simplicity, let's assume that we have a search tree that looks as follows:

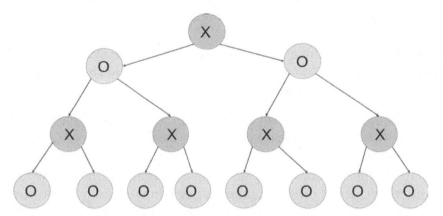

Figure 2.8: Example of search tree up to a certain depth

The AI plays with X, and the player plays with O. A node with X means that it's X's turn to move. A node with O means it's O's turn to act.

Suppose there are all O leaves at the bottom of the tree, and we didn't compute any more values because of resource limitations. Our task is to evaluate the utility of the leaves:

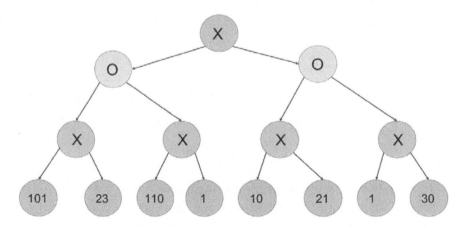

Figure 2.9: Example of search tree with possible moves

We have to select the best possible move from our perspective, because our goal is to maximize the utility of our move. This aspiration to maximize our gains represents the Max part in the Minmax algorithm:

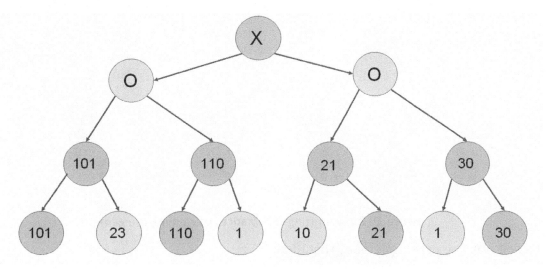

Figure 2.10: Example of search tree with best possible move

If we move one level higher, it is our opponent's turn to act. Our opponent picks the value that is the least beneficial to us. This is because our opponent's job is to minimize our chances of winning the game. This is the Min part of the Minmax algorithm:

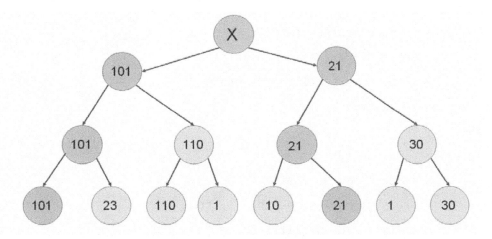

Figure 2.11: Minimizing the chances of winning the game

At the top, we can choose between a move with utility 101 and another move with utility 21. As we are maximizing our value, we should pick 101.

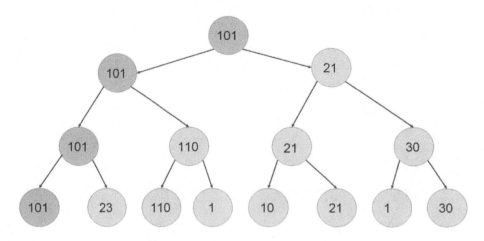

Figure 2.12: Maximizing the chances of winning the game

Let's see how we can implement this idea:

```
def min_max( state, depth, is_maximizing):
    if depth == 0 or is_end_state( state ):
     return utility( state )
    if is_maximizing:
        utility = 0
        for s in successors( state ):
            score = MinMax( s, depth - 1, false )
            utility = max( utility, score )
        return utility
    else
        utility = infinity
        for s in successors( state ):
            score = MinMax( s, depth - 1, true )
            utility = min( utility, score )
        return utility
```

This is the Minmax algorithm. We evaluate the leaves from our perspective. Then, from the bottom-up, we apply a recursive definition:

- Our opponent plays optimally by selecting the worst possible node from our perspective.

- We play optimally by selecting the best possible node from our perspective.

We need a few more considerations to understand the application of the Minmax algorithm on the Tic-Tac-Toe game:

- `is_end_state` is a function that determines whether the state should be evaluated instead of digging deeper, either because the game has ended, or because the game is about to end using forced moves. Using our utility function, it is safe to say that as soon as we reach a score of 1,000 or higher, we have effectively won the game. Therefore, `is_end_state` can simply check the score of a node and determine whether we need to dig deeper.

- Although the `successors` function only depends on the state, it is practical to pass the information of whose turn it is to make a move. Therefore, don't hesitate to add an argument if needed; you don't have to follow the pseudocode.

- We want to minimize our efforts in implementing the Minmax algorithm. For this reason, we will evaluate existing implementations of the algorithm, and we will also simplify the duality of the description of the algorithm in the rest of this topic.

- The suggested utility function is quite accurate compared to utility functions that we could be using in this algorithm. In general, the deeper we go, the less accurate our utility function has to be. For instance, if we could go nine steps deep into the Tic-Tac-Toe game, all we would need to do is award 1 point for a win, zero for a draw, and -1 point for a loss. Given that, in nine steps, the board is complete, and we have all of the necessary information to make the evaluation. If we could only look four steps deep, this utility function would be completely useless at the start of the game, because we need at least five steps to win the game.

- The Minmax algorithm could be optimized further by pruning the tree. Pruning is an act where we get rid of branches that don't contribute to the end result. By eliminating unnecessary computations, we save precious resources that could be used to go deeper into the tree.

Optimizing the Minmax Algorithm with Alpha-Beta Pruning

The last consideration in the previous thought process primed us to explore possible optimizations on reducing the search space by focusing our attention on nodes that matter.

There are a few constellations of nodes in the tree, where we can be sure that the evaluation of a subtree does not contribute to the end result. We will find, examine, and generalize these constellations to optimize the Minmax algorithm.

Let's examine pruning through the previous example of nodes:

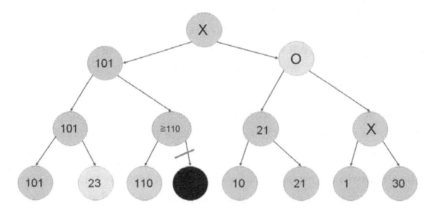

Figure 2.13: Search tree demonstrating pruning nodes

After computing the nodes with values 101, 23, and 110, we can conclude that two levels above, the value 101 will be chosen. Why?

- Suppose X <= 110. Then the maximum of 110 and X will be chosen, which is 110, and X will be omitted.

- Suppose X > 110. Then the maximum of 110 and X is X. One level above, the algorithm will choose the lowest value out of the two. The minimum of 101 and X will always be 101, because X > 110. Therefore, X will be omitted a level above.

This is how we prune the tree.

On the right-hand side, suppose we computed branches 10 and 21. Their maximum is 21. The implication of computing these values is that we can omit the computation of nodes Y1, Y2, and Y3, and we will know that the value of Y4 is less than or equal to 21. Why?

The minimum of 21 and Y3 is never greater than 21. Therefore, Y4 will never be greater than 21.

We can now choose between a node with utility 101, and another node with a maximal utility of 21. It is obvious that we have to choose the node with utility 101.

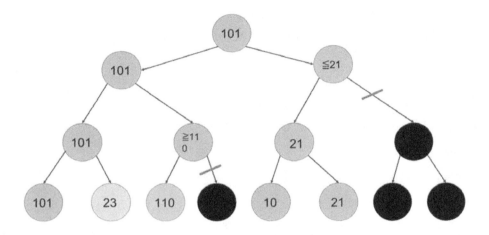

Figure 2.14: Example of pruning a tree

This is the idea behind alpha-beta pruning. We prune subtrees that we know are not going to be needed.

Let's see how we can implement alpha-beta pruning in the Minmax algorithm.

First, we will add an alpha and a beta argument to the argument list of Minmax:

```
def min_max(state, depth, is_maximizing, alpha, beta):
    if depth == 0 or is_end_state(state):
     return utility(state)
    if is_maximizing:
        utility = 0
        for s in successors(state):
            score = MinMax(s, depth - 1, false, alpha, beta)
            utility = max(utility, score)
        return utility
    else
```

```
        utility = infinity
        for s in successors(state):
            score = MinMax(s, depth - 1, true, alpha, beta)
            utility = min(utility, score)
        return utility
```

For the **isMaximizing** branch, we calculate the new alpha score, and break out of the loop whenever **beta <= alpha**:

```
def min_max(state, depth, is_maximizing, alpha, beta):
    if depth == 0 or is_end_state(state):
     return utility(state)
    if is_maximizing:
        utility = 0
        for s in successors(state):
            score = MinMax(s, depth - 1, false, alpha, beta)
            utility = max(utility, score)
            alpha = max(alpha, score)
            if beta <= alpha:
                break
        return utility
    else
        utility = infinity
        for s in successors(state):
            score = MinMax(s, depth - 1, true, alpha, beta)
            utility = min(utility, score)
        return utility
```

We need to do the dual for the minimizing branch:

```
def min_max(state, depth, is_maximizing, alpha, beta):
    if depth == 0 or is_end_state( state ):
     return utility(state)
    if is_maximizing:
        utility = 0
```

```
        for s in successors(state):
            score = min_max(s, depth - 1, false, alpha, beta)
            utility = max(utility, score)
            alpha = max(alpha, score)
            if beta <= alpha: break
        return utility
    else
        utility = infinity
        for s in successors(state):
            score = min_max(s, depth - 1, true, alpha, beta)
            utility = min(utility, score)
            beta = min(beta, score)
            if beta <= alpha: break
        return utility
```

We are done with the implementation. It is recommended that you mentally execute the algorithm on our example tree step-by-step to get a feel for the implementation.

One important piece is missing that's preventing us from doing the execution properly: the initial values for alpha and beta. Any number that's outside the possible range of utility values will do. We will use positive and negative infinity as initial values to call the Minmax algorithm:

```
alpha = infinity
beta = -infinity
```

DRYing up the Minmax Algorithm – The NegaMax Algorithm

The Minmax algorithm works great, especially with alpha-beta pruning. The only problem is that we have an if and an else branch in the algorithm that essentially negate each other.

As we know, in computer science, there is DRY code and WET code. DRY stands for Don't Repeat Yourself. Wet stands for We Enjoy Typing. When we write the same code twice, we double our chance of making a mistake while writing it. We also double our chances of each maintenance effort being executed in the future. Hence, it's better to reuse our code.

When implementing the Minmax algorithm, we always compute the utility of a node from the perspective of the AI player. This is why we have to have a utility-maximizing branch and a utility-minimizing branch in the implementations that are dual in nature. As we prefer clean code that describes the problem only once, we could get rid of this duality by changing the point of view of the evaluation.

Whenever the AI player's turn comes, nothing changes in the algorithm.

Whenever the opponent's turn comes, we negate the perspective. Minimizing the AI player's utility is equivalent to maximizing the opponent's utility.

This simplifies the Minmax algorithm:

```
def Negamax(state, depth, is_players_point_of_view):
    if depth == 0 or is_end_state(state):
        return utility(state, is_players_point_of_view)
    utility = 0
    for s in successors(state):
        score = Negamax(s,depth-1,not is_players_point_of_view)
    return score
```

There are necessary conditions for using the Negamax algorithm: the evaluation of the board state has to be symmetric. If a game state is worth +20 from the first player's perspective, it is worth -20 from the second player's perspective. Therefore, we often normalize the scores around zero.

Using the EasyAI Library

We have seen the **simpleai** library that helped us execute searches on pathfinding problems. We will now use the EasyAI library, which can easily handle AI search on two player games, reducing the implementation of the Tic-Tac-Toe problem to writing a few functions on scoring the utility of a board and determining when the game ends.

You can read the documentation of the library on GitHub at https://github.com/Zulko/easyAI.

To install the EasyAI library, run the following command:

```
pip install easyai
```

> **Note**
>
> As always, if you are using Anaconda, you must execute this command in the Anaconda prompt, and not in the Jupyter QtConsole.

Once EasyAI is available, it makes sense to follow the structure of the documentation to describe the Tic-Tac-Toe problem. This implementation was taken from https://zulko. github.io/easyAI/examples/games.html, where the Tic-Tac-Toe problem is described in a compact and elegant way:

```python
from easyAI import TwoPlayersGame
from easyAI.Player import Human_Player


class TicTacToe( TwoPlayersGame ):
    """ The board positions are numbered as follows:
            7 8 9
            4 5 6
            1 2 3
    """

    def __init__(self, players):
        self.players = players
        self.board = [0 for i in range(9)]
        self.nplayer = 1 # player 1 starts.

    def possible_moves(self):
        return [i+1 for i,e in enumerate(self.board) if e==0]
```

```python
    def make_move(self, move):
        self.board[int(move)-1] = self.nplayer


    def unmake_move(self, move): # optional method (speeds up the AI)
        self.board[int(move)-1] = 0


    def lose(self):
        """ Has the opponent "three in line ?" """
        return any( [all([(self.board[c-1]== self.nopponent)
                    for c in line])
                    for line in [[1,2,3],[4,5,6],[7,8,9],
                                 [1,4,7],[2,5,8],[3,6,9],
                                 [1,5,9],[3,5,7]]])


    def is_over(self):
        return (self.possible_moves() == []) or self.lose()


    def show(self):
        print ('\n'+'\n'.join([
                    ' '.join([['.','O','X'][self.board[3*j+i]]
                    for i in range(3)])
                for j in range(3)]) )


    def scoring(self):
        return -100 if self.lose() else 0



if __name__ == "__main__":

    from easyAI import AI_Player, Negamax
    ai_algo = Negamax(6)
    TicTacToe( [Human_Player(),AI_Player(ai_algo)]).play()
```

In this implementation, the computer player never loses thanks to the Negamax algorithm exploring the search criterion in a depth of 6.

Notice the simplicity of the scoring function. Wins or losses can guide the AI player to reach the goal of never losing a game.

Activity 4: Connect Four

In this section, we will practice using the **EasyAI** library and develop a heuristic. We will be using the game Connect 4 for this. The game board is seven cells wide and seven cells high. When you make a move, you can only select the column in which you drop your token. Then, gravity pulls the token down to the lowest possible empty cell. Your objective is to connect four of your own tokens horizontally, vertically, or diagonally, before your opponent does, or you run out of empty spaces. The rules of the game can be found at https://en.wikipedia.org/wiki/Connect_Four.

We can leave a few functions from the definition intact. We have to implement the following methods:

- __init__
- possible_moves
- make_move
- unmake_move (optional)
- lose
- show

1. We will reuse the basic scoring function from Tic-Tac-Toe. Once you test out the game, you will see that the game is not unbeatable, but plays surprisingly well, even though we are only using basic heuristics.

2. Then, let's write the **init** method. We will define the board as a one-dimensional list, like the Tic-Tac-Toe example. We could use a two-dimensional list too, but modeling will not get much easier or harder. We will generate all of the possible winning combinations in the game and save them for future use.

3. Let's handle the moves. The possible moves function is a simple enumeration. Notice that we are using column indices from 1 to 7 in the move names, because it is more convenient to start column indexing with 1 in the human player interface than with zero. For each column, we check whether there is an unoccupied field. If there is one, we will make the column a possible move.

4. Making a move is similar to the possible moves function. We check the column of the move and find the first empty cell, starting from the bottom. Once we find it, we occupy it. You can also read the implementation of the dual of the `make_move` function: `unmake_move`. In the `unmake_move` function, we check the column from top to bottom, and we remove the move at the first non-empty cell. Notice that we rely on the internal representation of `easyAi` so that it does not undo moves that it has not made. If we didn't, this function would remove one of the other player's tokens without checking whose token was removed.

5. As we already have the tuples that we have to check, we can mostly reuse the lose function from the Tic-Tac-Toe example.

6. Our last task is to implement the show method that prints the board. We will reuse the Tic-Tac-Toe implementation and just change the variables.

7. Now that all of the functions are complete, you can try out the example. Feel free to play a round or two against the opponent. You can see that the opponent is not perfect, but it plays reasonably well. If you have a strong computer, you can increase the parameter of the Negamax algorithm. I encourage you to come up with a better heuristic.

> **Note**
>
> The solution for this activity can be found on page 265.

Summary

In this chapter, we learned how to apply search techniques to play games.

First, we created a static approach that played the Tic-Tac-Toe game based on predefined rules without looking ahead. Then, we quantified these rules into a number we called heuristics. In the next topic, we learned how to use heuristics in the A* search algorithm to find an optimal solution to a problem.

Finally, we got to know the Minmax and the NegaMax algorithms so that the AI could win two-player games.

Now that you know the fundamentals of writing game AI, it is time to learn about a different field within artificial intelligence: machine learning. In the next chapter, you will learn about regression.

3

Regression

Learning Objectives

By the end of this chapter, you will be able to:

- Describe the mathematical logic involved in regression
- Illustrate the use of the NumPy library for Regression
- Identify linear regression with one variable and with multiple variables
- Use polynomial regression

This chapter covers the fundamentals of linear and polynomial regression.

Introduction

Regression is a broad topic that connects mathematical statistics, data science, machine learning, and artificial intelligence. As the basics of regression are rooted in mathematics, we will start by exploring the mathematical fundamentals.

Most of this topic will deal with different forms of linear regression, including linear regression with one variable, linear regression with multiple variables, polynomial regression with one variable, and polynomial regression with multiple variables. Python provides a lot of support for performing regression operations.

We will also use alternative regression models while comparing and contrasting support vector Regression with forms of Linear Regression. Throughout this chapter, we will use stock price data loaded from an online service provider. The models in this chapter are not intended to provide trading or investment advice.

> **Note**
>
> Although it is not suggested to use the models in this chapter to provide trading or investment advice, it is a very exciting and interesting journey that explains the fundamentals of regression.

Linear Regression with One Variable

A general regression problem can be defined as follows. Suppose we have a set of data points. We need to figure out a best fit curve to approximately fit the given data points. This curve will describe the relationship between our input variable x, which is the data points, and output variable y, which is the curve.

In real life, we often have multiple input variables determining one output variable. Regression helps us understand how the output variable changes when we keep all but one input variable fixed, and we change the remaining input variable.

What Is Regression?

In this chapter, we will work with regression on the two-dimensional plane. This means that our data points are two-dimensional, and we are looking for a curve to approximate how to calculate one variable from another.

We will learn about the following types of regression:

- **Linear regression with one variable using a polynomial of degree 1**: This is the most basic form of regression, where a straight line approximates the trajectory of future datasets.

- **Linear regression with multiple variables using a polynomial of degree 1**: We will be using equations of degree 1, but we will now allow multiple input variables, also known as features.

- **Polynomial regression with one variable**: This is a generic form of linear regression of one variable. As the polynomial used to approximate the relationship between the input and the output is of an arbitrary degree, we can create curves that fit the data points better than a straight line. The regression is still linear – not because the polynomial is linear, but because the regression problem can be modeled using linear algebra.

- **Polynomial regression with multiple variables**: This is the most generic regression problem using higher degree polynomials and multiple features to predict the future.

- **Support vector regression**: This form of regression uses support vector machines to predict data points. This type of regression is included to compare its usage to the other four regression types.

In this topic, we will deal with the first type of linear regression: we will use one variable, and the polynomial of the regression will describe a straight line.

On the two-dimensional plane, we will use the Déscartes coordinate system, more commonly known as the Cartesian coordinate system. We have an X and a Y axis, and the intersection of these two axes is the origin. We denote points by their X and Y coordinates.

For instance, the point (2, 1) corresponds to the orange point on the following coordinate system:

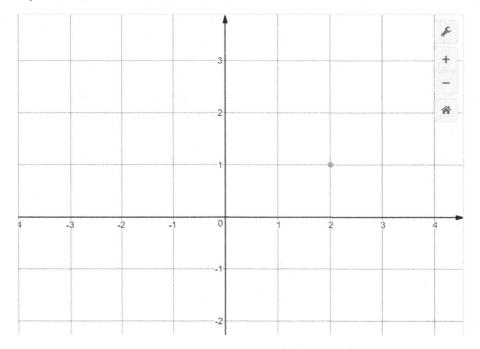

Figure 3.1: Representation of point (2,1) on the coordinate system

A straight line can be described with the equation **y = a*x + b**, where a is the slope of the equation, determining how steeply the equation climbs up, and b is a constant determining where the line intersects the Y axis

In the following diagram, you can see three equations:

- The blue line is described with the y = 2*x + 1 equation.

- The orange line is described with the y = x + 1 equation.

- The purple line is described with the y = 0.5*x + 1 equation.

You can see that all three equations intersect the y-axis at 1, and their slope is determined by the factor by which we multiply x.

If you know x, you can figure out y. If you know y, you can figure out x:

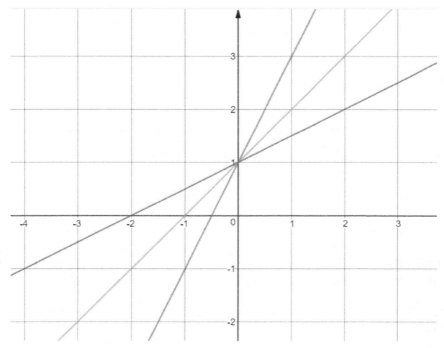

Figure 3.2: Representation of the equations y = 2*x + 1, y = x + 1, and y = 0.5*x + 1 on the coordinate system

We can describe more complex curves with equations too:

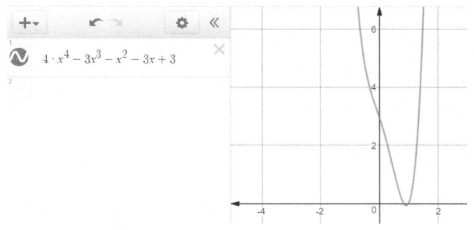

Figure 3.3: Image showing a complex curve

> **Note**
>
> If you would like to experiment more with the Cartesian coordinate system, you can use the following plotter: https://s3-us-west-2.amazonaws.com/oerfiles/ College+Algebra/calculator.html.

Features and Labels

In machine learning, we differentiate between features and labels. Features are considered our input variables, and labels are our output variables.

When talking about regression, the possible values of labels is a continuous set of rational numbers.

Think about features as values on the X-axis, and labels as the value on the Y-axis.

The task of regression is to predict label values based on feature values. We often create a label by shifting values of a feature forward. For instance, if we would like to predict stock prices in 1 month, and we create the label by shifting the stock price feature 1 month to the future, then:

- For each stock price feature value that's at least 1 month old, training data is available that shows the predicted stock price data 1 month in the future

- For the last month, prediction data is not available, so these values are all NaN (not a number)

We must drop the last month, because we cannot use these values for the prediction.

Feature Scaling

At times, we have multiple features that may have values within completely different ranges. Imagine comparing micrometers on a map to kilometers in the real world. They won't be easy to handle because of the magnitudinal difference of nine zeros.

A less dramatic difference is the difference between imperial and metric data. Pounds and kilograms, and centimeters and inches, don't compare that well.

Therefore, we often scale our features to normalized values that are easier to handle, as we can compare values of this range more easily. We scale training and testing data together. Ranges are typically scaled within [-1;1].

We will demonstrate two types of scaling:

- Min-Max normalization
- Mean normalization

Min-max scaling is calculated as follows:

```
x_scaled[n] = (x[n] - min(x)) / (max(x)-min(x))
```

Mean normalization is calculated as follows:

```
avg = sum(x) / len(x)
x_scaled[n] = (x[n] - avg) / (max(x)-min(x))
 [(float(i)-avg)/(max(fibonacci)-min(fibonacci)) for i in fibonacci]
```

Here's an example of Min-Max and min-max:

```
fibonacci = [0, 1, 1, 2, 3, 5, 8, 13, 21, 34, 55, 89, 144]
# Min-Max scaling:
[(float(i)-min(fibonacci))/(max(fibonacci)-min(fibonacci)) for i in fibonacci]
[0.0,
 0.006944444444444444,
 0.006944444444444444,
 0.013888888888888888,
 0.020833333333333332,
 0.034722222222222224,
 0.05555555555555555,
 0.09027777777777778,
 0.14583333333333334,
```

```
 0.2361111111111111,
 0.3819444444444444,
 0.6180555555555556,
 1.0]
# Mean normalization:
avg = sum(fibonacci) / len(fibonacci)
# 28.923076923076923
[(float(i)-avg)/(max(fibonacci)-min(fibonacci)) for i in fibonacci]
[-0.20085470085470086,
 -0.19391025641025642,
 -0.19391025641025642,
 -0.18696581196581197,
 -0.18002136752136752,
 -0.16613247863247863,
 -0.1452991452991453,
 -0.11057692307692307,
 -0.05502136752136752,
 0.035256410256410256,
 0.18108974358974358,
 0.4172008547008547,
 0.7991452991452992]
```

Scaling could add to the processing time, but often it is a sensible step to add.

In the scikit-learn library, we have access to a function that scales NumPy arrays:

```
import numpy as np
from sklearn import preprocessing
preprocessing.scale(fibonacci)
array([-0.6925069 , -0.66856384, -0.66856384, -0.64462079, -0.62067773,
       -0.57279161, -0.50096244, -0.38124715, -0.18970269,  0.12155706,
        0.62436127,  1.43842524,  2.75529341])
```

The scale method performs mean normalization. Notice that the result is a NumPy array.

Cross-Validation with Training and Test Data

Cross-validation measures the predictive performance of a statistical model. The better the cross-validation result, the more you can trust that your model can be used to predict the future.

During cross-validation, we test our model's ability to predict the future on real **test data**. Test data is not used in the prediction process.

Training data is used to construct the model that predicts our results.

Once we load data from a data source, we typically separate data into a larger chunk of training data, and a smaller chunk of test data. This separation shuffles the entries of training and test data randomly. Then, it gives you an array of training features, their corresponding training labels, testing features, and their corresponding testing labels.

We can do the training-testing split using the `model_selection` library of scikit-learn.

Suppose in our dummy example that we have scaled Fibonacci data and its indices as labels:

```
features = preprocessing.scale(fibonacci)
label = np.array(range(13))
```

Let's use 10% of the data as test data.

```
from sklearn import model_selection
(x_train, x_test, y_train, y_test) =
model_selection.train_test_split(features, label, test_size=0.1)
x_train
array([-0.66856384,  0.12155706, -0.18970269, -0.64462079,  1.43842524,
        2.75529341, -0.6925069 , -0.38124715, -0.57279161, -0.62067773,
       -0.66856384])


x_test
array([-0.50096244,  0.62436127])


y_train
array([1, 9, 8, 3, 11, 12, 0, 7, 5, 4, 2])
```

```
y_test
array([6, 10])
```

With training and testing, if we get the ratios wrong, we run the risk of overfitting or underfitting the model.

Overfitting occurs when we train the model too well, and it fits the training dataset too well. The model will be very accurate on the training data, but it will not be usable in real life, because its accuracy decreases when used on any other data. The model adjusts to the random noise in the training data and assumes patterns on this noise that yield false predictions. Underfitting occurs when the model does not fit the training data well enough to recognize important characteristics of the data. As a result, it cannot make the necessary predictions on new data. One example for this is when we attempt to do linear regression on data that is not linear. For instance, Fibonacci numbers are not linear, therefore, a model on a Fibonacci-like sequence cannot be linear either.

> **Note**
>
> If you remember the Cartesian coordinate system, you know that the horizontal axis is the X axis, and that the vertical axis is the Y axis. Our features are on the X axis, while our labels are on the Y axis. Therefore, we use features and X as synonyms, while labels are often denoted by Y. Therefore, x_test denotes feature test data, x_train denotes feature training data, y_test denotes label test data, and y_train denotes label training data.

Fitting a Model on Data with scikit-learn

We are illustrating the process of regression on a dummy example, where we only have one feature and very limited data.

As we only have one feature, we have to format **x_train** by reshaping it with **x_train.reshape (-1,1)** to a NumPy array containing one feature.

Therefore, before executing the code on fitting the best line, execute the following code:

```
x_train = x_train.reshape(-1, 1)

x_test = x_test.reshape(-1, 1)

# array([a, b, c]).reshape(-1, 1) becomes:

# array([[a, b, c]])
```

Suppose we have train and test data for our features and labels.

We can fit a model on this data for performing prediction. We will now use linear regression for this purpose:

```
from sklearn import linear_model
linear_regression = linear_model.LinearRegression()
model = linear_regression.fit(x_train, y_train)
model.predict(x_test)
array([4.16199119, 7.54977143])
```

We can also calculate the score associated with the model:

```
model.score(x_test, y_test)
-0.17273705326696565
```

This score is the mean square error and represents the accuracy of the model. It represents how well we can predict features from labels.

This number indicates a very bad model. The best possible score is 1.0. A score of 0.0 can be achieved if we constantly predict the labels by ignoring the features. We will omit the mathematical background of this score in this book.

Our model does not perform well for two reasons:

- 11 training data and 2 testing data are simply not enough to perform proper predictive analysis.

- Even if we ignore the number of points, the Fibonacci x -> y function does not describe a linear relationship between x and y. Approximating a non-linear function with a line is only useful if we are very close to the training interval.

We will see a lot of more accurate models in the future, and we may even reach model scores of 0.9.

Linear Regression Using NumPy Arrays

One reason why NumPy arrays are handier than Python lists is that they can be treated as vectors. There are a few operations defined on vectors that can simplify our calculations. We can perform operations on vectors of similar lengths. The sum and the (vectorial) product of two vectors equals a vector, where each coordinate is the sum or (vectorial) product of the corresponding coordinates.

For example:

```
import numpy as np
v1 = np.array([1,2,3])
v2 = np.array([2,0,2])
v1 + v2  # array([3, 2, 5])
v1 * v2   # array([2, 0, 6])
```

The product of a vector and a scalar is a vector, where each coordinate is multiplied by the scalar:

```
v1 * 2 # array([2, 4, 6])
```

The second power of a vector equals the vectorial product of the vector with itself. The double asterisk denotes the power operator:

```
v1 ** 2 # array([1, 4, 9], dtype=int32)
```

Suppose we have a set of points in the plane. Our job is to find the best fit line.

Let's see two examples.

Our first example contains 13 values that seem linear in nature. We are plotting the following data:

```
[2, 8, 8, 18, 25, 21, 32, 44, 32, 48, 61, 45, 62]
```

If you wanted to draw a line that is the closest to these dots, your educated guess would be quite close to reality:

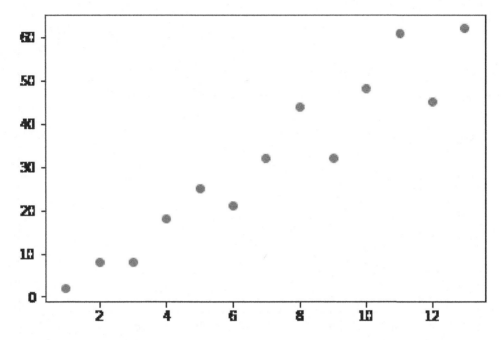

Figure 3.4: Plotted graph of values [2, 8, 8, 18, 25, 21, 32, 44, 32, 48, 61, 45, 62]

Our second example is the first 13 values of the Fibonacci sequence, after scaling. Although we can define a line that fits these points the closest, we can see from the distribution of the points that our model will not be too useful:

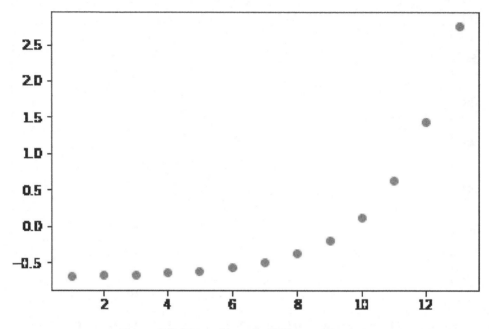

Figure 3.5: Plotted graph of Fibonacci values

We have already learned what the equation of a straight line is: y = a * x + b

In this equation, **a** is the slope, and **b** is the **y**-intercept. To find the line of best fit, we have to find the co-efficients **a** and **b**.

Our job is to minimize the sum of distances from the line of best fit.

In this book, we will save the thought process behind calculating the coefficients **a** and **b**, because you will find little practical use for it. We would rather utilize the mean as the arithmetic mean of the values in a list. We can use the mean function provided by NumPy for this.

Let's find the line of best fit for these two examples:

```
import numpy as np

from numpy import mean

x = np.array(range(1, 14))

y = np.array([2, 8, 8, 18, 25, 21, 32, 44, 32, 48, 61, 45, 62])

a = (mean(x)*mean(y) - mean(x*y)) / (mean(x) ** 2 - mean( x ** 2 ))

4.857142857142859

b = mean(y) - a*mean(x)

-2.7692307692307843
```

Once we plot the line y = a*x + b with the preceding coefficients, we get the following graph:

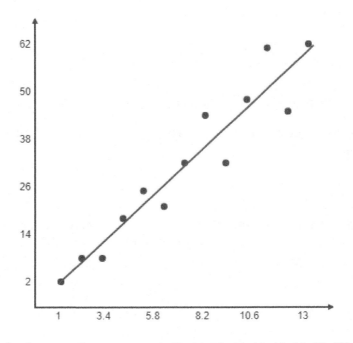

Figure 3.6: Plotted graph of array values [2, 8, 8, 18, 25, 21, 32, 44, 32, 48, 61, 45, 62] and the line y=a*x+b

> **Note**
>
> You can find a linear regression calculator at http://www.endmemo.com/statistics/lr.php. You can also check the calculator to get an idea of what lines of best fit look like on a given dataset.

Regarding the scaled Fibonacci values, the line of best fit looks as follows:

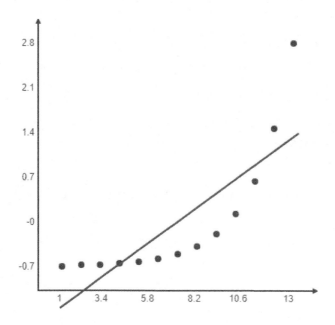

Figure 3.7: Plotted graph showing Fibonacci values and the line y=a*x+b

The best fit line of the second dataset clearly appears more off from anywhere outside the trained interval.

> **Note**
>
> We don't have to use this method to perform linear regression. Many libraries, including scikit-learn, will help us automatize this process. Once we perform linear regression with multiple variables, we are better off using a library to perform regression for us.

Fitting a Model Using NumPy Polyfit

NumPy Polyfit can also be used to create a line of best fit for linear regression with one variable.

Recall the calculation for the line of best fit:

```
import numpy as np
from numpy import mean
x = np.array(range(1, 14))
y = np.array([2, 8, 8, 18, 25, 21, 32, 44, 32, 48, 61, 45, 62])
a = (mean(x)*mean(y) - mean(x*y)) / (mean(x) ** 2 - mean( x ** 2 ))
4.857142857142859
b = mean(y) - a*mean(x)
-2.7692307692307843
```

The equation for finding the coefficients a and b is quite long. Fortunately, **numpy.polyfit** performs these calculations to find the coefficients of the line of best fit. The **polyfit** function accepts three arguments: the array of **x** values, the array of **y** values, and the degree of polynomial to look for. As we are looking for a straight line, the highest power of **x** is 1 in the polynomial:

```
import numpy as np
x = np.array(range(1, 14))
y = np.array([2, 8, 8, 18, 25, 21, 32, 44, 32, 48, 61, 45, 62])
[a, b] = np.polyfit(x, y, 1)
[4.857142857142858, -2.769230769230769]
```

Plotting the Results in Python

Suppose you have a set of data points and a regression line. Our task is to plot the points and the line together so that we can see the results with our own eyes.

We will use the **matplotlib.pyplot** library for this. This library has two important functions:

- **Scatter:** This displays scattered points on the plane, defined by a list of x coordinates and a list of y coordinates.

- **Plot:** Along with two arguments, this function plots a segment defined by two points, or a sequence of segments defined by multiple points. Plot is like scatter, except that instead of displaying the points, they are connected by lines.

A plot with three arguments plots a segment and/or two points formatted according to the third argument

A segment is defined by two points. As **x** ranges between 1 and 14, it makes sense to display a segment between 0 and 15. We must substitute the value of **x** in the equation **a*x+b** to get the corresponding **y** values:

```
import matplotlib.pyplot as plot


x = np.array(range(1, 14))
y = np.array([2, 8, 8, 18, 25, 21, 32, 44, 32, 48, 61, 45, 62])
a = (mean(x)*mean(y) - mean(x*y)) / (mean(x) ** 2 - mean(x ** 2))
4.857142857142859
b = mean(y) - a*mean(x)
-2.7692307692307843


# Plotting the points
plot.scatter(x, y)
# Plotting the line
plot.plot([0, 15], [b, 15*a+b])
```

The output is as follows:

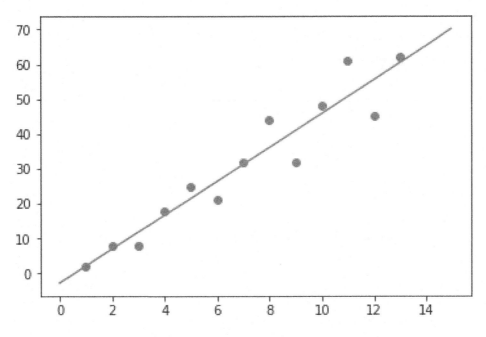

Figure 3.8: Graph displaying how data points fit a regression line

You might have to call **plot.show()** to display the preceding graph. In the IPython console, the coordinate system shows up automatically.

The segment and the scattered data points are displayed as expected.

Plot has an advanced signature. You can use one call of plot to draw scattered dots, lines, and any curves on this diagram. These variables are interpreted in groups of three:

- X values
- Y values
- Formatting options in the form of a string

Let's create a function for deriving an array of approximated y values from an array of approximated x values:

```
def fitY( arr ):
    return [4.857142857142859 * x - 2.7692307692307843 for x in arr]
```

We will use the **fit** function to plot values:

```
plot.plot(
    x, y, 'go',
    x, fitY(x), 'r--o'
)
```

The output is as follows:

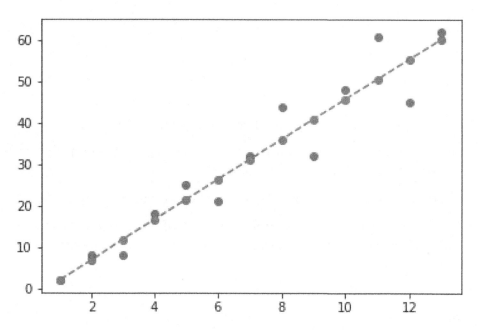

Figure 3.9: Graph for the plot function using the fit function

The Python plotter library offers a simple solution for most of your graphing problems. You can draw as many lines, dots, and curves as you want on this graph.

Every third variable is responsible for formatting. The letter g stands for green, while the letter r stands for red. You could have used b for blue, y for yellow, and so on. In the absence of a color, each triple will be displayed using a different color. The o character symbolizes that we want to display a dot where each data point lies. Therefore, 'go' has nothing to do with movement – it requests the plotter to plot green dots. The '-' characters are responsible for displaying a dashed line. If you just use one minus, a straight line appears instead of the dashed line.

If we simplify this formatting, we can specify that we only want dots of an arbitrary color, and straight lines of another arbitrary color. By doing this, we can simply write the following plot call:

```
plot.plot(
    x, y, 'o',
    x, fitY(x), '-'
)
```

The output is as follows:

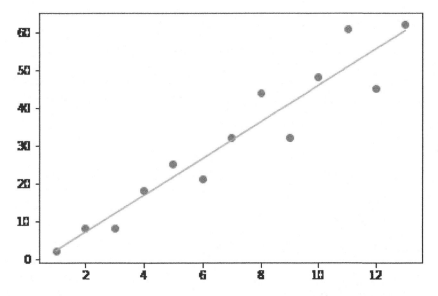

Figure 3.10: Graph for plot function with dashed line

When displaying curves, the plotter connects the dots with segments. Also, keep in mind that even a complex sequence of curves is an approximation that connects the dots. For instance, if you execute the code from https://gist.github.com/traeblain/1487795, you will recognize the segments of the batman function as connected lines:

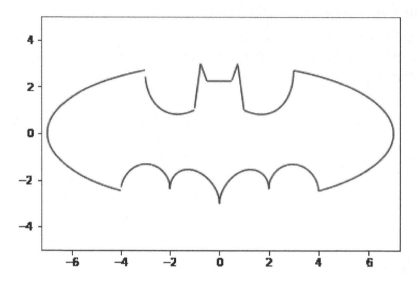

Figure 3.11: Graph for the batman function

There is a wide variety of ways to plot curves. We have seen that the `polyfit` method of the NumPy library returns an array of coefficients to describe a linear equation:

```
import numpy as np

x = np.array(range(1, 14))

y = np.array([2, 8, 8, 18, 25, 21, 32, 44, 32, 48, 61, 45, 62])

np.polyfit(x, y, 1)

# array([ 4.85714286, -2.76923077])
```

This array describes the equation `4.85714286 * x - 2.76923077`.

Suppose we now want to plot a curve, `y = -x**2 + 3*x - 2`. This quadratic equation is described by the coefficient array `[-1, 3, -2]`. We could write our own function to calculate the y values belonging to x values. However, the NumPy library already has a feature to do this work for us: `np.poly1d`:

```
import numpy as np

x = np.array(range( -10, 10, 0.2 ))

f = np.poly1d([-1,3,-2])
```

The f function that's created by the poly1d call not only works with single values, but also with lists or NumPy arrays:

```
f(5)
# -12
f(x)
# array([-132, -110,  -90,  -72,  -56,  -42,  -30,  -20,  -12,   -6,   -2,
0,    0,   -2,   -6,  -12,  -20,  -30,  -42,  -56])
```

We can now use these values to plot a non-linear curve:

```
import matplotlib.pyplot as plot

plot.plot(x, f(x))
```

The output is as follows:

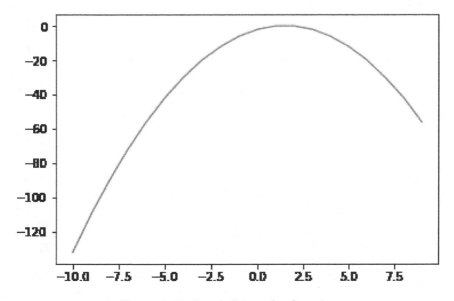

Figure 3.12: Graph for pyplot function

Predicting Values with Linear Regression

Suppose we are interested in the **y** value belonging to the **x** coordinate **20**. Based on the linear regression model, all we need to do is substitute the value of **20** in the place of **x**:

```
# Plotting the points
plot.scatter(x, y)
# Plotting the prediction belonging to x = 20
plot.scatter(20, a * 20 + b, color='red')
# Plotting the line
plot.plot([0, 25], [b, 25*a+b])
```

The output is as follows:

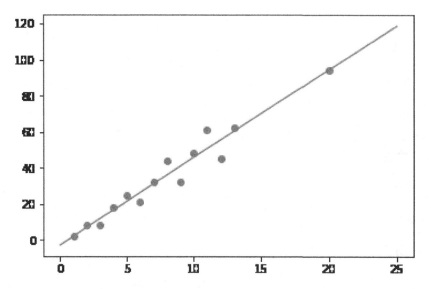

Figure 3.13: Graph showing the predicted value using Linear Regression

Here, we denoted the predicted value with red. This red point is on the best fit line.

Activity 5: Predicting Population

You are working at the government office of Metropolis, trying to forecast the need for elementary school capacity. Your task is to figure out a 2025 and 2030 prediction for the number of children starting elementary school. The past data is as follows:

2001	147026
2002	144272
2003	140020
2004	143801
2005	146233
2006	144539
2007	141273
2008	135389
2009	142500
2010	139452
2011	139722
2012	135300
2013	137289
2014	136511
2015	132884
2016	125683
2017	127255
2018	124275

Figure 3.14: A table representing number of kids starting elementary school from 2001 to 2018

Plot these tendencies on a two-dimensional chart. To do this, you must:

1. Use linear regression. Features are the years ranging from 2001 to 2018. For simplicity, we can indicate 2001 as year 1, and 2018 as year 18.

2. Use **np.polyfit** to determine the coefficients of the regression line.

3. Plot the results using **matplotlib.pyplot** to determine future tendencies.

> **Note**
>
> The solution to this activity is available at page 269.

Linear Regression with Multiple Variables

In the previous topic, we dealt with linear regression with one variable. Now we will learn an extended version of linear regression, where we will use multiple input variables to predict the output.

We will rely on examples where we will load and predict stock prices. Therefore, we will experiment with the main libraries used for loading stock prices.

Multiple Linear Regression

If you recall the formula for the line of best fit in linear regression, it was defined as **y = a*x + b**, where **a** is the slope of the line, **b** is the y-intercept of the line, **x** is the feature value, and **y** is the calculated label value.

In multiple regression, we have multiple features and one label. Assuming that we have three features, **x1**, **x2**, and **x3**, our model changes as follows:

```
y = a1 * x1 + a2 * x2 + a3 * x3 + b
```

In NumPy array format, we can write this equation as follows:

```
y = np.dot(np.array([a1, a2, a3]), np.array([x1, x2, x3])) + b
```

For convenience, it makes sense to define the whole equation in a vector multiplication form. The coefficient of **b** is going to be **1**:

```
y = np.dot(np.array([b, a1, a2, a3]) * np.array([1, x1, x2, x3]))
```

Multiple linear regression is a simple scalar product of two vectors, where the coefficients **b**, **a1**, **a2**, and **a3** determine the best fit equation in four-dimensional space.

To understand the formula of multiple linear regression, you will need the scalar product of two vectors. As the other name for a scalar product is dot product, the NumPy function performing this operation is called dot:

```
import numpy as np
v1 = [1, 2, 3]
v2 = [4, 5, 6]
np.dot( v1, v2 ) = 1 * 4 + 2 * 5 + 3 * 6 = 32
```

We simply sum the product of each respective coordinate.

We can determine these coefficients by minimizing the error between data points and the nearest points described by the equation. For simplicity, we will omit the mathematical solution of the best fit equation, and use scikit-learn instead.

> **Note**
>
> In n-dimensional spaces, where n is greater than 3, the number of dimensions determines the different variables that are in our model. In the preceding example, we have three features and one label. This yields four dimensions. If you want to imagine a four-dimensional space, you can imagine three-dimensional space and time for simplification. A five-dimensional space can be imagined as a four-dimensional space, where each point in time has a temperature. Dimensions are just features (and labels); they do not necessarily correlate with our concept of three-dimensional space.

The Process of Linear Regression

We will follow the following simple steps to solve Linear Regression problems:

1. Load data from data sources.

2. Prepare data for prediction (normalize, format, filter).

3. Compute the parameters of the regression line. Regardless of whether we use linear regression with one variable or with multiple variables, we will follow these steps.

Importing Data from Data Sources

There are multiple libraries that can provide us with access to data sources. As we will be working with stock data, let's cover two examples that are geared toward retrieving financial data, Quandl and Yahoo Finance:

- scikit-learn comes with a few datasets that can be used for practicing your skills.

- Quandl.com provides you with free and paid financial datasets.

- pandas.io helps you load any .csv, .excel, .json, or SQL data.

- Yahoo Finance provides you with financial datasets.

Loading Stock Prices with Yahoo Finance

The process of loading stock data with Yahoo Finance is straightforward. All you need to do is install the fix_yahoo_finance package using the following command in the CLI::

```
pip install fix_yahoo_finance
```

We will download a dataset that has open, high, low, close, adjusted close, and volume values of the S&P 500 index, starting from 2015:

```
import fix_yahoo_finance as yahoo
spx_data_frame = yahoo.download("^GSPC", "2015-01-01")
```

That's all you need to do. The data frame containing the S&P 500 index is ready.

You can plot the index prices with the plot method:

```
spx_data_frame.Close.plot()
```

The output is as follows:

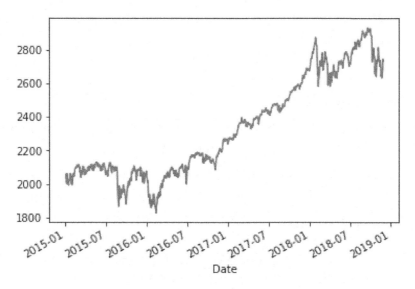

Figure 3.15: Graph showing stock prices for Yahoo Finance

It is also possible to save data to a CSV file using the following command:

```
spx.to_csv("spx.csv")
```

Loading Files with pandas

Suppose a CSV file containing stock data is given. We will now use pandas to load data from this file:

```
import pandas as pd

spx_second_frame = pd.read_csv("spx.csv", index_col="Date", header=0, parse_dates=True)
```

To properly parse data, we must set the index column name, specify the absence of headers, and make sure that dates are parsed as dates.

Loading Stock Prices with Quandl

Quandl.com is a reliable source of financial and economic datasets.

Exercise 8: Using Quandl to Load Stock Prices

1. Open the Anaconda prompt and install Quandl using the following command:

    ```
    pip install quandl
    ```

2. Go to https://www.quandl.com/.

3. Click on the Financial data.

4. Among the filters, click the checkbox next to the **Free** label. If you have a Quandl subscription, you can use that to download stock data.

5. Select a stock or index you would like to use. For our example, we will use the S&P Composite index data that was collected by the Yale Department of Economics. The link for this is https://www.quandl.com/data/YALE/SPCOMP-S-P-Composite.

6. Find the Quandl ticker belonging to your instrument you would like to load. Our Quandl code for the S&P 500 data is "**YALE/SPCOMP**".

7. Load the data from the Jupyter QtConsole:

    ```
    import quandl
    data_frame = quandl.get("YALE/SPCOMP")
    ```

8. All the columns of the imported values are features:

    ```
    data_frame.head()
    ```

9. The output is as follows:

    ```
                    S&P Composite  Dividend  Earnings        CPI  Long Interest
    Rate  \
    Year
    1871-01-31              4.44      0.26       0.4  12.464061
    5.320000
    1871-02-28              4.50      0.26       0.4  12.844641
    5.323333
    1871-03-31              4.61      0.26       0.4  13.034972
    5.326667
    1871-04-30              4.74      0.26       0.4  12.559226
    5.330000
    1871-05-31              4.86      0.26       0.4  12.273812
    5.333333


                    Real Price  Real Dividend  Real Earnings  \
    Year
    ```

1871-01-31	89.900119	5.264421	8.099110
1871-02-28	88.415295	5.108439	7.859137
1871-03-31	89.254001	5.033848	7.744382
1871-04-30	95.247222	5.224531	8.037740
1871-05-31	99.929493	5.346022	8.224650

	Cyclically Adjusted PE Ratio
Year	
1871-01-31	NaN
1871-02-28	NaN
1871-03-31	NaN
1871-04-30	NaN
1871-05-31	NaN
	...
2016-02-29	24.002607
2016-03-31	25.372299

Preparing Data for Prediction

Before we perform regression, we must choose the features we are interested in, and we also have to figure out the data range on which we do the regression.

Preparing the data for prediction is the second step in the regression process. This step also has several sub-steps. We will go through these sub-steps in the following order:

1. Suppose a data frame is given with preloaded data.

2. Select the columns from the dataset you are interested in.

3. Replace NaN values with a numeric value to avoid getting rid of data.

4. Determine the forecast interval T, determining the amount of time or number of data rows you wish to look into the future.

5. Create a label column out of the value you wish to forecast. For row i of the data frame, the value of the label should belong to the time instant, i+T.

6. For the last T rows, the label value is NaN. Drop these rows from the data frame.

7. Create NumPy arrays from the features and the label.

8. Scale the features array.

9. Separate the training and testing data.

A few features highly correlate to each other. For instance, the Real Dividend column proportionally grows with Real Price. The ratio between them is not always similar, but they do correlate.

As regression is not about detecting correlation between features, we would rather get rid of a few attributes we know are redundant and perform regression on the features that are non-correlated.

If you have gone through the Loading stock prices with Quandl section, you already have a data frame containing historical data on the S&P 500 Index. We will keep the Long Interest Rate, Real Price, and Real Dividend columns:

```
data_frame[['Long Interest Rate', 'Real Price', 'Real Dividend', 'Cyclically
Adjusted PE Ratio']]
```

As you cannot work with NaN data, you can replace it by filling in numbers in place of NaNs. In general, you have two choices:

- Get rid of the data

- Replace the data with a default value that makes sense

```
data_frame.fillna(-100, inplace=True)
```

We can check the length of the data frame by using the **len** function, as shown in the following code:

```
len(data_frame)
```

```
1771
```

The length of our data frame is 1771.

If we want to predict the Real Price for the upcoming 20 years, we will have to predict 240 values. This is approximately 15% of the length of the data frame, which makes perfect sense.

We will therefore create a Real Price Label by shifting the Real Price values up by 240 units:

```
data_frame['Real Price Label'] = data_frame['Real Price'].shift( -240 )
```

This way, each Real Price Label value will be the Real Price value in 20 years.

The side effect of shifting these values is that NaN values appear in the last 240 values:

```
data_frame.tail()
```

The output is as follows:

	S&P Composite	Dividend	Earnings	CPI	Long Interest Rate \
Year					
2018-03-31	2702.77	50.00	NaN	249.5540	2.840
2018-04-30	2653.63	50.33	NaN	250.5460	2.870
2018-05-31	2701.49	50.66	NaN	251.5880	2.976
2018-06-30	2754.35	50.99	NaN	252.1090	2.910
2018-07-31	2736.61	NaN	NaN	252.3695	2.830

	Real Price	Real Dividend	Real Earnings \
Year			
2018-03-31	2733.262995	50.564106	NaN
2018-04-30	2672.943397	50.696307	NaN
2018-05-31	2709.881555	50.817364	NaN
2018-06-30	2757.196024	51.042687	NaN
2018-07-31	2736.610000	NaN	NaN

	Cyclically Adjusted PE Ratio	Real Price Label
Year		
2018-03-31	31.988336	NaN
2018-04-30	31.238428	NaN
2018-05-31	31.612305	NaN
2018-06-30	32.091415	NaN
2018-07-31	31.765318	NaN

We can get rid of them by executing dropna on the data frame:

```
data_frame.dropna(inplace=True)
```

This way, we have data up to 1998 July, and we have the future values up to 2018 in the Real Price Label column:

```
data_frame.tail()
```

The output is as follows:

	S&P Composite	Dividend	Earnings	CPI	Long Interest Rate \
Year					
1998-03-31	1076.83	15.6400	39.5400	162.2	5.65
1998-04-30	1112.20	15.7500	39.3500	162.5	5.64
1998-05-31	1108.42	15.8500	39.1600	162.8	5.65
1998-06-30	1108.39	15.9500	38.9700	163.0	5.50
1998-07-31	1156.58	16.0167	38.6767	163.2	5.46

	Real Price	Real Dividend	Real Earnings \
Year			
1998-03-31	1675.456527	24.334519	61.520900
1998-04-30	1727.294510	24.460428	61.112245
1998-05-31	1718.251850	24.570372	60.705096
1998-06-30	1716.097117	24.695052	60.336438
1998-07-31	1788.514193	24.767932	59.808943

	Cyclically Adjusted PE Ratio	Real Price Label
Year		
1998-03-31	36.296928	2733.262995
1998-04-30	37.276934	2672.943397
1998-05-31	36.956599	2709.881555
1998-06-30	36.802293	2757.196024
1998-07-31	38.259645	2736.610000

Let's prepare our features and labels for regression.

For the features, we will use the drop method of the data frame. The drop method returns a new data frame that doesn't contain the column that was dropped:

```
import numpy as np
features = np.array(data_frame.drop('Real Price Label', 1))
label = np.array(data_frame['Real Price Label'])
```

The 1 in the second argument specifies that we are dropping columns. As the original data frame was not modified, the label can be directly extracted from it.

It is now time to scale the features with the preprocessing module of Scikit Learn:

```
from sklearn import preprocessing
scaled_features = preprocessing.scale(features)
```

```
features
array([[6.19000000e+00, 2.65000000e-01, 4.85800000e-01, ...,
         7.10000389e+00, 1.30157807e+01, 1.84739523e+01],
        [6.17000000e+00, 2.70000000e-01, 4.81700000e-01, ...,
         7.16161179e+00, 1.27768459e+01, 1.81472582e+01],
        [6.24000000e+00, 2.75000000e-01, 4.77500000e-01, ...,
         7.29423423e+00, 1.26654431e+01, 1.82701191e+01],
        ...,
        [1.10842000e+03, 1.58500000e+01, 3.91600000e+01, ...,
         2.45703721e+01, 6.07050959e+01, 3.69565985e+01],
        [1.10839000e+03, 1.59500000e+01, 3.89700000e+01, ...,
         2.46950523e+01, 6.03364381e+01, 3.68022935e+01],
        [1.15658000e+03, 1.60167000e+01, 3.86767000e+01, ...,
         2.47679324e+01, 5.98089427e+01, 3.82596451e+01]])
scaled_features
array([[-0.47564285, -0.62408514, -0.57496262, ..., -1.23976862,
         -0.84099698,  0.6398416 ],
        [-0.47577027, -0.62273749, -0.5754623 , ..., -1.22764677,
         -0.85903686,  0.57633607],
        [-0.47532429, -0.62138984, -0.57597417, ..., -1.20155224,
```

```
     -0.86744792,   0.60021881],
   ...,
   [ 6.54690076,   3.57654404,   4.13838295,  ...,   2.19766676,
     2.75960615,   4.23265262],
   [ 6.54670962,   3.60349707,   4.11522706,  ...,   2.22219859,
     2.73177202,   4.20265751],
   [ 6.85373845,   3.62147473,   4.07948167,  ...,   2.23653834,
     2.69194545,   4.48594968]])
```

As you can see, the scaled features are easier to read and interpret. While scaling data, we must scale all data together, including training and testing data.

Performing and Validating Linear Regression

Now that scaling is done, our next task is to separate the training and testing data from each other. We will be using 90% of the data as training data, and the rest (10%) will be used as test data:

```
from sklearn import model_selection
(features_train, features_test, label_train, label_test) =
    model_ selection.train_test_split(
        scaled_features, label, test_size=0.1
    )
```

The train_test_split function shuffles the lines of our data, keeping the correspondence, and puts approximately 10% of all data in the test variables, keeping 90% for the training variables. This will help us evaluate how good our model is.

We can now create the linear regression model based on the training data:

```
from sklearn import linear_model
model = linear_model.LinearRegression()
model.fit(features_train, label_train)
```

Once the model is ready, we can use it to predict the labels belonging to the test feature values:

```
label_predicted = model.predict(features_test)
```

If you are interested in the relationship between the predicted feature values and the accurate test feature values, you can plot them using a Python two-dimensional graph plotter utility:

```
from matplotlib import pyplot as plot
plot.scatter(label_test, label_predicted)
```

This gives you an image of a graph where the test data is compared to the results of the prediction. The closer these values are to the **y = x** line, the better.

You can see from the following graph that the predictions do center around the **y=x** line with a degree of error. This error is obvious, as otherwise, we would be able to make a lot of money with such a simple prediction, and everyone would pursue predicting stock prices instead of working in their own field of expertise:

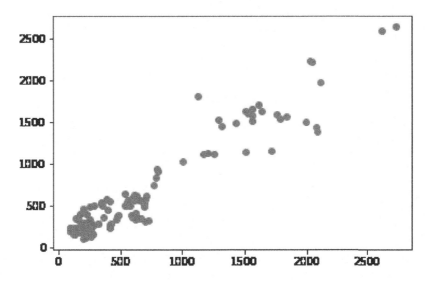

Figure 3.16: Graph for the plot scatter function

We can conclude that there is a degree of error in the model. The question is, how can we quantify this error? The answer is simple: we can score the model using a built-in utility that calculates the mean square error of the model:

```
model.score(features_test, label_test)
```

```
0.9051697119010782
```

We can conclude that the model is very accurate. This is not a surprise, because every single financial advisor scammer tends to tell us that the market grows at around 6-7% a year. This is a linear growth, and the model essentially predicts that the markets will continue growing at a linear rate. Making a conclusion that markets tend to go up in the long run is not rocket science.

Predicting the Future

We have already used prediction on test data. Now, it's time to use the actual data to see into the future.

```
import quandl

import numpy as np

from sklearn import preprocessing

from sklearn import model_selection

from sklearn import linear_model


data_frame = quandl.get("YALE/SPCOMP")


data_frame[['Long Interest Rate', 'Real Price', 'Real Dividend', 'Cyclically
Adjusted PE Ratio']]


data_frame.fillna(-100, inplace=True)


data_frame['Real Price Label'] = data_frame['Real Price'].shift(-240)


data_frame.dropna(inplace=True)


features = np.array(data_frame.drop('Real Price Label', 1))
label = np.array(data_frame['Real Price Label'])


scaled_features = preprocessing.scale(features)


(features_train, features_test, label_train, label_test) =
    model_ selection.train_test_split(
        scaled_features, label, test_size=0.1
```

```
    )

model = linear_model.LinearRegression()
model.fit(features_train, label_train)


label_predicted = model.predict(features_test)
```

The trick to predicting the future is that we have to save the values belonging to the values we dropped when building the model. We built our stock price model based on historical data from 20 years ago. Now, we have to keep this data, and we also have to include this data in scaling:

```
import quandl
import numpy as np
from sklearn import preprocessing
from sklearn import model_selection
from sklearn import linear_model


data_frame = quandl.get("YALE/SPCOMP")
data_frame[['Long Interest Rate', 'Real Price', 'Real Dividend', 'Cyclically
Adjusted PE Ratio']]
data_frame.fillna(-100, inplace=True)
# We shift the price data to be predicted 20 years forward
data_frame[ 'Real Price Label'] = data_frame['Real Price'].shift(-240)


# Then exclude the label column from the features
features = np.array(data_frame.drop('Real Price Label', 1))


# We scale before dropping the last 240 rows from the
# features
scaled_features = preprocessing.scale(features)


# Save the last 240 rows before dropping them
scaled_features_latest_240 = scaled_features[-240:]
```

```
# Exclude the last 240 rows from the data used for model
# building
scaled_features = scaled_features[:-240]


# Now we can drop the last 240 rows from the data frame
data_frame.dropna(inplace=True)


# Then build the labels from the remaining data
label = np.array(data_frame['Real Price Label'])


# The rest of the model building stays
(features_train, features_test, label_train, label_test) =
    model_ selection.train_test_split(
        scaled_features, label, test_size=0.1
    )


model = linear_model.LinearRegression()
model.fit(features_train, label_train)
```

Now that we have access to the scaled values of the features from the last 20 years, we can now predict the index prices of the next 20 years using the following code:

```
label_predicted = model.predict(scaled_features_latest_240)
```

This sounds great in theory, but in practice, using this model for making money by betting on the forecast is by no means better than gambling in a casino. This is just an example model to illustrate prediction; it is definitely not sufficient to be used for short-term or long-term speculation on market prices.

If you look at the values, you can see why this prediction may easily backfire. First, there are a few negative values, which are impossible for indices. Then, due to a few major market crashes, linear regression made a doomsday forecast a point in the future, where the index will drop from more than 3,000 to literally zero within a year. Linear regression is not a perfect tool to look ahead 20 years based on limited data. Also, note that stock prices are meant to be close to time invariant systems. This means that the past does not imply any patterns in the future.

Let's output the prediction belonging to the first ten years:

```
from matplotlib import pyplot as plot

plot.plot(list(range(1,241)), label_predicted[:240])
```

The output is as follows:

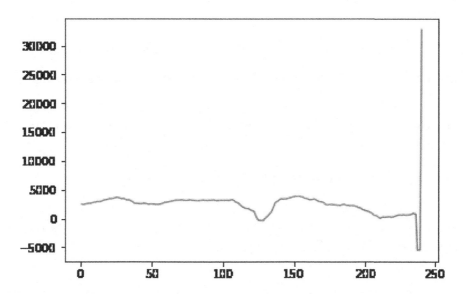

Figure 3.17: Graph for the plot function with a range of 1 to 241 and the label predicted as 240

The graph is hard to read near the end due to extreme values. Let's draw our conclusions by omitting the last five years and just plotting the first 180 months out of the predictions:

```
plot.plot(list(range(1,181)), label_predicted[:180])
```

The output is as follows:

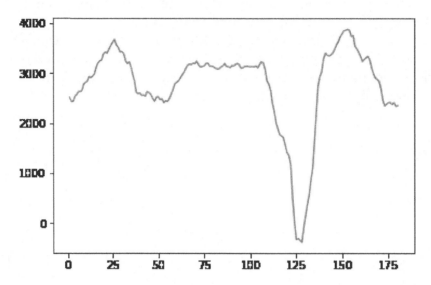

Figure 3.18: Graph for the plot function with a range of 1 to 181 and the label predicted as 180

This is a scary future for the American economy. According to this model, the S&P 500 has a bull run for about 2.5-3 years and doesn't recover for a long time. Also, notice that our model does not know that index values cannot be negative.

Polynomial and Support Vector Regression

When performing polynomial regression, the relationship between x and y, or using their other names, features and labels, is not a linear equation, but a polynomial equation. This means that instead of the **y** = **a*x+b** equation, we can have multiple coefficients and multiple powers of x in the equation.

To make matters even more complicated, we can perform polynomial regression using multiple variables, where each feature may have coefficients multiplying different powers of the feature.

Our task is to find a curve that best fits our dataset. Once polynomial regression is extended to multiple variables, we will learn the Support Vector Machines model to perform polynomial regression.

Polynomial Regression with One Variable

As a recap, we have performed two types of regression so far:

- Simple linear regression: y = a*x + b

- Multiple linear regression: y = b + a1 * x1 + a2 * x2 + … + an * xn

We will now learn how to do polynomial linear regression with one variable. The equation for polynomial linear regression is as follows:

y = b + a1*x + a2*(x ** 2) + a3*(x ** 3) + … + an * (x ** n)

have a vector of coefficients (b, a1, a2, …, an) multiplying a vector of degrees of x in the polynomial, (1, x**1, x**2, …, x**n).

At times, polynomial regression works better than linear regression. If the relationship between labels and features can be described using a linear equation, then using linear equation makes perfect sense. If we have a non-linear growth, polynomial regression tends to approximate the relationship between features and labels better.

The simplest implementation of linear regression with one variable was the **polyfit** method of the NumPy library. In the next exercise, we will perform multiple polynomial linear regression with degrees of 2 and 3.

> **Note**
>
> Even though our polynomial regression has an equation containing coefficients of x ** n, this equation is still referred to as polynomial linear regression in the literature. Regression is made linear not because we restrict the usage of higher powers of x in the equation, but because the coefficients a1, a2, …, and so on are linear in the equation. This means that we use the toolset of linear algebra, and work with matrices and vectors to find the missing coefficients that minimize the error of the approximation.

Exercise 9: 1st, 2nd, and 3rd Degree Polynomial Regression

Perform a 1st, 2nd, and 3rd degree polynomial regression on the following two datasets:

```
Declare the two datasets

import numpy as np

from matplotlib import pyplot as plot

# First dataset:

x1 = np.array(range(1, 14))

y1 = np.array([2, 8, 8, 18, 25, 21, 32, 44, 32, 48, 61, 45, 62])

# Second dataset:

x2 = np.array(range(1, 14))

y2 = np.array([0, 1, 1, 2, 3, 5, 8, 13, 21, 34, 55, 89, 144])
```

Then plot your results on the graph:

Let's start with plotting the first example:

```
import matplotlib.pyplot as plot
deg1 = np.polyfit(x1, y1, 1)
# array([ 4.85714286, -2.76923077])
f1 = np.poly1d(deg1)

deg2 = np.polyfit(x1, y1, 2)
# array([-0.03196803,  5.3046953 , -3.88811189])
f2 = np.poly1d(deg2)

deg3 = np.polyfit(x1, y1, 3)
# array([-0.01136364,  0.20666833,  3.91833167, -1.97902098])
f3 = np.poly1d(deg3)

plot.plot(
    x1, y1, 'o',
    x1, f1(x1),
    x1, f2(x1),
    x1, f3(x1)
 )
plot.show()
```

The output is as follows:

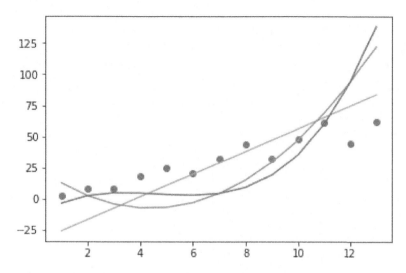

Figure 3.19: Graph showing the first dataset with linear curves

As the coefficients are enumerated from left to right in order of decreasing degree, we can see that the higher degree coefficients stay close to negligible. In other words, the three curves are almost on top of each other, and we can only detect a divergence near the right edge. This is because we are working on a dataset that can be very well approximated with a linear model.

In fact, the first dataset was created out of a linear function. Any nonzero coefficients for x**2 and x**3 are the results of overfitting the model based on the available data. The linear model is better for predicting values outside the range of the training data than any higher degree polynomial.

Let's contrast this behavior with the second example. We know that the Fibonacci sequence is non-linear. So, using a linear equation to approximate it is a clear case for underfitting. Here, we expect a higher degree polynomic to perform better:

```
deg1 = np.polyfit(x2, y2, 1)
# array([  9.12087912, -34.92307692])
f1 = np.poly1d(deg1)

deg2 = np.polyfit(x2, y2, 2)
# array([  1.75024975, -15.38261738,  26.33566434])
f2 = np.poly1d(deg2)

deg3 = np.polyfit(x2, y2, 3)
# array([0.2465035, -3.42632368, 14.69080919,
# -15.07692308])
```

```
f3 = np.poly1d(deg3)

plot.plot(
    x2, y1, 'o',# blue dots
    x2, f1(x2), # orange
    x2, f2(x2), # green
    x2, f3(x2)  # red
)
```

The output is as follows:

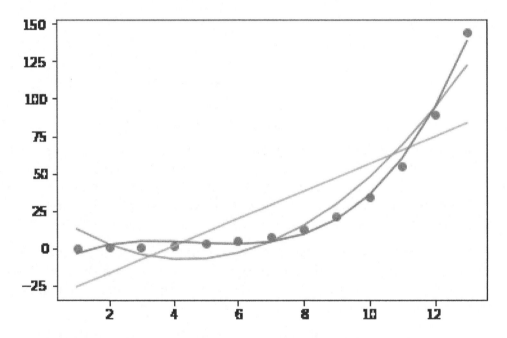

Figure 3.20: Graph showing second dataset points and three polynomial curves

The difference is clear. The quadratic curve fits the points a lot better than the linear one. The cubic curve is even better.

If you research Binet's formula, you will find out that the Fibonacci function is an exponential function, as the xth Fibonacci number is calculated as the xth power of a constant. Therefore, the higher degree polynomial we use, the more accurate our approximation will be.

Polynomial Regression with Multiple Variables

When we have one variable of degree n, we have n+1 coefficients in the equation:

```
y = b + a1*x + a2*(x ** 2) + a3*(x ** 3) + … + an * (x ** n)
```

Once we deal with multiple features x1, x2, …, xm, and their powers of up to the nth degree, we get an m * (n+1) matrix of coefficients. The math will become quite lengthy once we start exploring the details and prove how a polynomial model works. We will also lose the nice visualizations of two-dimensional curves.

Therefore, we will apply the chapters learned in previous section on polynomial regression with one variable and omit the math. When training and testing a Linear Regression model, we can calculate the mean square error to see how good an approximation a model is.

In scikit-learn, the degree of the polynomials used in the approximation is a simple parameter in the model.

As polynomial regression is a form of linear regression, we can perform polynomial regression without changing the regression model. All we need to do is transform the input and keep the linear regression model.

The transformation of the input is performed by the **fit_transform** method of the **PolynomialFeatures** package:

```
import numpy as np
import quandl
from sklearn import preprocessing
from sklearn import model_selection
from sklearn import linear_model
from matplotlib import pyplot as plot
from sklearn.preprocessing import PolynomialFeatures
```

```python
data_frame = quandl.get("YALE/SPCOMP")


data_frame.fillna(-100, inplace=True)


# We shift the price data to be predicted 20 years forward
data_frame['Real Price Label'] = data_frame['Real Price'].shift(-240)
# Then exclude the label column from the features
features = np.array(data_frame.drop('Real Price Label', 1))


# We scale before dropping the last 240 rows from the features
scaled_features = preprocessing.scale(features)


# Save the last 240 rows before dropping them
scaled_features_latest_240 = scaled_features[-240:]


# Exclude the last 240 rows from the data used for model building
scaled_features = scaled_features[:-240]


# Now we can drop the last 240 rows from the data frame
data_frame.dropna(inplace=True)


# Then build the labels from the remaining data
label = np.array(data_frame['Real Price Label'])


# Create a polynomial regressor model and fit it to the training data
poly_regressor = PolynomialFeatures(degree=3)
poly_scaled_features = poly_regressor.fit_transform(scaled_features)


# Split to training and testing data
(
```

```
    poly_features_train, poly_features_test,
    poly_label_train, poly_label_test
) = model_selection.train_test_split(
    poly_scaled_ features,
    label, test_size=0.1
)


# Apply linear regression
model = linear_model.LinearRegression()
model.fit(poly_features_train, poly_label_train)


# Model score
print('Score: ', model.score(poly_features_test, poly_label_test))


# Prediction
poly_label_predicted = model.predict(poly_features_test)
plot.scatter(poly_label_test, poly_label_predicted)
```

The model scores too well. Chances are, the polynomial model is overfitting the dataset.

There is another model in scikit-learn that performs polynomial regression called the SVM model, which stands for Support Vector Machines.

Support Vector Regression

Support Vector Machines are binary classifiers defined on a vector space. Vector Machines divide the state space with a surface. An SVM classifier takes classified data and tries to predict where unclassified data belongs. Once the classification of a data point is determined, it gets labeled.

Support Vector Machines can also be used for regression. Instead of labeling data, we can predict future values in a series. The Support Vector Regression model uses the space between our data as a margin of error. Based on the margin of error, it makes predictions regarding future values.

If the margin of error is too small, we risk overfitting the existing dataset. If the margin of error is too big, we risk underfitting the existing dataset.

A kernel describes the surface dividing the state space in the case of a classifier. A kernel is also used to measure the margin of error in the case of a regressor. This kernel can use a linear model, a polynomial model, or many other possible models. The default kernel is **RBF**, which stands for **Radial Basis Function**.

Support Vector Regression is an advanced topic, which is outside the scope of this book. Therefore, we will only stick to a walkthrough of how easy it is to try out another regression model on our test data.

Suppose we have our features and labels in two separate NumPy arrays. Let's recall how we performed linear regression on them:

```
from sklearn import model_selection
from sklearn import linear_model


(features_train, features_test, label_train,
 label_test) = model_selection.train_test_split(scaled_features, label,
test_size=0.1)


model = linear_model.LinearRegression()
model.fit(features_train, label_train)
```

We can perform regression with Support Vector Machines by changing the linear model to a support vector model:

```
from sklearn import model_selection
from sklearn import svm
from matplotlib import pyplot as plot


# The rest of the model building stays the same
(features_train, features_test, label_train,
 label_test) = model_selection.train_test_split(scaled_features, label,
test_size=0.1)
```

```
model = svm.SVR()
model.fit(features_train, label_train)


label_predicted = model.predict(features_test)


print('Score: ', model.score(features_test, label_test))


plot.plot(label_test, label_predicted, 'o')
```

The output is as follows:

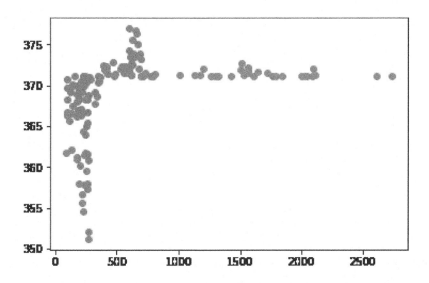

Figure 3.21: Graph showing Support Vector regression with a linear model

The output is as follows:

```
-0.19365084431020874
```

The model score is quite low, and the points don't align on the **y=x** line. Prediction with the default values is quite low.

The output of the model describes the parameters of the Support Vector Machine:

```
SVR(C=1.0, cache_size=200, coef0=0.0, degree=3, epsilon=0.1, gamma='auto',
kernel='rbf', max_iter=-1, shrinking=True, tol=0.001, verbose=False)
```

We could fiddle with these parameters to increase the accuracy of the prediction by creating a better algorithm.

Support Vector Machines with a 3 Degree Polynomial Kernel

Let's switch the kernel of the Support Vector Machine to poly. The default degree of the polynomial is 3:

```
model = svm.SVR(kernel='poly')

model.fit(features_train, label_train)

label_predicted = model.predict(features_test)

plot.plot(label_test, label_predicted, 'o')
```

The output is as follows:

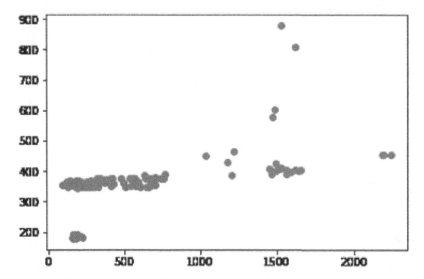

Figure 3.22: Graph showing Support Vector regression with a polynomial kernel of degree 3

```
model.score(features_test, label_test)
```

The output is as follows:

```
0.06388628722032952
```

With Support Vector Machines, we often end up with points concentrated in small areas. We could change the margin of error to separate the points a bit more.

Activity 6: Stock Price Prediction with Quadratic and Cubic Linear Polynomial Regression with Multiple Variables

In this section, we will discuss how to perform linear, polynomial, and support vector regression with scikit-learn. We will also learn how to find the best fit model for a given task. We will be assuming that you are a software engineer at a financial institution and your employer wants to know whether linear regression or support vector regression is a better fit for predicting stock prices. You will have to load all of the data of the S&P 500 from a data source. Then, you will need to build a regressor using linear regression, cubic polynomial linear regression, and a support vector regression with a polynomial kernel of degree 3 before separating the training and test data. Plot the test labels and the prediction results and compare them with the y=x line. Finally, compare how well the three models score.

1. Load the S&P 500 index data using Quandl, and then prepare the data for prediction.

2. Use a polynomial of degree 1 for the evaluation of the model and for the prediction.

   The closer the dots are to the y=x line, the less error the model works with.

   Perform a linear multiple regression with quadratic polynomials. The only change is in the Linear Regression model.

3. Perform Support Vector regression with a polynomial kernel of degree 3.

The model does not look efficient at all. For some reason, this model clearly prefers lower values for the S&P 500 that are completely unrealistic, assuming that the stock market does not lose 80% of its value within a day.

> **Note**
>
> The solution to this activity is available at page 271.

Summary

In this chapter, we have learned the fundamentals of Linear Regression.

After going through some basic mathematics, we dived into the mathematics of linear regression using one variable and multiple variables.

Challenges occurring with regression include loading data from external sources such as a .csv file, Yahoo Finance, or Quandl were dealt with. After loading the data, we learned how to identify the features and labels, how to scale data, and how to format data to perform regression.

We learned how to train and test a linear regression engine, and how to predict the future. Our results were visualized by an easy-to-use Python graph plotting library called `pyplot`.

A more complex form of linear regression is a linear polynomial regression of arbitrary degree. We learned how to define these regression problems on multiple variables. We compared their performance to each other on stock price prediction problems. As an alternative to polynomial regression, we also introduced Support Vector Machines as a regression model and experimented with two kernels.

You will soon learn about another field inside machine learning. The setup and code structure of this machine learning method will be very similar to regression, while the problem domain is somewhat different. In the next chapter, you will learn the ins and outs of classification.

Classification

Learning Objectives

By the end of this chapter, you will be able to:

- Describe the fundamental concepts of classification

- Load and preprocess data for classification

- Implement k-nearest neighbor and support vector machine classifiers

In chapter will focus on the goals of classification, and learn about k-nearest neighbors and support vector machines.

Introduction

In this chapter, we will learn about classifiers, especially the k-nearest neighbor classifier and support vector machines. We will use this classification to categorize data. Just as we did for regression, we will build a classifier based on training data, and test the performance of our classifier using testing data.

The Fundamentals of Classification

While regression focuses on creating a model that best fits our data to predict the future, classification is all about creating a model that separates our data into separate classes.

Assuming that you have some data belonging to separate classes, classification helps you predict the class a new data point belongs to. A classifier is a model that determines the label value belonging to any data point in the domain. Suppose you have a set of points, P = {p1, p2, p3, ..., pm}, and another set of points, Q = {q1, q2, q3, ..., qn}. You treat these points as members of different classes. For simplicity, we could imagine that P contains credit-worthy individuals, and Q contains individuals that are risky in terms of their credit repayment tendencies.

You can divide the state space so that all points in P are on one cluster of the state space, and then disjoint from the state space cluster containing all points in Q. Once you find these bounded spaces, called **clusters**, inside the state space, you have successfully performed **clustering**.

Suppose we have a point, x, that's not equal to any of the previous points. Does point x belong to cluster P or cluster Q? The answer to this question is a **classification exercise**, because we classify point x.

Classification is usually determined by proximity. The closer point x is to points in cluster P, the more likely it is that it belongs to cluster P . This is the idea behind nearest neighbor classification. In the case of k-nearest neighbor classification, we find the k-nearest neighbor of point x and classify it according to the maximum number of the nearest neighbors from the same class. Besides k-nearest neighbor, we will also use support vector machines for classification. In this chapter, we will be covering this credit scoring method in detail.

We could either assemble random dummy data ourselves, or we could choose to use an online dataset with hundreds of data points. To make this learning experience as realistic as possible, we will choose the latter. Let's continue with an exercise that lets us download some data that we can use for classification. A popular place for downloading machine learning datasets is https://archive.ics.uci.edu/ml/datasets.html. You can find five different datasets on credit approval. We will now load the dataset on German credit approvals, because the size of 1,000 data points is perfect for an example, and its documentation is available.

The german dataset is available in the CSV format

CSV stands for comma-separated values. A CSV file is a simple text file, where each line of the file contains a data point in your dataset. The attributes of the data point are given in a fixed order, separated by a separator character such as a comma. This character may not occur in the data, otherwise we would not know if the separator character is part of the data or serves as a separator. Although the name comma-separated values suggests that the separator character is a comma, it is not always the case. For instance, in our example, the separator character is a space. CSV files are used in many applications, including Excel. CSV is a great, lean interface between different applications.

Exercise 10: Loading Datasets

1. Visit https://archive.ics.uci.edu/ml/datasets/ Statlog+%28German+Credit+Data%29. The data files are located at https://archive. ics.uci.edu/ml/machine-learning-databases/statlog/german/.

   Load the data from the space-separated **german.data** file. Make sure that you add headers to your DataFrame so that you can reference your features and labels by name instead of column number.

   Save the **german.data** file locally. Insert header data into your CSV file.

   The first few lines of the dataset are as follows:

   ```
   A11 6 A34 A43 1169 A65 A75 4 A93 A101 4 A121 67 A143 A152 2 A173 1 A192
   A201 1
   A12 48 A32 A43 5951 A61 A73 2 A92 A101 2 A121 22 A143 A152 1 A173 1 A191
   A201 2
   A14 12 A34 A46 2096 A61 A74 2 A93 A101 3 A121 49 A143 A152 1 A172 2 A191
   A201 1
   ```

The explanation to interpret this data is in the `german.doc` file, where you can see the list of attributes. These attributes are: Status of existing checking account (A11 – A14), Duration (numeric, number of months), Credit history (A30 - A34), Purpose of credit (A40 – A410), Credit amount (numeric), Savings account/bonds (A61 – A65), Present employment since (A71 – A75), Disposable income percent rate (numeric), Personal status and sex (A91 – A95), Other debtors and guarantors (A101 – A103), Present residence since (numeric), Property (A121 – A124), Age (numeric, years), Other installment plans (A141 – A143), Housing (A151 – A153), Number of existing credits at this bank, Job (A171 – A174), Number of people being liable to provide maintenance for (numeric) Telephone (A191 – A192) and Foreign worker (A201 – A202).

The result of classification would be as follows: `1 means good debtor, while 2 means bad debtor`.

Our task is to determine how to separate the state space of twenty input variables into two clusters: good debtors and bad debtors.

2. We will use the pandas library to load the data. Before loading the data, though, I suggest adding a header to the `german.data` file. Insert the following header line before the first line:

```
CheckingAccountStatus DurationMonths CreditHistory CreditPurpose
CreditAmount SavingsAccount EmploymentSince DisposableIncomePercent
PersonalStatusSex OtherDebtors PresentResidenceMonths Property Age
OtherInstallmentPlans Housing NumberOfExistingCreditsInBank Job
LiabilityNumberOfPeople Phone ForeignWorker CreditScore
```

Notice that the preceding header is just one line, which means that there is no newline character until the end of the 21st label, `CreditScore`.

> **Note**
>
> The header is of help because pandas can interpret the first line as the column name. In fact, this is the default behavior of the **read_csv** method of pandas. The first line of the `.csv` file is going to be the header, and the rest of the lines are the actual data.

Let's import the CSV data using the **pandas.read_csv** method:

```
import pandas
data_frame = pandas.read_csv('german.data', sep=' ')
```

3. The first argument of **read_csv** is the file path. If you saved it to the E drive of your Windows PC, for instance, then you can also write an absolute path there: *e:\ german.data.*

Attributes	Cells
Status of existing checking account	(A11 – A14)
Duration	(numeric, number of months)
Credit history	(A30 - A34)
Purpose of credit	(A40 – A410)
Credit amount	(numeric)
Savings account/bonds	(A61 – A65)
Present employment since	(A71 – A75)
Disposable income percent rate	(numeric)
Personal status and sex	(A91 – A95)
Other debtors and guarantors	(A101 – A103)
Present residence since	(numeric)
Property	(A121 – A124)
Age	(numeric, years)
Other installment plans	(A141 – A143)
Housing	(A151 – A153)
Number of existing credits at this bank	(numeric)
Job	(A171 – A174)
Number of people being liable to provide maintenance for	(numeric)
Telephone	(A191 – A192)
Foreign worker	(A201 – A202)

Figure 4.1: Table displaying list of attributes in respective cells

Let's see the format of the data. The **data_frame.head()** call prints the first five rows of the CSV file, structured by the pandas DataFrame:

```
data_frame.head()
```

The output will be as follows:

```
   CheckingAccountStatus  DurationMonths CreditHistory CreditPurpose  \
0                    A11               6           A34           A43
. .
4                    A11              24           A33           A40

   CreditAmount SavingsAccount EmploymentSince  DisposableIncomePercent  \
0          1169            A65             A75                        4
. .
4          4870            A61             A73                        3

  PersonalStatusSex OtherDebtors    ...     Property Age  \
0               A93         A101    ...         A121  67
. .
```

```
4               A93      A101     . . .           A124  53

     OtherInstallmentPlans Housing NumberOfExistingCreditsInBank   Job  \
0                    A143    A152                              2  A173
. .
4                    A143    A153                              2  A173

     LiabilityNumberOfPeople  Phone ForeignWorker CreditScore
0                          1   A192          A201           1
. .
4                          2   A191          A201           2
```

[5 rows x 21 columns]

We have successfully loaded the data into the DataFrame.

Data Preprocessing

Before building a classifier, we are better off formatting our data so that we can keep relevant data in the most suitable format for classification, and removing all data that we are not interested in.

1. Replacing or dropping values

For instance, if there are **N/A** (or **NA**) values in the dataset, we may be better off substituting these values with a numeric value we can handle. NA stands for Not Available. We may choose to ignore rows with NA values or replace them with an outlier value. An outlier value is a value such as -1,000,000 that clearly stands out from regular values in the dataset. The replace method of a DataFrame does this type of replacement. The replacement of NA values with an outlier looks as follows:

```
data_frame.replace('NA', -1000000, inplace=True)
```

The replace method changes all NA values to numeric values.

This numeric value should be far from any reasonable values in the DataFrame. Minus one million is recognized by the classifier as an exception, assuming that only positive values are there.

The alternative to replacing unavailable data with extreme values is dropping the rows that have unavailable data:

```
data_frame.dropna(0, inplace=True)
```

The first argument specifies that we drop rows, not columns. The second argument specifies that we perform the drop operation, without cloning the DataFrame. Dropping the NA values is less desirable, as you often lose a reasonable chunk of your dataset.

2. Dropping columns

If there is a column we do not want to include in the classification, we are better off dropping it. Otherwise, the classifier may detect false patterns in places where there is absolutely no correlation. For instance, your phone number itself is very unlikely to correlate with your credit score. It is a 9 to 12-digit number that may very easily feed the classifier with a lot of noise. So we drop the phone column.

```
data_frame.drop(['Phone'], 1, inplace=True)
```

The second argument indicates that we drop columns, not rows. The first argument is an enumeration of the columns we would like to drop. The **inplace** argument is so that the call modifies the original DataFrame.

3. Transforming data

Oftentimes, the data format we are working with is not always optimal for the classification process. We may want to transform our data into a different format for multiple reasons, such as the following:

- To highlight aspects of data we are interested in (for example, Minmax scaling or normalization)

- To drop aspects of data we are not interested in (for example, Binarization)

- Label encoding

Minmax scaling can be performed by the **MinMaxScaler** method of the scikit preprocessing utility:

```
from sklearn import preprocessing
data = np.array([
    [19, 65],
    [4, 52],
    [2, 33]
])
preprocessing.MinMaxScaler(feature_range=(0,1)).fit_transform(data)
```

The output is as follows:

```
array([[1.          , 1.          ],
       [0.11764706, 0.59375    ],
       [0.          , 0.          ]])
```

MinMaxScaler scales each column in the data so that the lowest number in the column becomes 0, the highest number becomes 1, and all of the values in between are proportionally scaled between zero and one.

Binarization transforms data into ones and zeros based on a condition:

```
preprocessing.Binarizer(threshold=10).transform(data)
array([[1, 1],
       [0, 1],
       [0, 1]])
```

Label encoding is important for preparing your features for scikit-learn to process. While some of your features are string labels, scikit-learn expects this data to be numbers.

This is where the preprocessing library of scikit-learn comes into play.

> **Note**
>
> You might have noticed that in the credit scoring example, there were two data files. One contained labels in string form, and the other in integer form. I asked you to load the data with string labels on purpose so that you got some experience of how to preprocess data properly with the label encoder.

Label encoding is not rocket science. It creates a mapping between string labels and numeric values so that we can supply numbers to scikit-learn:

```
from sklearn import preprocessing
labels = ['Monday', 'Tuesday', 'Wednesday', 'Thursday', 'Friday']
label_encoder = preprocessing.LabelEncoder()
label_encoder.fit(labels)
```

Let's enumerate the encoding:

```
[x for x in enumerate(label_encoder.classes_)]
```

The output will be as follows:

```
[(0, 'Friday'),
 (1, 'Monday'),
 (2, 'Thursday'),
 (3, 'Tuesday'),
 (4, 'Wednesday')]
```

We can use the encoder to transform values:

```
encoded_values = label_encoder.transform(['Wednesday', 'Friday'])
```

The output will be as follows:

```
array([4, 0], dtype=int64)
```

The inverse transformation that transforms encoded values back to labels is performed by the **inverse_transform** function:

```
label_encoder.inverse_transform([0, 4])
```

The output will be as follows:

```
array(['Wednesday', 'Friday'], dtype='<U9')
```

Exercise 11: Pre-Processing Data

In this exercise, we will use a dataset with pandas.

1. Load the CSV data of the 2017-2018 January kickstarter projects from https://github.com/TrainingByPackt/Artificial-Intelligence-and-Machine-Learning-Fundamentals/blob/master/Lesson04/Exercise%2011%20Pre-processing%20Data/ks-projects-201801.csv and apply the preprocessing steps on the loaded data.

> **Note**
>
> Note that you need a working internet connection to complete this exercise.

2. If you open the file, you will see that you don't have to bother adding a header, because it is included in the CSV file:

```
ID,name,category,main_
category,currency,deadline,goal,launched,pledged,state,
backers,country,usd pledged,usd_pledged_real,usd_goal_real
```

3. Import the data and create a DataFrame using pandas:

```
import pandas
data_frame = pandas.read_csv('ks-projects-201801.csv', sep=',')
data_frame.head()
```

4. The previous command prints the first five entries belonging to the dataset. We can see the name and format of each column. Now that we have the data, it's time to perform some preprocessing steps.

5. Suppose you have some NA or N/A values in the dataset. You can replace them with the following **replace** operations:

```
data_frame.replace('NA', -1000000, inplace=True)
data_frame.replace('N/A', -1000000, inplace=True)
```

6. When performing classification or regression, keeping the ID column is just asking for trouble. In most cases, the ID does not correlate with the end result. Therefore, it makes sense to drop the ID column:

```
data_frame.drop(['ID'], 1, inplace=True)
```

7. Suppose we are only interested in whether the projects had backers or not. This is a perfect case for binarization:

```
from sklearn import preprocessing
preprocessing.Binarizer(threshold=1).transform([data_frame['backers']])
```

8. The output will be as follows:

```
array([[0, 1, 1, ..., 0, 1, 1]], dtype=int64)
```

> **Note**
>
> We are discarding the resulting binary array. To make use of the binary data, we would have to replace the backers column with it. We will omit this step for simplicity.

9. Let's encode the labels so that they become numeric values that can be interpreted by the classifier:

```
labels = ['AUD', 'CAD', 'CHF', 'DKK', 'EUR', 'GBP', 'HKD', 'JPY', 'MXN',
'NOK', 'NZD', 'SEK', 'SGD', 'USD']
label_encoder = preprocessing.LabelEncoder()
label_encoder.fit(labels)
label_encoder.transform(data_frame['currency'])
```

10. The output will be as follows:

```
array([ 5, 13, 13, ..., 13, 13, 13], dtype=int64)
```

You have to know about all possible labels that can occur in your file. The documentation is responsible for providing you with the available options. In the unlikely case that the documentation is not available for you, you have to reverse engineer the possible values from the file.

Once the encoded array is returned, the same problem holds as in the previous point: we have to make use of these values by replacing the **currency** column of the DataFrame with these new values.

Minmax Scaling of the Goal Column

When Minmax scaling was introduced, you saw that instead of scaling the values of each vector in a matrix, the values of each coordinate in each vector were scaled together. This is how the matrix structure describes a dataset. One vector contains all attributes of a data point. When scaling just one attribute, we have to transpose the column we wish to scale.

You learned about the transpose operation of NumPy in *Chapter 1, Principles of Artificial Intelligence*:

```
import numpy as np

values_to_scale = np.mat([data_frame['goal']]).transpose()
```

Then, we have to apply the **MinMaxScaler** to scale the transposed values. To get the results in one array, we can transpose the results back to their original form:

```
preprocessing

    .MinMaxScaler(feature_range=(0,1))

    .fit_transform(values_to_scale)

    .transpose()
```

The output is as follows:

```
array([[9.999900e-06, 2.999999e-04, 4.499999e-04, ..., 1.499999e-04,
1.499999e-04, 1.999990e-05]])
```

The values look weird because there were some high goals on Kickstarter, possibly using seven figure values. Instead of linear Minmax scaling, it is also possible to use the magnitude and scale logarithmically, counting how many digits the goal price has. This is another transformation that could make sense for reducing the complexity of the classification exercise.

As always, you have to place the results in the corresponding column of the DataFrame to make use of the transformed values.

We will stop preprocessing here. Hopefully, the usage of these different methods is now clear, and you will have a strong command of using these preprocessing methods in the future.

Identifying Features and Labels

Similar to regression, in classification, we must also separate our features and labels. Continuing from the original example, our features are all columns, except the last one, which contains the result of the credit scoring. Our only label is the credit scoring column.

We will use NumPy arrays to store our features and labels:

```
import numpy as np

features = np.array(data_frame.drop(['CreditScore'], 1))

label = np.array(data_frame['CreditScore'])
```

Now that we are ready with our features and labels, we can use this data for cross-validation.

Cross-Validation with scikit-learn

Another pertinent point about regression is that we can use cross-validation to train and test our model. This process is exactly the same as in the case of regression problems:

```
from sklearn import model_selection

features_train, features_test, label_train, label_test =
    model_selection.train_test_split(
        features,
        label,
```

```
    test_size=0.1
)
```

The **train_test_split** method shuffles and then splits our features and labels into a training dataset and a testing dataset. We can specify the size of the testing dataset as a number between **0** and **1**. A **test_size** of **0.1** means that **10%** of the data will go into the testing dataset.

Activity 7: Preparing Credit Data for Classification

In this section, we will discuss how to prepare data for a classifier. We will be using **german.data** from https://archive.ics.uci.edu/ml/machine-learning-databases/statlog/german/ as an example and will prepare the data for training and testing a classifier. Make sure that all of your labels are numeric, and that the values are prepared for classification. Use 80% of the data points as training data:

1. Save **german.data** from https://archive.ics.uci.edu/ml/machine-learning-databases/statlog/german/ and open it in a text editor such as Sublime Text or Atom. Add the header row to it.

2. Import the data file using pandas and replace the NA values with an outlier value.

3. Perform label encoding. Transform all of the labels in the data frame into integers.

4. Separate features from labels. We can apply the same method as the one we saw in the theory section.

5. Perform scaling of the training and testing data together. Use **MinMaxScaler** from Scikit's Preprocessing library.

6. The final step is cross-validation. Shuffle our data and use 80% of all data for training and 20% for testing.

> **Note**
>
> The solution to this activity is available at page 276.

The k-nearest neighbor Classifier

We will continue from where we left off in the first topic. We have training and testing data, and it is now time to prepare our classifier to perform k-nearest neighbor classification. After introducing the K-Nearest Neighbor algorithm, we will use scikit-learn to perform classification.

Introducing the K-Nearest Neighbor Algorithm

The goal of classification algorithms is to divide data so that we can determine which data points belong to which region. Suppose that a set of classified points is given. Our task is to determine which class a new data point belongs to.

The k-nearest neighbor classifier receives classes of data points with given feature and label values. The goal of the algorithm is to classify data points. These data points contain feature coordinates, and the objective of the classification is to determine the label values. Classification is based on proximity. Proximity is defined as a Euclidean distance. Point A is closer to point B than to point C if the Euclidean distance between A and B is shorter than the Euclidean distance between A and C.

The k-nearest neighbor classifier gets the k-nearest neighbors of a data point. The label belonging to point A is the most frequently occurring label value among the k-nearest neighbors of point A. Determining the value of K is a non-obvious task. Obviously, if there are two groups, such as credit-worthy and not credit-worthy, we need K to be 3 or greater, because otherwise, with K=2, we could easily have a tie between the number of neighbors. In general, though, the value of K does not depend on the number of groups or the number of features.

A special case of k-nearest neighbors is when K=1. In this case, the classification boils down to finding the nearest neighbor of a point. K=1 most often gives us significantly worse results than K=3 or greater.

Distance Functions

Many distance metrics could work with the k-nearest neighbor algorithm. We will now calculate the Euclidean and the Manhattan distance of two data points. The Euclidean distance is a generalization of the way we calculate the distance of two points in the plane or in a three-dimensional space.

The distance between points A = (a1, a2, …, an) and B=(b1, b2, …, bn) is the length of the line segment connecting these two points:

$$\text{distance}(a, b) = \sqrt{\sum_{i=1}^{n} (a_i - b_i)^2}$$

Figure 4.2: Distance between points A and B

Technically, we don't need to calculate the square root when we are just looking for the nearest neighbors, because the square root is a monotone function.

As we will use the Euclidean distance in this book, let's see how to calculate the distance of multiple points using one scikit-learn function call. We have to import **euclidean_distances** from **sklearn.metrics.pairwise**. This function accepts two sets of points and returns a matrix that contains the pairwise distance of each point from the first and the second sets of points:

```
from sklearn.metrics.pairwise import euclidean_distances
points = [[2,3], [3,7], [1,6]]
euclidean_distances([[4,4]], points)
```

The output is as follows:

```
array([[2.23606798, 3.16227766, 3.60555128]])
```

For instance, the distance of (4,4) and (3,7) is approximately 3.162.

We can also calculate the Euclidean distances between points in the same set:

```
euclidean_distances(points)
array([[0.        , 4.12310563, 3.16227766],
       [4.12310563, 0.        , 2.23606798],
       [3.16227766, 2.23606798, 0.        ]])
```

The Manhattan/Hamming Distance

The Hamming and Manhattan distances represent the same formula.

The Manhattan distance relies on calculating the absolute value of the difference of the coordinates of the data points:

$$\text{distance}(a, b) = \sum_{i=1}^{n} |a_i - b_i|$$

Figure 4.3: The Manhattan and Hamming Distance

The Euclidean distance is a more accurate generalization of distance, while the Manhattan distance is slightly easier to calculate.

Exercise 12: Illustrating the K-nearest Neighbor Classifier Algorithm

Suppose we have a list of employee data. Our features are the numbers of hours worked per week and yearly salary. Our label indicates whether an employee has stayed with our company for more than two years. The length of stay is represented by a zero if it is less than two years, and a one in case it is greater than or equal to two years.

We would like to create a 3-nearest neighbor classifier that determines whether an employee stays with our company for at least two years.

Then, we would like to use this classifier to predict whether an employee with a request to work 32 hours a week and earning 52,000 dollars per year is going to stay with the company for two years or not.

The dataset is as follows:

```
employees = [
      [20, 50000, 0],
      [24, 45000, 0],
      [32, 48000, 0],
      [24, 55000, 0],
      [40, 50000, 0],
      [40, 62000, 1],
      [40, 48000, 1],
      [32, 55000, 1],
      [40, 72000, 1],
      [32, 60000, 1]
]
```

1. Scale the features:

```
import matplotlib.pyplot as plot
from sklearn import preprocessing
import numpy as np
from sklearn.preprocessing import MinMaxScaler
scaled_employees = preprocessing.MinMaxScaler(feature_range=(0,1))

    .fit_transform(employees)
```

The scaled result is as follows:

```
array([[0.       , 0.18518519, 0.       ],
       [0.2      , 0.       , 0.       ],
       [0.6      , 0.11111111, 0.       ],
       [0.2      , 0.37037037, 0.       ],
       [1.       , 0.18518519, 0.       ],
       [1.       , 0.62962963, 1.       ],
       [1.       , 0.11111111, 1.       ],
       [0.6      , 0.37037037, 1.       ],
       [1.       , 1.        , 1.       ],
       [0.6      , 0.55555556, 1.       ]])
```

It makes sense to scale our requested employee as well at this point: [32, 52000] becomes [(32-24)/(40 - 24), (52000-45000)/(72000 - 45000)] = [0.5, 0.25925925925925924].

2. Plot these points on a two-dimensional plane such that the first two coordinates represent a point on the plane, and the third coordinate determines the color of the point:

```
import matplotlib.pyplot as plot
[
    plot.scatter(x[0], x[1], color = 'g' if x[2] > 0.5 else 'r')
    for x in scaled_employees
] + [plot.scatter(0.5, 0.25925925925925924, color='b')]
```

The output is as follows:

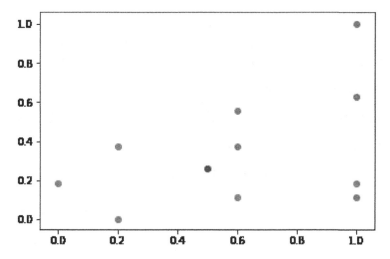

Figure 4.4: Points plotted on a two-dimensional plane

3. To calculate the distance of the blue point and all the other points, we will apply the transpose function from *Chapter 1, Principles of AI*. If we transpose the **scaledEmployee** matrix, we get three arrays of ten. The feature values are in the first two arrays. We can simply use the **[:2]** index to keep them. Then, transposing this matrix back to its original form gives us the array of feature data points:

```
scaled_employee_features = scaled_employees.transpose()[:2].transpose()
scaled_employee_features
```

The output is as follows:

```
array([[0.        , 0.18518519],
       [0.2       , 0.        ],
       [0.6       , 0.11111111],
       [0.2       , 0.37037037],
       [1.        , 0.18518519],
       [1.        , 0.62962963],
       [1.        , 0.11111111],
       [0.6       , 0.37037037],
       [1.        , 1.        ],
       [0.6       , 0.55555556]])
```

4. Calculate the Euclidean distance using:

```
from sklearn.metrics.pairwise import euclidean_distances
euclidean_distances(
    [[0.5, 0.25925925925925924]],
    scaled_employee_features
)
```

The output is as follows:

```
array([[0.50545719, 0.39650393, 0.17873968, 0.31991511, 0.50545719,
        0.62223325, 0.52148622, 0.14948471, 0.89369841, 0.31271632]])
```

The shortest distances are as follows:

- **0.14948471** for the point **[0.6, 0.37037037, 1.]**

- **0.17873968** for the point **[0.6, 0.11111111, 0.]**

- **0.31271632** for the point **[0.6, 0.55555556, 1.]**

As two out of the three points have a label of 1, we found two green points and one red point. This means that our 3-nearest neighbor classifier classified the new employee as being more likely to stay for at least two years than not at all.

> **Note**
>
> Although, the fourth point just missed the top three by a very small margin. In fact, our algorithm would have found a tie if there were two points of a different color that had the third smallest distance from the target. In case of a race condition in distances, there could be a tie. This is an edge case, though, which should almost never occur in real-life problems.

Exercise 13: k-nearest Neighbor Classification in scikit-learn

1. Split our data into four categories: **training** and **testing**, **features**, and **labels**:

    ```
    from sklearn import model_selection
    import pandas
    import numpy as np
    from sklearn import preprocessing
    features_train, features_test, label_train, label_test =
    model_selection.train_test_split(
        scaled_features,
        label,
        test_size=0.2
    )
    ```

2. Create a K-Nearest Neighbor classifier to perform this classification:

    ```
    from sklearn import neighbors
    classifier = neighbors.KNeighborsClassifier()
    classifier.fit(features_train, label_train)
    ```

    Since we have not mentioned the value of K, the default is 5.

3. Check how well our classifier performs on the test data:

    ```
    classifier.score(features_test, label_test)
    ```

    The output is **0.665**.

You might find higher ratings with other datasets, but it is understandable that more than 20 features may easily contain some random noise that makes it difficult to classify data.

Exercise 14: Prediction with the k-nearest neighbors classifier

This code is built on the code of previous exercise.

1. We'll create a data point that we will classify by taking the ith element of the ith test data point:

    ```
    data_point = [None] * 20
    for i in range(20):
        data_point[i] = features_test[i][i]
    data_point = np.array(data_point)
    ```

2. We have a one-dimensional array. The classifier expects an array containing data point arrays. Therefore, we must reshape our data point into an array of data points:

    ```
    data_point = data_point.reshape(1, -1)
    ```

3. With this, we have created a completely random persona, and we are interested in whether they are classified as credit-worthy or not:

    ```
    credit_rating = classifier.predict(data_point)
    ```

    Now, we can safely use prediction to determine the credit rating of the data point:

    ```
    classifier.predict(data_point)
    ```

    The output is as follows:

    ```
    array([1], dtype=int64)
    ```

We have successfully rated a new user based on input data.

Parameterization of the k-nearest neighbor Classifier in scikit-learn

You can access the documentation of the k-nearest neighbor classifier here: http://scikit-learn.org/stable/modules/generated/sklearn.neighbors.KNeighborsClassifier.html.

The parameterization of the classifier may fine-tune the accuracy of your classifier. Since we haven't learned all of the possible variations of k-nearest neighbor, we will concentrate on the parameters that you already understand based on this topic.

n_neighbors: This is the k value of the k-nearest neighbor algorithm. The default value is 5.

metric: When creating the classifier, you will see a weird name – "Minkowski". Don't worry about this name – you have learned about the first and second order Minkowski metric already. This metric has a power parameter. For $p=1$, the Minkowski metric is the same as the Manhattan metric. For $p=2$, the Minkowski metric is the same as the Euclidean metric.

p: This is the power of the Minkowski metric. The default value is 2.

You have to specify these parameters once you create the classifier:

```
classifier = neighbors.KNeighborsClassifier(n_neighbors=50)
```

Activity 8: Increasing the Accuracy of Credit Scoring

In this section, we will learn how the parameterization of the k-nearest neighbor classifier affects the end result. The accuracy of credit scoring is currently quite low: 66.5%. Find a way to increase it by a few percentage points. To ensure that this happens correctly, you will need to have done the previous exercises.

There are many ways to complete this exercise. In this solution, I will show you one way to increase the credit score, which will be done by changing the parameterization:

1. Increase the k-value of the k-nearest neighbor classifier from the default 5 to 10, 15, 25, and 50.

2. Run this classifier for all four **n_neighbors** values and observe the results.

3. Higher K values do not necessarily mean a better score. In this example, though, **K=50** yielded a better result than **K=5**.

> **Note**
>
> The solution to this activity is available at page 280.

Classification with Support Vector Machines

We first used support vector machines for regression in Chapter 3, *Regression*. In this topic, you will find out how to use support vector machines for classification. As always, we will use scikit-learn to run our examples in practice.

What are Support Vector Machine Classifiers?

The goal of a support vector machines defined on an n-dimensional vector space is to find a surface in that n-dimensional space that separates the data points in that space into multiple classes.

In two dimensions, this surface is often a straight line. In three dimensions, the support vector machines often finds a plane. In general, the support vector machines finds a hyperplane. These surfaces are optimal in the sense that, based on the information available to the machine, it optimizes the separation of the n-dimensional spaces.

The optimal separator found by the support vector machines is called the **best separating hyperplane**.

A support vector machines is used to find one surface that separates two sets of data points. In other words, support vector machines are **binary classifiers**. This does not mean that support vector machines can only be used for binary classification. Although we were only talking about one plane, support vector machines can be used to partition a space into any number of classes by generalizing the task itself.

The separator surface is optimal in the sense that it maximizes the distance of each data point from the separator surface.

A vector is a mathematical structure defined on an n-dimensional space having a magnitude (length) and a direction. In two dimensions, you draw the vector (x, y) from the origin to the point (x, y). Based on geometry, you can calculate the length of the vector using the Pythagorean theorem, and the direction of the vector by calculating the angle between the horizontal axis and the vector.

For instance, in two dimensions, the vector (3, -4) has the following magnitude:

```
sqrt( 3 * 3 + 4 * 4 ) = sqrt( 25 ) = 5
```

And it has the following direction:

```
np.arctan(-4/3) / 2 / np.pi * 360 = -53.13010235415597 degrees
```

Understanding Support Vector Machines

Suppose that two sets of points, **Red** and **Blue**, are given. For simplicity, we can imagine a two-dimensional plane with two features: one mapped on the horizontal axis, and one on the vertical axis.

The objective of the support vector machine is to find the best separating line that separates points **A**, **D**, **C**, **B**, and **H** from points **E**, **F**, and **G**:

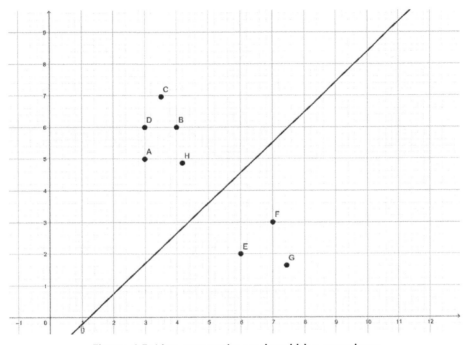

Figure 4.5: Line separating red and blue members

Separation is not always that obvious. For instance, if there is a blue point in between
E, F, and G, there is no line that could separate all points without errors. If points in the
blue class form a full circle around the points in the red class, there is no straight line
that could separate the two sets:

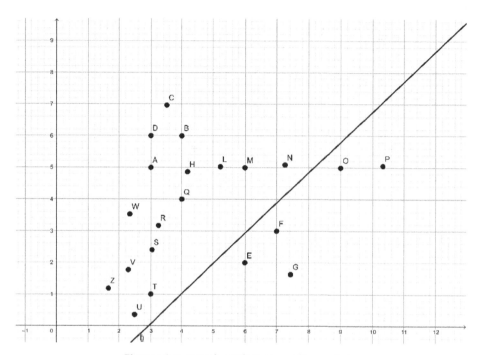

Figure 4.6: Graph with two outlier points

For instance, in the preceding graph, we tolerate two outlier points, O and P.

In the following solution, we do not tolerate outliers, and instead of a line, we create a best separating path consisting of two half lines:

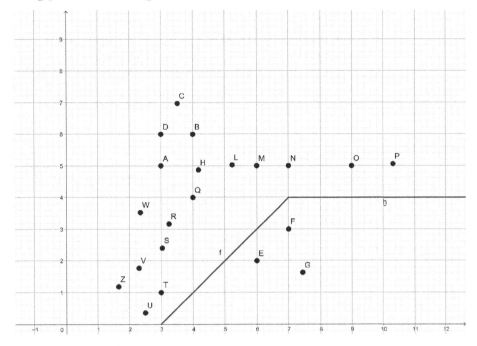

Figure 4.7: Graph removing the separation of the two outliers

A perfect separation of all data points is rarely worth the resources. Therefore, the support vector machine can be regularized to simplify and restrict the definition of the best separating shape and to allow outliers.

The **regularization parameter** of a support vector machine determines the rate of error to allow or forbid misclassifications.

A support vector machine has a kernel parameter. A linear kernel strictly uses a linear equation for describing the best separating hyperplane. A polynomial kernel uses a polynomial, while an exponential kernel uses an exponential expression to describe the hyperplane.

A margin is an area centered around the separator and is bounded by the points closest to the separator. A balanced margin has points from each class that are equidistant from the line.

When it comes to defining the allowed error rate of the best separating hyperplane, a gamma parameter decides whether only the points near the separator count in determining the position of the separator, or whether the points farthest from the line count, too. The higher the gamma, the lower the amount of points that influence the location of the separator.

Support Vector Machines in scikit-learn

Our entry point is the end result of previous activity. Once we have split the training and test data, we are ready to set up the classifier:

```
features_train, features_test, label_train, label_test = model_selection
    .train_test_split(
        scaled_features,
        label,
        test_size=0.2
    )
```

Instead of using the K-Nearest Neighbor classifier, we will use the **svm.SVC()** classifier:

```
from sklearn import svm
classifier = svm.SVC()
classifier.fit(features_train, label_train)
# Let's can check how well our classifier performs on the
# test data:
classifier.score(features_test, label_test)
```

The output is **0.745**.

It seems that the default support vector machine classifier of scikit-learn does a slightly better job than the k-nearest neighbor classifier.

Parameters of the scikit-learn SVM

The following are the parameters of the scikit-learn SVM:

Kernel: This is a string or callable parameter specifying the kernel used in the algorithm. The predefined kernels are linear, poly, rbf, sigmoid, and precomputed. The default value is rbf.

Degree: When using a polynomial, you can specify the degree of the polynomial. The default value is 3.

Gamma: This is the kernel coefficient for rbf, poly, and sigmoid. The default value is auto, computed as 1/`number_of_features`.

C: This is a floating-point number with a default of 1.0 describing the penalty parameter of the error term.

You can read about rest parameters in the reference documentation at http://scikit-learn.org/stable/modules/generated/sklearn.svm.SVC.html.

Here is an example of SVM:

```
classifier = svm.SVC(kernel="poly", C=2, degree=4, gamma=0.05)
```

Activity 9: Support Vector Machine Optimization in scikit-learn

In this section, we will discuss how to use the different parameters of a support vector machine classifier. We will be using, comparing, and contrasting the different support vector regression classifier parameters you have learned about and will find a set of parameters resulting in the highest classification data on the training and testing data that we loaded and prepared in the previous activity. To ensure that you can complete this activity, you will need to have completed the first activity of this chapter.

We will try out a few combinations. You may have to choose different parameters and check the results:

1. Let's first choose the linear kernel and check the classifier's fit and score.

2. Once you are done with that, choose the polynomial kernel of degree 4, C=2, and gamma=0.05 and check the classifier's fit and score.

3. Then, choose the polynomial kernel of degree 4, C=2, and gamma=0.25 and check the classifier's fit and score.

4. After that, select the polynomial kernel of degree 4, C=2, and gamma=0.5 and check the classifier's fit and score.

5. Choose the next classifier as sigmoid kernel.

6. Lastly, choose the default kernel with a gamma of 0.15 and check the classifier's fit and score.

> **Note**
>
> The solution for this activity can be found on page 280.

Summary

In this chapter, we learned the basics of classification. After discovering the goals of classification, and loading and formatting data, we discovered two classification algorithms: K-Nearest Neighbors and support vector machines. We used custom classifiers based on these two methods to predict values. In the next chapter, we will use trees for predictive analysis.

5

Using Trees for Predictive Analysis

Learning Objectives

By the end of this chapter, you will be able to:

- Understand the metrics used for evaluating the utility of a data model
- Classify datapoints based on decision trees
- Classify datapoints based on the random forest algorithm

In this chapter, we will learn about two types of supervised learning algorithm in detail. The first algorithm will help us to classify data points using decision trees, while the other algorithm will help us classify using random forests.

Introduction to Decision Trees

In decision trees, we have input and corresponding output in the training data. A decision tree, like any tree, has leaves, branches, and nodes. Leaves are the end nodes like a yes or no. Nodes are where a decision is taken. A decision tree consists of rules that we use to formulate a decision on the prediction of a data point.

Every node of the decision tree represents a feature and every edge coming out of an internal node represents a possible value or a possible interval of values of the tree. Each leaf of the tree represents a label value of the tree.

As we learned in the previous chapters, data points have features and labels. A task of a decision tree is to predict the label value based on fixed rules. The rules come from observing patterns on the training data.

Let's consider an example of determining the label values

Suppose the following training dataset is given. Formulate rules that help you determine the label value:

Employed	Income	LoanType	LoanAmount	CreditWorthy
true	75000	car	30000	No
false	25000	studies	15000	No
true	125000	car	30000	Yes
false	75000	car	30000	Yes
true	100000	studies	25000	Yes
true	100000	house	125000	Yes
false	80000	house	150000	Yes

Figure 5.1: Dataset to formulate the rules

In this example, we predict the label value based on four features. To set up a decision tree, we have to make observations on the available data. Based on the data that's available to us, we can conclude the following:

- All house loans are determined as credit-worthy.

- Studies loans are credit-worthy as long as the debtor is employed. If the debtor is not employed, he/she is not creditworthy.

- Loans are credit-worthy above 75,000/year income.

- At or below 75,000/year, car loans are credit-worthy whenever the debtor is not employed.

Depending on the order of how we take these rules into consideration, we can build a tree and describe one possible way of credit scoring. For instance, the following tree maps the preceding four rules:

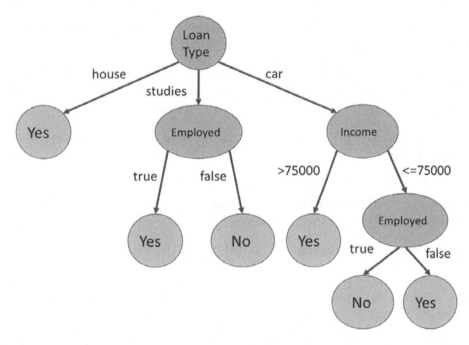

Figure 5.2: Decision Tree for the loan type

We first determine the loan type. House loans are automatically credit-worthy according to the first rule. Studies loans are described by the second rule, resulting in a subtree containing another decision on employment. As we have covered both house and studies loans, there are only car loans left. The third rule describes an income decision, while the fourth rule describes a decision on employment.

Whenever we have to score a new debtor to determine if he/she is credit-worthy, we have to go through the decision tree from top to bottom and observe the true or false value at the bottom.

Obviously, a model based on seven data points is highly inaccurate, because we can generalize rules that simply do not match reality. Therefore, rules are often determined based on large amounts of data.

This is not the only way that we can create a decision tree. We can build decision trees based on other sequences of rules, too. Let's extract some other rules from the Dataset in Figure 5.1.

Observation 1: Notice that individual salaries that are strictly greater than 75,000 are all credit-worthy. This means that we can classify four out of seven data points with one decision.

Rule 1: Income > 75,000 => CreditWorthy is true.

Rule 1 classifies four out of seven data points; we need more rules for the remaining three data points.

Observation 2: Out of the remaining three data points, two are not employed. One is employed and is not credit worthy. With a vague generalization, we can claim the following rule:

Rule 2: Assuming Income <= 75,000, the following holds: Employed == true => CreditWorthy is false.

The first two rules classify five data points. Only two data points are left. We know that their income is less than or equal to 75,000 and that none of them are employed. There are some differences between them, though:

- The credit-worthy person makes 75,000, while the non-credit-worthy person makes 25,000.

- The credit-worthy person took a car loan, while the non-credit-worthy person took a studies loan.

- The credit-worthy person took a loan of 30,000, while the non-credit-worthy person took a loan of 15,000

Any of these differences can be extracted into a rule. For discrete ranges, such as car, studies, and house, the rule is a simple membership check. In the case of continuous ranges such as salary and loan amount, we need to determine a range to branch off.

Let's suppose that we chose the loan amount as a basis for our third rule.

Rule 3:

Assuming `Income <= 75,000` and `Employed == false`,

If `LoanAmount <= AMOUNT`

Then `CreditWorthy` is `false`

Else `CreditWorthy` is `true`

The first line describes the path that leads to this decision. The second line formulates the condition, and the last two lines describe the result.

Notice that there is a constant AMOUNT in the rule. What should AMOUNT be equal to?

The answer is, any number is fine in the range 15,000 <= AMOUNT < 30,000. We are free to select any number. In this example, we chose the bottom end of the range:

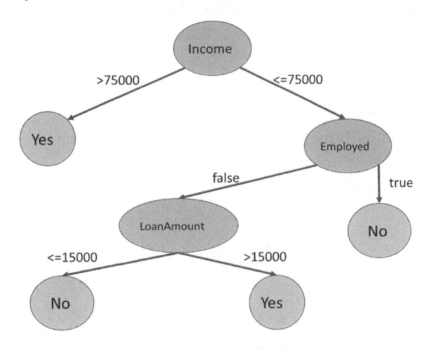

Figure 5.3: Decision Tree for Income

The second decision tree is less complex. At the same time, we cannot overlook the fact that the model says, "higher loan amounts are more likely to be repaid than lower loan amounts." It is also hard to overlook the fact that employed people with a lower income never pay back their loans. Unfortunately, there is not enough training data available, which makes it likely that we end up with false conclusions.

Overfitting is a frequent problem in decision trees when making a decision based on a few data points. This decision is rarely representative.

Since we can build decision trees in any possible order, it makes sense to define the desired way of algorithmically constructing a decision tree. Therefore, we will now explore a good measure for optimally ordering the features in the decision process.

Entropy

In information theory, entropy measures how randomly distributed the possible values of an attribute are. The higher the degree of randomness, the higher the entropy of the attribute.

Entropy is the highest possibility of an event. If we know beforehand what the outcome will be then the event has no randomness. So, entropy is zero.

When measuring the entropy of a system to be classified, we measure the entropy of the label.

Entropy is defined as follows:

- `[v1, v2, ..., vn]` are the possible values of an attribute

- `[p1, p2, ..., pn]` is the probability of these values occurring for that attribute assuming the values are equally distributed

- `p1 + p2 + ... + pn = 1`

$$H(\text{distribution}) = \sum_{i=0}^{n} -p_i \log_i p_i$$

Figure 5.4: Entropy Formula

The symbol of entropy is H in information theory. Not because entropy has anything to do with the h sound, but because H is the symbol for the upper-case Greek letter eta. Eta is, the symbol of entropy.

> **Note**
>
> We use entropy to order the nodes in the decision tree because the lower the entropy, the less randomly its values are distributed. The less randomness there is in the distribution, the more likely it is that the value of the label can be determined.

To calculate the entropy of a distribution in Python, we have to use the NumPy library:

```
import numpy as np
distribution = list(range(1,4))
minus_distribution = [-x for x in distribution]
log_distribution = [x for x in map(np.log2,distribution)]
entropy_value = np.dot(minus_distribution, log_distribution)
```

The distribution is given as a NumPy array or a regular list. On line 2, you have to insert your own distribution in place of [p1, p2, …, pn].

We need to create a vector of the negated values of the distribution in line 3.

On line 4, we must take the base 2 logarithm of each value in the distribution list

Finally, we calculate the sum with the scalar product, also known as the dot product of the two vectors.

Let's define the preceding calculation in the form of a function:

```
def entropy(distribution):
    minus_distribution = [-x for x in distribution]
    log_distribution = [x for x in map(np.log2, distribution)]
    return np.dot(minus_distribution, log_distribution)
```

> **Note**
>
> You first learned about the dot product in *Chapter 3, Regression*. The dot product of two vectors is calculated by multiplying the ith coordinate of the first vector by the ith coordinate of the second vector, for each i. Once we have all of the products, we sum the values:
>
> `np.dot([1, 2, 3], [4, 5, 6]) # 1*4 + 2*5 + 3*6 = 32`

Exercise 15: Calculating the Entropy

Calculate the entropy of the features in the dataset in *Figure 5.1*.

We will calculate entropy for all features.

1. We have four features: **Employed**, **Income**, **LoanType**, and **LoanAmount**. For simplicity, we will treat the values in **Income** and **LoanAmount** as discrete values for now.

2. The following is the distribution of values for **Employed**:

   `true 4/7 times`

   `false 3/7 times`

3. Let's use the entropy function to calculate the entropy of the Employed column:

   `H_employed = entropy([4/7, 3/7])`

   The output is `0.9852`.

4. The following is the distribution of values for **Income**:

   `25,000 1/7 times`

   `75,000 2/7 times`

   `80,000 1/7 times`

   `100,000 2/7 times`

   `125,000 1/7 times`

5. Let's use the entropy function to calculate the entropy of the Income column:

   `H_income = entropy([1/7, 2/7, 1/7, 2/7, 1/7])`

   The output is `2.2359`.

6. The following is the distribution of values for **LoanType**:

   `car 3/7 times`

   `studies 2/7 times`

   `house 2/7 times`

7. Let's use the entropy function to calculate the entropy of the LoanType column:

   `H_loanType = entropy([3/7, 2/7, 2/7])`

   The output is `1.5567`.

8. The following is the distribution of values for **LoanAmount**:

   `15,000 1/7 times`

   `25,000 1/7 times`

   `30,000 3/7 times`

   `125,000 1/7 times`

   `150,000 1/7 times`

9. Let's use the entropy function to calculate the entropy of the LoanAmount column:

   ```
   H_LoanAmount = entropy([1/7, 1/7, 3/7, 1/7, 1/7])
   ```

   The output is **2.1281**.

10. As you can see, the closer the distribution is to the uniform distribution, the higher the entropy.

11. In this exercise, we were cheating a bit, because these are not the entropies that we will be using to construct the tree. In both trees, we had conditions like "greater than 75,000". We will therefore calculate the entropies belonging to the decision points we used in our original trees as well.

12. The following is the distribution of values for **Income>75000**

    `true 4/7 times`

    `false 3/7 times`

13. Let's use the entropy function to calculate the entropy of the Income>75,000 column:

    ```
    H_incomeMoreThan75K = entropy([4/7, 3/7])
    ```

    The output is **0.9852**.

14. The following is the distribution of values for **LoanAmount>15000**

    `true 6/7 times`

    `false 1/7 times`

15. Let's use the entropy function to calculate the entropy of the **LoanAmount**
    >15,000 column:

    ```
    H_loanMoreThan15K = entropy([6/7, 1/7])
    ```

    The output is `0.5917`.

Intuitively, the distribution [1] is the most deterministic distribution. This is because we know for a fact that there is 100% chance that the value of a feature stays fixed.

```
H([1]) = 1 * np.log2( 1 ) # 1*0 =0
```

We can conclude that the entropy of a distribution is strictly non-negative.

Information Gain

When we partition the data points in a dataset according to the values of an attribute, we reduce the entropy of the system.

To describe information gain, we can calculate the distribution of the labels. Initially, we have five credit-worthy and two not credit-worthy individuals in our dataset. The entropy belonging to the initial distribution is as follows:

```
H_label = entropy([5/7, 2/7])
0.863120568566631
```

Let's see what happens if we partition the dataset based on whether the loan amount is greater than 15,000 or not.

- In group 1, we get one data point belonging to the 15,000 loan amount. This data point is not credit-worthy.

- In group 2, we have 5 credit-worthy and 1 non-credit-worthy individuals.

The entropy of the labels in each group is as follows:

```
H_group1 = entropy([1]) #0
H_group2 = entropy([5/6, 1/6]) #0.65
```

To calculate the information gain, let's calculate the weighted average of the group entropies:

```
H_group1 * 1/7 + H_group2 * 6/7 #0.55

Information_gain = 0.8631 - 0.5572 #0.30
```

When creating the decision tree, on each node, our job is to partition the dataset using a rule that maximizes the information gain.

We could also use Gini Impurity instead of entropy-based information gain to construct the best rules for splitting decision trees.

Gini Impurity

Instead of entropy, there is another widely used metric that can be used to measure the randomness of a distribution: Gini Impurity.

Gini Impurity is defined as follows:

$$\text{Gini(distribution)} = 1 - \sum_{i=0}^{n} p_i{}^2 |$$

Fig 5.5: Gini Impurity

For two variables, the Gini Impurity is:

$$\text{Gini}([p_1, p_2]) = 1 - (p_1^2 + p_2^2)$$

Fig 5.6: Gini Impurity for two variables

Entropy may be a bit slower to calculate because of the usage of the logarithm. Gini Impurity, on the other hand, is less precise when it comes to measuring randomness.

> **Note**
>
> Is information gain with entropy or Gini Impurity better for creating a decision tree?
>
> Some people prefer Gini Impurity, because you don't have to calculate with logarithms. Computation-wise, none of the solutions are particularly complex, and so both of them can be used. When it comes to performance, the following study concluded that there are often just minimal differences between the two metrics: https://www.unine.ch/files/live/sites/imi/files/shared/documents/papers/ Gini_index_fulltext.pdf.

We have learned that we can optimize a decision tree based on information gain or Gini Impurity. Unfortunately, these metrics are only available for discrete values. What if the label is defined on a continuous interval such as a price range or salary range?

We have to use other metrics. You can technically understand the idea behind creating a decision tree based on a continuous label, which was about regression. The metric we can reuse from this chapter is the mean squared error. Instead of Gini Impurity or information gain, we have to minimize the mean squared error to optimize the decision tree. As this is a beginner's book, we will omit this metric.

Exit Condition

We can continuously split the data points according to rule values until each leaf of the decision tree has an entropy of zero. The question is whether this end state is desirable.

Often, this state is not desirable, because we risk overfitting the model. When our rules for the model are too specific and too nitpicky, and the sample size on which the decision was made is too small, we risk making a false conclusion, thus recognizing a pattern in the dataset that simply does not exist in real life.

For instance, if we spin a roulette wheel three times and we get 12, 25, 12, concluding that every odd spin result in the value 12 is not a sensible strategy. By assuming that every odd spin equals 12, we find a rule that is exclusively due to random noise.

Therefore, posing a restriction on the minimum size of the dataset that we can still split is an exit condition that works well in practice. For instance, if you stop splitting as soon as you have a dataset that's lower than 50, 100, 200, or 500 in size, you avoid drawing conclusions on random noise, and so you minimize the risk of overfitting the model.

Another popular exit condition is a maximum restriction on the depth of the tree. Once we reach a fixed tree depth, we classify the data points in the leaves.

Building Decision Tree Classifiers using scikit-learn

We have already learned how to load data from a **.csv** file, how to apply preprocessing on the data, and how to split data into a training and testing dataset. If you need to refresh yourself on this knowledge, go back to previous chapters, where you go through this process in the context of regression and classification.

We will now assume that a set of training features, training labels, testing features, and testing labels are given as a return value of the scikit-learn train-test-split call.

Notice that, in older versions of scikit-learn, you have to import cross_validation instead of model selection:

```
features_train, features_test, label_train, label_test =
    model_selection.train_test_split(
        features,
        label,
        test_size=0.1
    )
```

We will not focus on how we got these data points, because the process is exactly the same as in the case of regression and classification.

It's time to import and use the decision tree classifier of scikit-learn:

```
from sklearn.tree import DecisionTreeClassifier
decision_tree = DecisionTreeClassifier(max_depth=6)
decision_tree.fit( features_train, label_train )
```

We set one optional parameter in the `DecisionTreeClassifier`, that is, `max_depth`, to limit the depth of the decision tree. You can read the official documentation for a full list of parameters: http://scikit-learn.org/stable/modules/generated/sklearn.tree. DecisionTreeClassifier.html. Some of the more important parameters are as follows:

- **criterion**: Gini stands for Gini Impurity, while entropy stands for information gain.

- **max_depth**: This is the maximum depth of the tree.

- **min_samples_split**: This is the minimum number of samples needed to split an internal node.

You can also experiment with all of the other parameters enumerated in the documentation. We will omit them in this topic.

Once the model has been built, we can use the decision tree classifier to predict data:

```
decision_tree.predict(features_test)
```

You will build a decision tree classifier in the activity at the end of this topic.

Evaluating the Performance of Classifiers

After splitting training and testing data, the decision tree model has a score method to evaluate how well testing data is classified by the model. We already learned how to use the score method in Chapters 3 and 4:

```
decision_tree.score(features_test, label_test)
```

The return value of the score method is a number that's less than or equal to 1. The closer we get to 1, the better our model is.

We will now learn another way to evaluate the model. Feel free to use this method on the models you constructed in the previous chapter as well.

Suppose we have one test feature and one test label:

```
# testLabel denotes the test label
predicted_label = decision_tree.predict(testFeature)
```

Suppose we are investigating a label value, positiveValue.

We will use the following definitions to define some metrics that help you evaluate how good your classifier is:

- **Definition (True Positive)**: `positiveValue == predictedLabel == testLabel`
- **Definition (True Negative)**: `positiveValue != predictedLabel == testLabel`
- **Definition (False Positive)**: `positiveValue == predictedLabel != testLabel`
- **Definition (False Negative)**: `positiveValue != predictedLabel != testLabel`

A false positive is a prediction that is equal to the positive value, but the actual label in the test data is not equal to this positive value. For instance, in a tech interview, a false positive is an incompetent software developer who got hired because he acted in a convincing manner, hiding his complete lack of competence.

Don't confuse a false positive with a false negative. Using the tech interview example, a false negative is a software developer who was competent enough to do the job, but he did not get hired.

Using the preceding four definitions, we can define three metrics that describe how well our model predicts reality. The symbol #(X) denotes the number of values in X. Using technical terms, #(X) denotes the cardinality of X:

Definition (Precision):

`#( True Positives ) / (#( True Positives ) + #( False Positives ))`

Definition (Recall):

`#( True Positives ) / (#( True Positives ) + #( False Negatives ))`

Precision centers around values that our classifier found to be positive. Some of these results are true positive, while others are false positive. A high precision means that the number of false positive results are very low compared to true positive results. This means that a precise classifier rarely makes a mistake when finding a positive result.

Recall that centers around values are positive among the test data. Some of these results are found by the classifier. These are the true positive values. Those positive values that are not found by the classifier are false negatives. A classifier with a high recall value finds most of the positive values.

Exercise 16: Precision and Recall

Find the precision and the recall value of the following two classifiers:

```
# Classifier 1
TestLabels1 = [True, True, False, True, True]
PredictedLabels1 = [True, False, False, False, False]
# Classifier 2
TestLabels2 = [True, True, False, True, True]
PredictedLabels = [True, True, True, True, True]
```

1. According to the formula let's calculate the number of true positives, false positives, and false negatives for classifier 1:

    ```
    TruePositives1 = 1 # both the predicted and test labels are true
    FalsePositives1 = 0 # predicted label is true, test label is false
    FalseNegatives1 = 3 # predicted label is false, test label is true
    Precision1 = TruePositives1 / (TruePositives1 + FalsePositives1)
    Precision1 # 1/1 = 1
    Recall1 = TruePositives1 / (TruePositives1 + FalseNegatives1)
    Recall1 #1/4 = 0.25
    ```

2. The first classifier has excellent precision, but bad recall. Let's calculate the same for the second classifier.

    ```
    TruePositives2 = 4
    FalsePositives2 = 1
    FalseNegatives2 = 0
    Precision2 = TruePositives2 / (TruePositives2 + FalsePositives2)
    Precision2 #4/5 = 0.8
    Recall2 = TruePositives2 / (TruePositives2 + FalseNegatives2)
    Recall2 # 4/4 = 1
    ```

3. The second classifier has excellent recall, but its precision is not perfect.

4. The F1 score is the harmonic mean of precision and recall. Its value ranges between 0 and 1. The advantage of the F1 score is that it considers both false positives and false negatives.

Exercise 17: Calculating the F1 Score

Calculate the F1 Score of the two classifiers from the previous exercise:

1. The formula for calculating the F1 Score is as follows:

    ```
    2*Precision*Recall / (Precision + Recall)
    ```

2. The first classifier has the following F1 Score:

    ```
    2 * 1 * 0.25 / (1 + 0.25) # 0.4
    ```

3. The second classifier has the following F1 Score:

    ```
    2 * 0.8 * 1 / (0.8 + 1) # 0.888888888888889
    ```

Now that we know what precision, recall, and F1 score mean, let's use a scikit-learn utility to calculate and print these values:

```
from sklearn.metrics import classification_report

print(
    classification_report(
        label_test,
        decision_tree.predict(features_test)
    )
)
```

The output will be as follows:

	precision	recall	f1-score	support
0	0.97	0.97	0.97	36
1	1.00	1.00	1.00	5
2	1.00	0.99	1.00	127
3	0.83	1.00	0.91	5
avg / total	0.99	0.99	0.99	173

In this example, there are four possible label values, denoted by 0, 1, 2, and 3. In each row, you get a precision, recall, and F1 score value belonging to each possible label value. You can also see in the support column how many of these label values exist in the dataset. The last row contains an aggregated precision, recall, and f1-score.

If you used label encoding to encode string labels to numbers, you may want to perform an inverse transformation to find out which row belongs to which label. In the following example, Class is the name of the label, and **labelEncoders['Class']** is the label encoder belonging to the Class label:

```
labelEncoders['Class'].inverse_transform([0, 1, 2, 3])

array(['acc', 'good', 'unacc', 'vgood'])
```

If you prefer calculating the precision, recall, and F1 Score on its own, you can use individual calls. Note that in the next example, we will call each score function twice: once with **average=None**, and once with **average='weighted'**.

When the average is specified as None, we get the score value belonging to each possible label value. You can see the same values rounded in the table if you compare the results to the first four values of the corresponding column.

When the average is specified as weighted, you get the cell value belonging to the column of the score name and the avg/total row:

```
from sklearn.metrics import recall_score, precision_score, f1_score

label_predicted = decision_tree.predict(features_test)
```

Calculating the precision score with no average can be done like so:

```
precision_score(label_test, label_predicted, average=None)
```

The output is as follows:

```
array([0.97222222, 1.        , 1.        , 0.83333333])
```

Calculating the precision score with a weighted average can be done like so:

```
precision_score(label_test, label_predicted, average='weighted')
```

The output is **0.989402697495183**.

Calculating the recall score with no average can be done like so:

```
recall_score(label_test, label_predicted, average=None)
```

The output is as follows:

```
array([0.97222222, 1.        , 0.99212598, 1.        ])
```

Calculating the recall score with a weighted average can be done like so:

```
recall_score(label_test, label_predicted, average='weighted')
```

The output is **0.9884393063583815**.

Calculating the f1_score with no average can be done like so:

```
f1_score(label_test, label_predicted, average=None)
```

The output is as follows:

```
array([0.97222222, 1.        , 0.99604743, 0.90909091])
```

Calculating the f1_score with a weighted average can be done like so:

```
f1_score(label_test, label_predicted, average='weighted')
```

The output is **0.988690625785373**.

There is one more score worth investigating: the accuracy score. Suppose #(Dataset) denotes the length of the total dataset, or in other words, the sum of true positives, true negatives, false positives, and false negatives.

Accuracy is defined as follows:

Definition (Accuracy): #(True Positives) + #(True Negatives) / #(Dataset)

Accuracy is a metric that's used for determining how many times the classifier gives us the correct answer. This is the first metric we used to evaluate the score of a classifier. Whenever we called the score method of a classifier model, we calculated its accuracy:

```
from sklearn.metrics import accuracy_score
accuracy_score(label_test, label_predicted )
```

The output is **0.9884393063583815**.

Calculating the decision tree score can be done like so:

```
decisionTree.score(features_test, label_test)
```

The output is **0.9884393063583815**.

Confusion Matrix

We will conclude this topic with one data structure that helps you evaluate the performance of a classification model: the confusion matrix.

A confusion matrix is a square matrix, where the number of rows and columns equals the number of distinct label values. In the columns of the matrix, we place each test label value. In the rows of the matrix, we place each predicted label value.

For each data point, we add one to the corresponding cells of the confusion matrix based on the predicted and actual label value.

Exercise 18: Confusion Matrix

Construct the confusion matrix of the following two distributions:

```
# Classifier 1
TestLabels1 = [True, True, False, True, True]
PredictedLabels1 = [True, False, False, False, False]
# Classifier 2
TestLabels2 = [True, True, False, True, True]
PredictedLabels = [True, True, True, True, True]
```

1. We will start with the first classifier. The columns determine the place of the test labels, while the rows determine the place of the predicted labels. The first entry is **TestLabels1[0]** and **PredictedLabels1[0]**. The values are true and true, and so we add 1 to the top-left column.

2. The second values are **TestLabels1[1] = True** and **PredictedLabels1[1] = False**. These values determine the bottom-left cell of the 2x2 matrix.

3. After finishing the placement of all five label pairs, we get the following confusion matrix:

	True	False
True	1	0
False	3	1

4. After finishing the placement of all five label pairs, we get the following confusion matrix:

	True	False
True	4	1
False	0	0

5. In a 2x2 matrix, we have the following distribution:

```
                 True              False
    True      TruePositives   FalsePositives
    False   FalseNegatives    TrueNegatives
```

6. The confusion matrix can be used to calculate precision, recall, accuracy, and f1_score metrics. The calculation is straightforward and is implied by the definitions of the metrics.

7. The confusion matrix can be calculated by scikit-learn:

```
from sklearn.metrics import confusion_matrix
confusion_matrix(label_test, label_predicted)
array([[ 25,   0,  11,   0],
       [  5,   0,   0,   0],
       [  0,   0, 127,   0],
       [  5,   0,   0,   0]])
```

8. Note that this is not the same example as the one we used in the previous section. Therefore, if you use the values inside the confusion matrix, you will get different precision, recall, and f1_score values.

9. You can also use pandas to create the confusion matrix:

```
import pandas
pandas.crosstab(label_test, label_predicted)


col_0   0     2
row_0
0       25    11
1        5     0
2        0   127
3        5     0
```

Let's verify these values by calculating the accuracy score of the model:

*   We have 127 + 25 = 152 data points that were classified correctly.

*   The total number of data points is 152 + 11 + 5 + 5 = 173.

*   152/173 is 0.8786127167630058.

Let's calculate the accuracy score by using the scikit-learn utility we used before:

```
from sklearn.metrics import accuracy_score

accuracy_score(label_test, label_predicted)
```

The output is as follows:

```
0.8786127167630058
```

We got the same value. All of the metrics can be derived from the confusion matrix.

Activity 10: Car Data Classification

In this section, we will discuss how to build a reliable decision tree model that's capable of aiding your company in finding cars that clients are likely to buy. We will be assuming that you are employed by a car rental agency who's focusing on building a lasting relationship with its clients. Your task is to build a decision tree model that classifies cars into one of four categories: unacceptable, acceptable, good, and very good.

The dataset for this activity can be accessed here: https://archive.ics.uci.edu/ml/datasets/Car+Evaluation. Click the Data Folder link to download the dataset. Then, click the Dataset Description link to access the description of the attributes.

Let's evaluate the utility of your decision tree model:

1. Download the car data file from here: https://archive.ics.uci.edu/ml/machine-learning-databases/car/car.data. Add a header line to the front of the CSV file so that you can reference it in Python easily. We simply call the label Class. We named the six features after their descriptions in https://archive.ics.uci.edu/ml/machine-learning-databases/car/car.names.

2. Load the dataset into Python and check if it has loaded properly.

   It's time to separate the training and testing data with the cross-validation (in newer versions, this is model-selection) feature of scikit-learn. We will use 10% test data.

   Note that the **train_test_split** method will be available in the **model_selection** module, and not in the **cross_validation** module, starting from scikit-learn 0.20. In previous versions, **model_selection** already contains the **train_test_split** method.

   Build the decision tree classifier.

3. Check the score of our model based on the test data.

4. Create a deeper evaluation of the model based on the `classification_report` feature.

> **Note**
>
> The solution to this activity is available at page 282.

Random Forest Classifier

If you think about the name Random forest classifier, it makes sense to conclude the following:

- A forest consists of multiple trees.

- These trees can be used for classification.

- Since the only tree we have used so far for classification is a decision tree, it makes sense that the random forest is a forest of decision trees.

- The random nature of the trees means that our decision trees are constructed in a randomized manner.

- As a consequence, we will base our decision tree construction on information gain or Gini Impurity.

Once you understand these basic concepts, you essentially know what a Random forest classifier is all about. The more trees you have in the forest, the more accurate prediction is going to be. When performing prediction, each tree performs classification. We collect the results, and the class that gets the most votes wins.

Random forests can be used for regression as well as for classification. When using random forests for regression, instead of counting the most votes for a class, we take the average of the arithmetic mean (average) of the prediction results and return it. Random forests are not as ideal for regression as they are for classification, though, because the models used to predict values are often out of control, and often return a wide range of values. The average of these values is often not too meaningful. Managing the noise in a regression exercise is harder than in classification.

Random forests are often better than one simple decision tree because they provide redundancy. They treat outlier values better and have a lower probability of overfitting the model. Decision trees seem to behave great as long as you are using them on data that you used when creating the model. Once you use them to predict new data, random forests lose their edge. Random forests are widely used for classification problems, whether it be customer segmentation for banks or e-commerce, classifying images, or medicine. If you own an Xbox with Kinect, your Kinect device contains a random forest classifier to detect your body parts.

Random Forest Classification and regression are ensemble algorithms. The idea behind ensemble learning is that we take an aggregated view over a decision of multiple agents that potentially have different weaknesses. Due to the aggregated vote, these weaknesses cancel out, and the majority vote likely represents the correct result.

Constructing a Random Forest

One way to construct the trees of a random forest is to limit the number of features used in the classification task. Suppose you have a feature set, F. The length of the feature set is #(F). The number of features in the feature set is dim(F), where dim stands for dimension.

Suppose we limit the training data to a different subset of size $s < \#(F)$, and each random forest receives a different training data set of size s. Suppose we specify that we will use $k < dim(F)$ features out of the possible features to construct a tree in the random forest. The selection of k features is chosen at random.

We construct each decision tree completely. Once we get a new data point to classify, we execute each tree in the random forest to perform the prediction. Once the prediction results are in, we count the votes, and the most voted class is going to be the class of the data point predicted by the random forest.

In random forest terminology, we describe the performance benefits of random forests with one word: bagging. Bagging is a technique that consists of bootstrapping and using aggregated decision making. Bootstrapping is responsible for creating a dataset that contains a subset of the entries of the original dataset. The size of the original dataset and the bootstrapped dataset is still the same because we are allowed to select the same data points multiple times in the bootstrapped dataset.

Out of bag data points are ones that don't end up in some bootstrapped datasets. To measure the out of bag error of a random forest classifier, we have to run all out of bag data points on trees of the random forest classifier that were built without considering the out of bag data points. The margin of error is the ratio between correctly classified out of bag data points and all out of bag data points.

Random Forest Classification Using scikit-learn

Our starting point is the result of the train-test splitting:

```
from sklearn import model_selection
features_train, features_test, label_train, label_test =
    model_selection.train_test_split(
        features,
        label,
        test_size=0.1
    )
```

The random forest classifier can be implemented as follows:

```
from sklearn.ensemble import RandomForestClassifier
random_forest_classifier = RandomForestClassifier(
    n_estimators=100,
    max_depth=6
)
randomForestClassifier.fit(features_train, label_train)
labels_predicted = random_forest_classifier.predict(features_test)
```

The interface of scikit-learn makes it easy to handle the random forest classifier. Throughout the last three chapters, we have already gotten used to this way of calling a classifier or a regression model for prediction.

Parameterization of the random forest classifier

As usual, consult the documentation for the full list of parameters. You can find the documentation here: http://scikit-learn.org/stable/modules/generated/sklearn.ensemble.RandomForestClassifier.html#sklearn.ensemble.RandomForestClassifier.

We will only consider a subset of the possible parameters, based on what you already know, which is based on the description of constructing random forests:

- **n_estimators**: The number of trees in the random forest. The default value is 10.

- **criterion**: Use Gini or entropy to determine whether you use Gini Impurity or information gain using entropy in each tree.

- **max_features**: The maximum number of features considered in any tree of the forest. Possible values include an integer. You can also add some strings such as "**sqrt**" for the square root of the number of features.

- **max_depth**: The maximum depth of each tree.

- **min_samples_split**: The minimum number of samples in the dataset in a given node to perform a split. This may also reduce the tree's size.

- **bootstrap**: A Boolean indicating whether to use bootstrapping on data points when constructing trees.

Feature Importance

A random forest classifier gives you information on how important each feature in data classification is. Remember, we use a lot of randomly constructed decision trees to classify data points. We can measure how accurately these data points behave, and we can also see which features are vital in decision making.

We can retrieve the array of feature importance scores with the following query:

```
random_forest_classifier.feature_importances_
```

The output is as follows:

```
array([0.12794765, 0.1022992 , 0.02165415, 0.35186759, 0.05486389,
       0.34136752])
```

In this six-feature classifier, the fourth and the sixth features are clearly a lot more important than any other features. The third feature has a very low importance score.

Feature importance scores come in handy when we have a lot of features and we want to reduce the feature size to avoid the classifier getting lost in the details. When we have a lot of features, we risk overfitting the model. Therefore, reducing the number of features by dropping the least significant ones is often helpful.

Extremely Randomized Trees

Extremely randomized trees increase randomization inside random forests by randomizing the splitting rules on top of the already randomized factors in random forests.

The parameterization is similar to the random forest classifier. You can see the full list of parameters here: http://scikit-learn.org/stable/modules/generated/sklearn.ensemble.ExtraTreesClassifier.html.

The Python implementation is as follows:

```
from sklearn.ensemble import ExtraTreesClassifier

extra_trees_classifier = ExtraTreesClassifier(
    n_estimators=100,
    max_depth=6
)

extra_trees_classifier.fit(features_train, label_train)

labels_predicted = extra_trees_classifier.predict(features_test)
```

Activity 11: Random Forest Classification for Your Car Rental Company

In this section, we will optimize your classifier so that you satisfy your clients more when selecting future cars for your car fleet. We will be performing random forest and Extreme random forest classification on the car dealership dataset that you worked on in previous activity of this chapter. Suggest further improvements for the model to improve the performance of the classifier:

1. Follow steps 1 to 5 of previous activity.

2. If you are using **IPython**, your variables may already be accessible in your console.

3. Create a random forest and an extremely randomized trees classifier and train the models.

4. Estimate how well the two models perform on the test data. We can also calculate the accuracy scores.

5. As a first optimization technique, let's see which features more important and which features are less important. Due to randomization, removing the least important features may reduce the random noise in the model.

6. Remove the third feature from the model and retrain the classifier. Compare how well the new models fare compared to the original ones.

7. Tweak the parameterization of the classifiers a bit more.

Note that we reduced the amount of nondeterminism by allowing the maximum number of features to go up to this could eventually lead to some degree of overfitting.

> **Note**
>
> The solution to this activity is available at page 285.

Summary

In this chapter, we have learned how to use decision trees for prediction. Using ensemble learning techniques, we created complex reinforcement learning models to predict the class of an arbitrary data point.

Decision trees on their own proved to be very accurate on the surface, but they were prone to overfitting the model. Random Forests and Extremely Randomized Trees combat overfitting by introducing some random elements and a voting algorithm, where the majority wins.

Beyond decision trees, random forests, and Extremely Randomized Trees, we also learned about new methods for evaluating the utility of a model. After using the well-known accuracy score, we started using the precision, recall, and F1 score metrics to evaluate how well our classifier works. All of these values were derived from the confusion matrix.

In the next chapter, we will describe the clustering problem and compare and contrast two clustering algorithms.

6

Clustering

Learning Objectives

By the end of this chapter, you will be able to:

- Summarize the basics of clustering

- Perform flat clustering with the k-means algorithm

- Perform hierarchical clustering with the mean shift algorithm

In this chapter, you will learn about the fundamentals of clustering, which will be illustrated with two unsupervised learning algorithms.

Introduction to Clustering

In the previous chapters, we dealt with supervised learning algorithms to perform classification and regression. We used training data to train our classification or regression model, and then we validated our model using testing data.

In this chapter, we will perform unsupervised learning by using clustering algorithms.

We may use clustering to analyze data to find certain patterns and create groups. Apart from that, clustering can be used for many purposes:

- Market segmentation detects the best stocks in the market you should be focusing on fundamentally. We can detect trends, segment customers, or recommend certain products to certain customer types using clustering.

- In computer vision, image segmentation is performed using clustering, where we find different objects in an image that a computer processes.

- Clustering can be combined with classification, where clustering may generate a compact representation of multiple features, which can then be fed to a classifier.

- Clustering may also filter data points by detecting outliers.

Regardless of whether we are applying clustering to genetics, videos, images, or social networks, if we analyze data using clustering, we may find similarities between data points that are worth treating uniformly.

We perform clustering without specified labels. Clustering defines clusters based on the distance between their data points. While; in classification, we define exact label classes to group classified data points, in clustering, there are no labels. We just give the machine learning model the features, and the model has to figure out the clusters in which those feature sets are grouped.

Defining the Clustering Problem

Suppose you are a store manager who's responsible for ensuring the profitability of your store. Your products are divided into categories. Different customers of the store prefer different items.

For instance, a customer interested in bio products tends to select products that are bio in nature. If you check out Amazon, you will also find suggestions for different groups of products. This is based on what users are likely to be interested in.

We will define the clustering problem in such a way that we will be able to find these similarities between our data points. Suppose we have a dataset that consists of points. Clustering helps us understand this structure by describing how these points are distributed.

Let's look at an example of data points in a two-dimensional space:

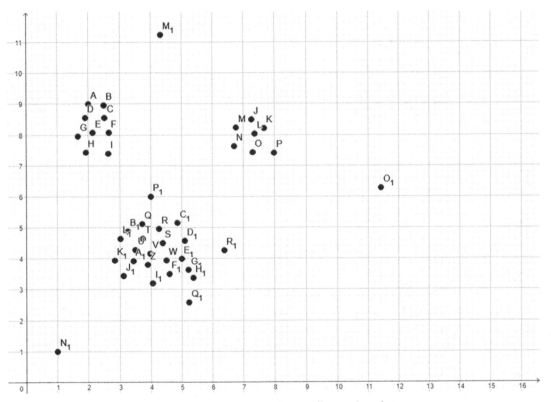

Figure 6.1: Data points in a two-dimensional space

In this example, it is evident that there are three clusters:

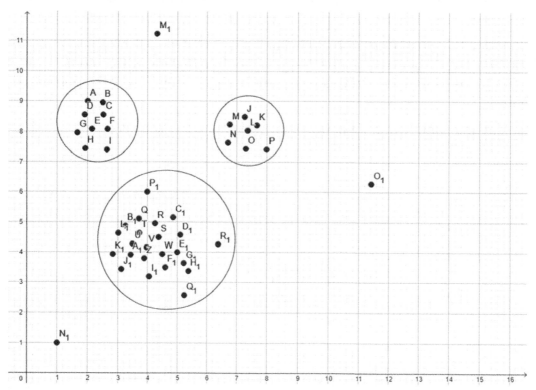

Figure 6.2: Three clusters formed using the data points in a two-dimensional space

The three clusters were easy to detect because the points are close to one another. Clustering determines data points that are close to each other. There are also some outlier points that do not belong to any cluster. The clustering algorithm should be prepared to treat these outlier points properly, without moving them into a cluster.

While it is easy to recognize clusters in a two-dimensional space, we normally have multidimensional data points. Therefore, it is important to know which data points are close to one other. Also, it is important to define distance metrics that detect whether data points are close to each other. One well-known distance metric is the Euclidean distance. In mathematics, we often use Euclidean distance to measure the distance between two points. Therefore, Euclidean distance is an intuitive choice when it comes to clustering algorithms so that we can determine the proximity of data points when locating clusters.

There is one drawback to most distance metrics, including Euclidean distance: the more we increase the dimensions, the more uniform these distances will become compared to each other. Therefore, getting rid of features that act as noise rather than useful information may greatly increase the accuracy of the clustering model.

Clustering Approaches

There are two types of clustering: **flat** and **hierarchical**.

In flat clustering, we specify the number of clusters we would like the machine to find. One example of flat clustering is the k-means algorithm, where K specifies the number of clusters, we would like the algorithm to use.

In hierarchical clustering, the machine learning algorithm finds out the number of clusters that are needed.

Hierarchical clustering also has two approaches:

- **Bottom-up hierarchical clustering** treats each point as a cluster. This approach unites clusters that are close to each other.

- **Top-down hierarchical clustering** treats data points as if they were in one cluster spanning the whole state space. Then, the clustering algorithm splits our clusters into smaller ones.

- **Point assignment clustering** assigns new data points to existing clusters based on how close the new data point is to these clusters.

Clustering Algorithms Supported by scikit-learn

In this chapter, we will learn about two clustering algorithms supported by scikit-learn: the **k-means** algorithm and the **mean shift** algorithm.

k-means is an example of flat clustering, where we have to specify the number of clusters in advance. k-means is a generic purpose clustering algorithm that performs well if the number of clusters is not too high and the size of the clusters is even.

Mean-shift is an example of hierarchical clustering, where the clustering algorithm determines the number of clusters. Mean shift is used when we don't know the number of clusters in advance. In contrast with k-means, mean shift supports use cases where many clusters are present, even if the size of the clusters greatly differs.

scikit-learn provides other clustering algorithms. These are as follows:

- **<u>Affinity Propagation</u>**: Performs similarly to Mean Shift

- **<u>Spectral clustering</u>**: Performs better if only a few clusters are present, with even cluster sizes

- **<u>Ward hierarchical clustering</u>**: Used when many clusters are expected

- **<u>Agglomerative clustering</u>**: Used when many clusters are expected

- **<u>DBSCAN clustering</u>**: Supports uneven cluster sizes and non-flat geometry of point distributions

- **<u>Gaussian mixtures</u>**: Uses flat geometry, which is good for density estimations

- **<u>Birch clustering</u>**: Supports large datasets, removes outliers, and supports data reduction

For a complete description of clustering algorithms, including performance comparisons, visit the clustering page of scikit-learn at <u>http://scikit-learn.org/stable/modules/clustering.html</u>.

The k-means Algorithm

The k-means algorithm is a flat clustering algorithm. It works as follows:

- Set the value of K.

- Choose K data points from the dataset that are initial centers of the individual clusters.

- Calculate the distance of each data point to the chosen center points, and group each point in the cluster whose initial center is the closest to the data point.

- Once all of the points are in one of the K clusters, calculate the center point of each cluster. This center point does not have to be an existing data point in the dataset; it is just an average.

- Repeat this process of assigning each data point into the cluster that has a center closest to the data point. Repetition continues until the center points no longer move.

To make sure that the k-means algorithm terminates, we need the following:

- A maximum level of tolerance when we exit in case the centroids move less than the tolerance value

- A maximum number of repetitions of shifting the moving points

Due to the nature of the k-means algorithm, it will have a hard time dealing with clusters that greatly differ in size.

The k-means algorithm has many use cases that are part of our everyday lives:

Market segmentation: Companies gather all sorts of data from their customer base. Performing k-means clustering analysis on the customer base of a company reveals market segments that have defined characteristics. Customers belonging to the same segment can be treated similarly. Different segments receive different treatment.

Classification of books, movies, or other documents: When influencers build their personal brand, authors write books and create books, or a company manages its social media accounts, content is king. Content is often described by hashtags and other data. This data can be used as a basis for clustering to locate groups of documents that are similar in nature.

Detection of fraud and criminal activities: Fraudsters often leaves clues in the form of unusual customer or visitor behavior. For instance, car insurance protects drivers from theft and damage arising from accidents. Real theft and fake theft are characterized by different feature values. Similarly, wrecking a car on purpose leaves different traces than wrecking a car by accident. Clustering can often detect fraud, helping industry professionals understand the behavior of their worst customers better.

Exercise 19: k-means in scikit-learn

To plot data points in a two-dimensional plane and execute the k-means algorithm on them to perform clustering, execute the following steps:

1. We will create an artificial dataset as a NumPy Array to demonstrate the k-means algorithm:

    ```
    import numpy as np
    data_points = np.array([
        [1, 1],
        [1, 1.5],
        [2, 2],
        [8, 1],
        [8, 0],
        [8.5, 1],
    ```

```
        [6, 1],
        [1, 10],
        [1.5, 10],
        [1.5, 9.5],
        [10, 10],
        [1.5, 8.5]
    ])
```

We can plot these data points in the two-dimensional plane using `matplotlib.pyplot`:

```
import matplotlib.pyplot as plot
plot.scatter(data_points.transpose()[0], data_points.transpose()[1])
```

The output is as follows:

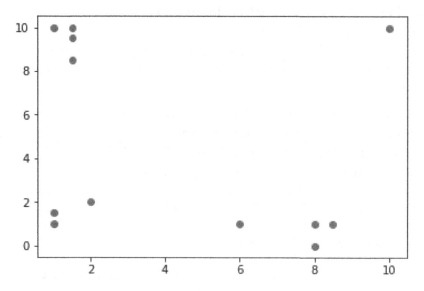

Figure 6.3: Graph showing the data points on a two-dimensional plane using matplotlib.pyplot

> Note
>
> We used the **transpose array** method to get the values of the first feature and the second feature. This is in alignment with the previous chapters. We could also use proper array indexing to access these columns: **dataPoints[:,0]** is equivalent to **dataPoints.transpose()[0]**.

2. Now that we have the data points, it's time to execute the k-means algorithm on them. If we define K as **3** in the k-means algorithm, we expect a cluster on the bottom-left, top-left, and bottom-right corner of the graph:

```
from sklearn.cluster import KMeans
k_means_model = KMeans(n_clusters=3)
k_means_model.fit(data_points)
```

3. Once the clustering is done, we can access the center point of each cluster:

```
k_means_model.cluster_centers_
```

The output will be as follows:

```
array([[1.33333333, 1.5        ],
       [3.1        , 9.6        ],
       [7.625      , 0.75       ]])
```

Indeed, the center points of the clusters appear to be in the bottom-left, top-left, and bottom-right corners of the graph. The X-coordinate of the top-left cluster is 3.1, most likely because it contains our outlier data point [10, 10].

4. Let's plot the clusters with different colors and their center points. To know which data point belongs to which cluster, we have to query the **labels_** property of the k-means classifier:

```
k_means_model.labels_
```

The output will be as follows:

```
array([0, 0, 0, 2, 2, 2, 2, 1, 1, 1, 1, 1])
```

5. The output array shows which data point belongs to which cluster. This is all we need to plot the data:

```
plot.scatter(
    k_means_model.cluster_centers_[:,0],
    k_means_model.cluster_centers_[:,1]
)
for i in range(len(data_points)):
    plot.plot(
        data_points[i][0],
        data_points[i][1],
        ['ro','go','yo'][k_means_model.labels_[i]]
    )
plot.show()
```

The output is as follows:

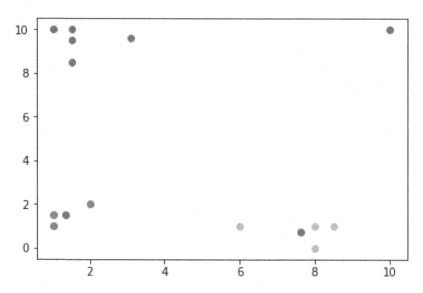

Figure 6.4: Graph showing the data points in red, green, and blue while selecting three clusters

The blue center points are indeed inside their clusters, which are represented by the red points, the green points, and the yellow points.

6. Let's see what happens if we choose only two clusters instead of three:

```
k_means_model = KMeans(n_clusters=2)
k_means_model.fit(data_points)
plot.scatter(
    k_means_model.cluster_centers_[:,0],
    k_means_model.cluster_centers_[:,1]
)
for i in range(len(data_points)):
    plot.plot(
        data_points[i][0],
        data_points[i][1],
        ['ro','go'][k_means_model.labels_[i]]
    )
plot.show()
```

The output is as follows:

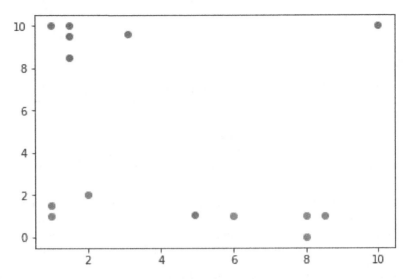

Figure 6.5: Graph showing the datapoints in red, blue, and green while selecting two clusters

This time, we only have red and green points, and we have a bottom cluster and a top cluster. Interestingly, the top red cluster in the second example contains the same points as the top cluster in the first example. The bottom cluster of the second example consists of the data points joining the bottom-left and the bottom-right clusters of the first example.

7. We can also use the k-means model for prediction. The output is an array containing the cluster numbers belonging to each data point:

```
k_means_model.predict([[5,5],[0,10]])
```

The output is as follows:

```
array([1, 0])
```

Parameterization of the k-means Algorithm in scikit-learn

Like the classification and regression models in Chapters 3, 4, and 5, the k-means algorithm can also be parameterized. The complete list of parameters can be found at http://scikit-learn.org/stable/modules/generated/sklearn.cluster.KMeans.html.

Some examples are as follows:

- **n_clusters**: The number of clusters in which the data points are separated. The default value is **8**.

- **max_iter**: The maximum number of iterations.

- **tol**: The tolerance for checking whether we can exit the k-means algorithm.

In the previous section, we used two attributes to retrieve the cluster center points and the clusters themselves:

cluster_centers_: This returns the coordinates of the cluster center points.

labels_: This returns an array of integers symbolizing the number of clusters the data point belongs to. Numbering starts from zero.

Exercise 20: Retrieving the Center Points and the Labels

To understand the usage of **cluster_centers_** and **labels_**, perform the following steps:

1. Recall the example that we had from executing the k-means algorithm in scikit-learn. We had 12 data points and three clusters:

```
data_points = np.array([
    [1, 1],
    [1, 1.5],
    [2, 2],
    [8, 1],
    [8, 0],
    [8.5, 1],
    [6, 1],
    [1, 10],
    [1.5, 10],
    [1.5, 9.5],
    [10, 10],
    [1.5, 8.5]
])
k_means_model.cluster_centers_
```

The output is as follows:

```
array([[1.33333333, 1.5       ],
       [3.1       , 9.6       ],
       [7.625     , 0.75      ]])
```

2. Apply the **labels_** property on the cluster:

```
k_means_model.labels_
```

The output is as follows:

```
array([0, 0, 0, 2, 2, 2, 2, 1, 1, 1, 1, 1])
```

The output of the **cluster_centers_** property is obvious: it shows the X and Y coordinates of the center points. The **labels_** property is an array of length 12, showing the cluster of each of the 12 data points it belongs to. The first cluster is associated with the number 0, the second is associated with 1, the third is associated with 2, and so on.

k-means Clustering of Sales Data

In the upcoming activity, we will be considering sales data and we will perform k-means clustering on that sales data.

Activity 12: k-means Clustering of Sales Data

In this section, we will detect product sales that perform similarly to recognize trends in product sales.

We will be using the Sales Transactions Weekly Dataset, found at the following URL:

https://archive.ics.uci.edu/ml/datasets/Sales_Transactions_Dataset_Weekly Perform clustering on the dataset using the k-means algorithm. Make sure that you prepare your data for clustering based on what you have learned in the previous chapters.

Use the default settings for the k-means algorithm:

1. Load the dataset using pandas. If you examine the data in the CSV file, you will realize that the first column contains product ID strings. These values just add noise to the clustering process. Also, notice that for weeks 0 to 51, there is a W-prefixed label and a normalized label. Using the normalized label makes more sense so that we can drop the regular weekly labels from the dataset.Create a k-means clustering model and fit the data points into 8 clusters.Retrieve the center points and the labels from the clustering algorithm.

2. The labels belonging to each data point can be retrieved using the **labels_** property. These labels determine the clustering of the rows of the original data frame. How are these labels beneficial?

Suppose that, in the original data frame, the product names are given. You can easily recognize the fact that similar types of products sell similarly. There are also products that fluctuate a lot, and products that are seasonal in nature. For instance, if some products promote fat loss and getting into shape, they tend to sell during the first half of the year, before the beach season.

> **Note**
>
> The solution to this activity is available at page 291.

Mean Shift Algorithm

Mean shift is a hierarchical clustering algorithm. Unlike the k-means algorithm, in mean shift, the clustering algorithm determines how many clusters are needed, and also performs the clustering. This is advantageous because we rarely know how many clusters we are looking for.

This algorithm also has many use cases in our everyday lives. For instance, the Xbox Kinect device detects human body parts using the mean shift algorithm. Some mobile phones also use the Mean Shift algorithm to detect faces. With the growth of social media platforms, image segmentation is a feature that many users have gotten used to. As image segmentation is also a basis of computer vision, some applications can be found there. The mean shift algorithm may also save lives, as it is built into the car detection software of many modern cars. Imagine that someone emergency brakes in front of you. The image segmentation software of your car detects that the car in front of you is getting alarmingly close to you and applies the emergency brake before you even realize the emergency situation. These driver aids are widespread in modern cars. Self-driving cars are just one step away.

Exercise 21: Illustrating Mean Shift in 2D

To learn clustering by using the mean shift algorithm, execute the following steps:

1. Let's recall the data points from the previous topic:

```
data_points = np.array([
    [1, 1],
    [1, 1.5],
    [2, 2],
    [8, 1],
    [8, 0],
    [8.5, 1],
    [6, 1],
    [1, 10],
    [1.5, 10],
    [1.5, 9.5],
    [10, 10],
    [1.5, 8.5]
])
r = 2;
```

2. Our task now is to find a point P (x, y), for which the number of data points within a radius R from point P is maximized. The points are distributed as follows:

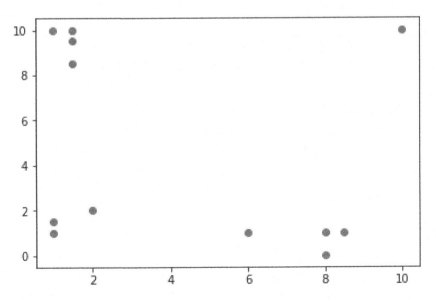

Figure 6.6: Graph showing the data points from the data_points array

3. Suppose we initially equate point P to the first data point, [1, 1]:

```
P = [1, 1]
```

4. Let's find the points that are within a distance of R from this point:

```
from scipy.spatial import distance
points = np.array([
    p0 for p0 in data_points if distance.euclidean(p0, P) <= r
])
points
```

The output will be as follows:

```
array([[1. , 1. ],
   [1. , 1.5],
   [2. , 2. ]])
```

5. Let's calculate the mean of the data points:

```
import numpy as np
P = [
    np.mean( points.transpose()[0] ),
    np.mean(points.transpose()[1] )
]
P
```

The output will be as follows:

```
[1.3333333333333333, 1.5]
```

6. Now that the new mean has been calculated, we can retrieve the points within the given radius again:

```
points = np.array([
    p0 for p0 in data_points if distance.euclidean( p0, P) <= r
])
points
```

The output will be as follows:

```
array([[1. , 1. ],
   [1. , 1.5],
   [2. , 2. ]])
```

7. These are the same three points, so we can stop here. Three points have been found around the mean of **[1.3333333333333333, 1.5]**. The points around this center within a radius of 2 form a cluster.

8. If we examined the data points [1, 1.5] and [2, 2], we would get the same result. Let's continue with the fourth point in our list, [8, 1]:

```
P = [8, 1]
points = np.array( [
    p0 for p0 in data_points if distance.euclidean(p0, P) <= r
])
points
```

The output will be as follows:

```
array([[8. , 1. ],
       [8. , 0. ],
       [8.5, 1. ],
       [6. , 1. ]])
```

9. This time, all four points in the area were found. Therefore, we can simply calculate their mean:

```
P = [
    np.mean(points.transpose()[0]),
    np.mean(points.transpose()[1])
]
```

The output will be as follows:

```
[7.625, 0.75]
```

This mean will not change, as in the next iteration, we will find the same data points.

10. Notice that we got lucky with the selection of the point [8, 1]. If we started with P = **[8, 0]** or P = **[8.5, 1]**, we would only find three points instead of four:

```
P = [8, 0]
points = np.array([
    p0 for p0 in data_points if distance.euclidean(p0, P) <= r
])
points
```

The output will be as follows:

```
array([[8. , 1. ],
    [8. , 0. ],
    [8.5, 1. ]])
```

11. After calculating the mean of these three points, we would have to rerun the distance calculation with the shifted mean:

```
P = [
    np.mean(points.transpose()[0]),
    np.mean(points.transpose()[1])
]
P
```

The output will be as follows:

```
[8.166666666666666, 0.6666666666666666]
```

12. The output for point P = [8.5, 1] is the following array:

```
array([[8. , 1. ],
    [8. , 0. ],
    [8.5, 1. ]])
```

We only found the same three points again. This means that starting from [8,1], we got a larger cluster than starting from [8, 0] or [8.5, 1]. Therefore, we have to take the center point that contains the maximum number of data points.

13. Now, let's examine what would happen if we started the discovery from the fourth data point, **[6, 1]**:

```
P = [6, 1]
points = np.array([
    p0 for p0 in data_points if distance.euclidean(p0, P) <= r
])
points
```

The output will be as follows:

```
array([[8., 1.],
    [6., 1.]])
```

14. We successfully found the data point [8, 1]. Therefore, we have to shift the mean from [6, 1] to the calculated new mean, [7, 1]:

```
P = [
    np.mean(points.transpose()[0]),
    np.mean(points.transpose()[1])
]
P
```

The output will be as follows:

```
[7.0, 1.0]
```

15. Let's check if we found more points:

```
points = np.array([
    p0 for p0 in data_points if distance.euclidean(p0, P) <= r
])
points
```

The output will be as follows:

```
array([[8. , 1. ],
    [8. , 0. ],
    [8.5, 1. ],
    [6. , 1. ]])
```

Yes – we successfully found all four points! Therefore, we have successfully defined a cluster of size 4. The mean will be the same as before: **[7.625, 0.75]**.

This was a simple clustering example that applied the mean shift algorithm. We only provided an illustration of what the algorithm considers to find the clusters. There is one remaining question, though: the value of the radius.

Note that if the radius of 2 was not set, we could simply start either with a huge radius including all data points and then reduce the radius or start with a very small radius, making sure that each data point is in its own cluster, and then increase the radius until we get the desired result.

Mean Shift Algorithm in scikit-learn

Let's use the same data points as in the k-means algorithm:

```
import numpy as np
data_points = np.array([
    [1, 1],
    [1, 1.5],
    [2, 2],
    [8, 1],
    [8, 0],
    [8.5, 1],
    [6, 1],
    [1, 10],
    [1.5, 10],
    [1.5, 9.5],
    [10, 10],
    [1.5, 8.5]
])
```

The syntax of the mean shift clustering algorithm is similar to the k-means clustering algorithm.

```
from sklearn.cluster import MeanShift
mean_shift_model = MeanShift()
mean_shift_model.fit(data_points)
```

Once clustering is done, we can access the center point of each cluster:

```
mean_shift_model.cluster_centers_
```

The output will be as follows:

```
array([[ 1.375     ,  9.5       ],
       [ 1.33333333,  1.5       ],
       [ 8.16666667,  0.66666667],
       [ 6.        ,  1.        ],
       [10.        , 10.        ]])
```

The Mean Shift model found 5 clusters with the centers shown in the preceding code.

Similar to k-means,, we can also get the labels:

```
mean_shift_model.labels_
```

The output will be as follows:

```
array([1, 1, 1, 2, 2, 2, 3, 0, 0, 0, 4, 0], dtype=int64)
```

The output array shows which data point belongs to which cluster. This is all we need to plot the data:

```
plot.scatter(
    mean_shift_model.cluster_centers_[:,0],
    mean_shift_model.cluster_centers_[:,1]
)
for i in range(len(data_points)):
    plot.plot(
        data_points[i][0],
        data_points[i][1],
        ['ro','go','yo', 'ko', 'mo'][mean_shift_model.labels_[i]]
    )
plot.show()
```

The output will be as follows:

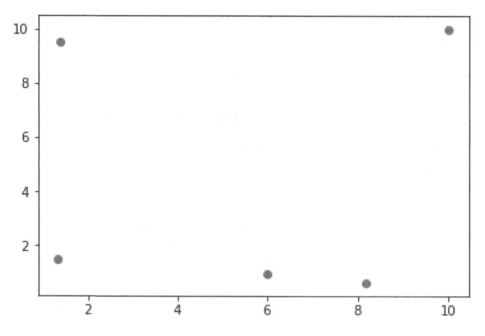

Figure 6.7: Graph based on k-means,

The three blue points are the center points of the red, green, and yellow clusters. There are two more single dot clusters in the coordinate system, belonging to the points (6,1) and (10,10).

Image Processing in Python

To solve the upcoming activity, you need to know how to process images in Python. We will use the SciPy library for this.

There are multiple ways that you can read an image file from a path.

The easiest one is the **Image** interface from the Python Imaging Library (PIL):

```
from PIL import Image

image = Image.open('file.jpg')
```

The preceding code assumes that the file path specified in the string argument of the **open** method points to a valid image file.

We can get the size of the image by querying the size property:

```
image.size
```

The output will be as follows:

```
(750, 422)
```

We can create a two-dimensional NumPy array from the image containing the RGB values of each pixel:

```
import numpy as np

pixel_array = np.array(image)
```

Once the pixel array has been constructed, we can easily retrieve and manipulate each pixel:

```
pixel_array[411][740]
```

The output will be as follows:

```
array([29, 33, 32], dtype=uint8)
```

The pixels of the image can also be made accessible using the **load()** method of the image. Once we get access to these pixels, we can get the RGB or RGBA values of each pixel, depending on the file format:

```
pixels = image.load()

pixels[740, 411]
```

The output will be as follows:

```
(29, 33, 32)
```

Notice that the order of pixel coordinates is the opposite, that is, **pixel_array[411][740]** when reading from left to right. We are reading the exact same pixel, but we have to supply the coordinates differently.

We can also set pixels to a new value:

```
pixels[740, 411] = (255, 0, 0)
```

If you want to save changes, use the **save()** method of the image:

```
image.save('test.jpg')
```

To perform clustering analysis on the pixels of the image, we need to convert the image to a data frame. This implies that we have to convert the pixels of the image to a tuple or array of ['x', 'y', 'red', 'green', 'blue'] values. Once we have a one-dimensional array of these values, we can convert them to a pandas DataFrame:

```
import pandas

data_frame = pandas.DataFrame(
    [[x,y,pixels[x,y][0], pixels[x,y][1], pixels[x,y][2]]
        for x in range(image.size[0])
        for y in range(image.size[1])
    ],
    columns=['x', 'y', 'r', 'g', 'b' ]
)
data_frame.head()
```

The output will be as follows:

	x	y	r	g	b
0	0	0	6	29	71
1	0	1	7	32	73
2	0	2	8	37	77
3	0	3	8	41	82
4	0	4	7	45	84

This is all you need to know to complete the activity on processing images using the Mean Shift algorithm.

Activity 13: Shape Recognition with the Mean Shift Algorithm

In this section, we will learn how images can be clustered. Imagine you are working for a company that detects human emotions from photos. Your task is to extract pixels making up a face in an avatar photo.

Create a clustering algorithm with Mean Shift to cluster pixels of images. Examine the results of the Mean Shift algorithm and check whether any of the clusters contain a face when used on avatar images.

Then, apply the k-means, algorithm with a fixed default number of clusters (8, in this case). Compare your results with the Mean Shift clustering algorithm:

1. Select an image you would like to cluster and load the image.

2. Transform the pixels into a data frame to perform clustering. Perform Mean Shift clustering on the image using scikit-learn. Note that, this time, we will skip normalizing the features, because the proximity of the pixels and the proximity of the color components are represented in a close to equal weight. The algorithm will find two clusters.

3. Depending on the image you use, notice how the Mean Shift algorithm treats human skin color, and what other parts of the image are placed in the same cluster. The cluster containing most of the skin in the avatar often includes data points that are very near and/or have a similar color as the color of the skin.

4. Let's use the k-means algorithm to formulate eight clusters on the same data.

You will see that the clustering algorithm indeed located data points that are close and contain similar colors.

> **Note**
>
> The solution to this activity is available at page 293.

Summary

In this chapter, we learned how clustering works. Clustering is a form of unsupervised learning, where the features are given, and the clustering algorithm finds the labels.

There are two types of clustering: flat and hierarchical.

The k-means algorithm is a flat clustering algorithm, where we determine K center points for our K clusters, and the algorithm finds the data points.

Mean Shift is an example of a hierarchical clustering algorithm, where the number of distinct label values is to be determined by the algorithm.

The final chapter will introduce a field that has become popular this decade due to the explosion of computation power and cheap, scalable online server capacity. This field is the science of neural networks and deep learning.

Deep Learning with Neural Networks

Learning Objectives

By the end of this chapter, you will be able to:

- Perform basic TensorFlow operations to solve various expressions
- Describe how aritifical neural networks work
- Train and test neural networks with TensorFlow
- Implement deep learning neural network models with TensorFlow

In this chapter, we'll detect a written digit using the TensorFlow library.

Introduction

In this chapter, we will learn about another supervised learning technique. However, this time, instead of using a simple mathematical model such as classification or regression, we will use a completely different model: **neural networks**. Although we will use Neural Networks for supervised learning, note that Neural Networks can also model unsupervised learning techniques. The significance of this model increased in the last century, because in the past, the computation power required to use this model for supervised learning was not enough. Therefore, neural networks have emerged in practice in the last century.

TensorFlow for Python

TensorFlow is one of the most important machine learning and open source libraries maintained by Google. The TensorFlow API is available in many languages, including Python, JavaScript, Java, and C. As TensorFlow supports supervised learning, we will use TensorFlow for building a graph model, and then use this model for prediction.

TensorFlow works with tensors. Some examples for tensors are:

- Scalar values such as a floating point number.

- A vector of arbitrary length.

- A regular matrix, containing p times q values, where p and q are finite integers.

- A p x q x r generalized matrix-like structure, where p, q, r are finite integers. Imagine this construct as a rectangular object in three dimensional space with sides p, q, and r. The numbers in this data structure can be visualized in three dimensions.

- Observing the above four data structures, more complex, n-dimensional data structures can also be valid examples for tensors.

We will stick to scalar, vector, and regular matrix tensors in this chapter. Within the scope of this chapter, think of tensors as scalar values, or arrays, or arrays of arrays.

TensorFlow is used to create artificial neural networks because it models its inputs, outputs, internal nodes, and directed edges between these nodes. TensorFlow also comes with mathematical functions to transform signals. These mathematical functions will also come handy when modeling when a neuron inside a neural network gets activated.

> **Note**
>
> Tensors are array-like objects. Flow symbolizes the manipulation of tensor data. So, essentially, TensorFlow is an array data manipulation library.

The main use case for TensorFlow is artificial neural networks, as this field requires operation on big arrays and matrices. TensorFlow comes with many deep learning-related functions, and so it is an optimal environment for neural networks. TensorFlow is used for voice recognition, voice search, and it is also the brain behind translate.google.com. Later in this chapter, we will use TensorFlow to recognize written characters.

Installing TensorFlow in the Anaconda Navigator

Let's open the Anaconda Prompt and install TensorFlow using **pip**:

```
pip install tensorflow
```

Installation will take a few minutes because the package itself is quite big. If you prefer using your video card GPU instead of your CPU, you can also use **tensorflow-gpu**. Make sure that you only use the GPU version if you have a good enough graphics card for it.

Once you are done with the installation, you can import TensorFlow in IPython:

```
import tensorflow as tf
```

First, we will use TensorFlow to build a graph. The execution of this model is separated. This separation is important because execution is resource intensive and may therefore run on a server specialized in solving computation heavy problems.

TensorFlow Operations

TensorFlow provides many operations to manipulate data. A few examples of these operations are as follows:

- **Arithmetic operations**: add and multiply
- **Exponential operations**: exp and log
- **Relational operations**: greater, less, and equal
- **Array operations**: concat, slice, and split
- **Matrix operations**: matrix_inverse, matrix_determinant, and matmul
- **Neural network-related operations**: sigmoid, ReLU, and softmax

Exercise 22: Using Basic Operations and TensorFlow constants

Use arithmetic operations in Tensorflow to solve the expression: 2 * 3 + 4

These operations can be used to build a graph. To understand more about TensorFlow constants and basic arithmetic operators, let's consider a simple expression 2 * 3 + 4 the graph for this expression would be as follows:

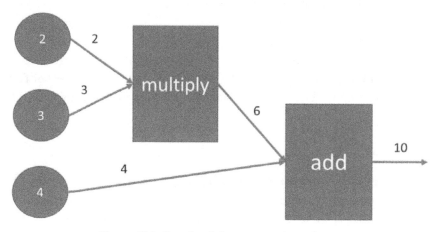

Figure 7.1: Graph of the expression 2*3+4

1. Model this graph in TensorFlow by using the following code:

```
import tensorflow as tf
input1 = tf.constant(2.0, tf.float32, name='input1')
input2 = tf.constant(3.0, tf.float32, name='input2')
input3 = tf.constant(4.0, tf.float32, name='input3')
product12 = tf.multiply(input1, input2)
sum = tf.add(product12, input3)
```

2. Once the graph is built, to perform calculations, we have to open a TensorFlow session and execute our nodes:

```
with tf.Session() as session:
    print(session.run(product12))
    print(session.run(sum))
```

The intermediate and final results are printed to the console:

```
6.0
10.0
```

Placeholders and Variables

Now that you can build expressions with TensorFlow, let's take things a step further and build placeholders and variables.

Placeholders are substituted with a constant value when the execution of a session starts. Placeholders are essentially parameters that are substituted before solving an expression. Variables are values that might change during the execution of a session.

Let's create a parametrized expression with TensorFlow:

```
import tensorflow as tf
input1 = tf.constant(2.0, tf.float32, name='input1')
input2 = tf.placeholder(tf.float32, name='p')
input3 = tf.Variable(0.0, tf.float32, name='x')
product12 = tf.multiply(input1, input2)
sum = tf.add(product12, input3)
with tf.Session() as session:
    initializer = tf.global_variables_initializer()
    session.run(initializer)
    print(session.run(sum, feed_dict={input2: 3.0}))
```

The output is **6.0**.

The **tf.global_variables_initializer()** call initialized the variable in **input3** to its default value, zero, after it was executed in **session.run**.

The sum was calculated inside another **session.run** statement by using the feed dictionary, thus using the constant **3.0** in place of the **input2** parameter.

Note that in this specific example, the variable x is initialized to zero. The value of x does not change during the execution of the TensorFlow session. Later, when we will use TensorFlow to describe neural networks, we will define an optimization target, and the session will optimize the values of the variables to meet this target.

Global Variables Initializer

As TensorFlow often makes use of matrix operations, it makes sense to learn how to initialize a matrix of random variables to a value that's randomly generated according to a normal distribution centered at zero.

Not only matrices, but all global variables are initialized inside the session by calling **tf.global_variables_initializer()**:

```
randomMatrix = tf.Variable(tf.random_normal([3, 4]))


with tf.Session() as session:
    initializer = tf.global_variables_initializer()
    print( session.run(initializer))
    print( session.run(randomMatrix))


None
[[-0.41974232  1.8810892  -1.4549098  -0.73987174]
 [ 2.1072254   1.7968426  -0.38310152  0.98115194]
 [-0.550108   -0.41858754  1.3511614   1.2387075 ]]
```

As you can see, the initialization of a **tf.Variable** takes one argument: the value of **tf.random_normal([3,4])**.

Introduction to Neural Networks

Neural networks are the newest branch of AI. Neural networks are inspired by how the human brain works. Originally, they were invented in the 1940s by Warren McCulloch and Walter Pitts. The neural network was a mathematical model that was used for describing how the human brain can solve problems.

We will use the phrase artificial neural network when talking about the mathematical model and use biological neural network when talking about the human brain. Artificial neural networks are supervised learning algorithms.

The way a neural network learns is more complex compared to other classification or regression models. The neural network model has a lot of internal variables, and the relationship between the input and output variables may go through multiple internal layers. Neural networks have higher accuracy as compared to other supervised learning algorithms.

> **Note**
>
> Mastering neural networks with TensorFlow is a complex process. The purpose of this section is to provide you with an introductory resource to get started.

In this chapter, the main example we are going to use is the recognition of digits from an image. We are considering this image since it is small, and we have around 70,000 images available. The processing power required to process these images, is similar to that of a regular computer.

Artificial neural network works similar to human brain works. Dendroid in a human brain is connected to the nucleus and the nucleus is connected to the axon. Here, the dendroid acts as the inputs, nucleus is where the calculations occurs (weighted sum and the activation function) and the axon acts similar to the output.

Then, we determine which neuron fires by passing the weighted sum to an activation function. If this function determines that a neuron has to fire, the signal appears in the output. This signal can be the input of other neurons in the network:

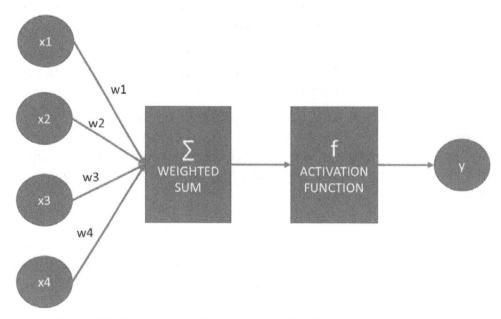

Figure 7.2: Diagram showing how the artificial neural network works

Suppose **f** is the activation function, **x1**, **x2**, **x3**, and **x4** are the inputs, and their sum is weighted with the weights **w1**, **w2**, **w3**, and **w4**:

```
y = f(x1*w1 + x2*w2 + x3*w3 + x4*w4)
```

Assuming vector **x** is (**x1**, **x2**, **x3**, **x4**) and vector **w** is (**w1**, **w2**, **w3**, **w4**), we can write this equation as the scalar or dot product of these two vectors:

```
y = f(x   w)
```

The construct we have defined is one neuron:

Let's hide the details of this neuron so that it becomes easier to construct a neural network:

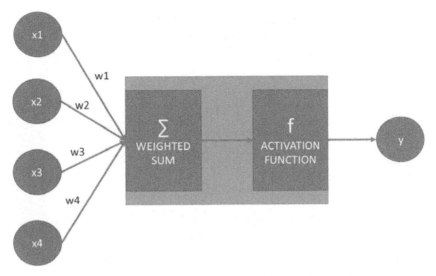

Figure 7.4: Diagram that represents the hidden layer of a neuron

We can create multiple boxes and multiple output variables that may get activated as a result of reading the weighted average of inputs.

Although in the following diagram there are arrows leading from all inputs to all boxes, bear in mind that the weights on the arrows might be zero. We still display these arrows in the diagram:

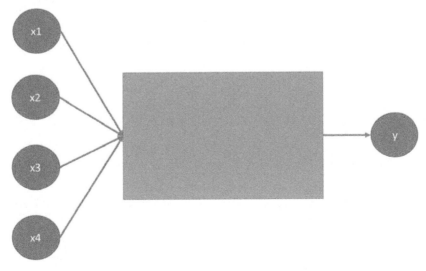

Figure 7.5: Diagram representing a neural network

The boxes describing the relationship between the inputs and the outputs are referred to as a hidden layer. A neural network with one hidden layer is called a **regular neural network**.

When connecting inputs and outputs, we may have multiple hidden layers. A neural network with multiple layers is called a **deep neural network**:

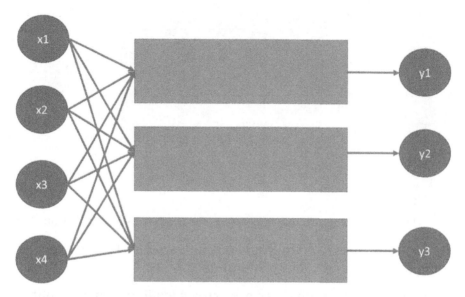

Figure 7.6: A diagram representing a deep neural network

The term deep learning comes from the presence of multiple layers. When creating an artificial neural network, we can specify the number of hidden layers.

Biases

Let's see the model of a neuron in a neural network again:

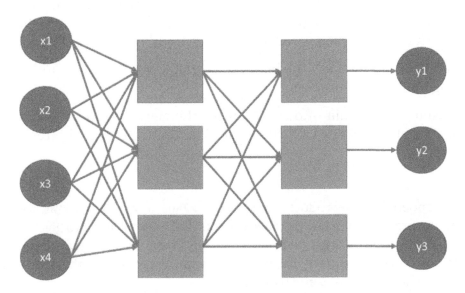

Figure 7.7: Diagram of neuron in neural network

We learned that the equation of this neuron is as follows:

```
y = f(x1*w1 + x2*w2 + x3*w3 + x4*w4)
```

The problem with this equation is that there is no constant factor that depends on the inputs x1, x2, x3, and x4. This implies that each neuron in a neural network, without bias, always produces this value whenever for each weight-input pair, their product is zero.

Therefore, we add bias to the equation:

```
y = f(x1*w1 + x2*w2 + x3*w3 + x4*w4 + b)
y = f(x   w + b)
```

The first equation is the verbose form, describing the role of each coordinate, weight coefficient, and bias. The second equation is the vector form, where x = (x1, x2, x3, x4) and w = (w1, w2, w3, w4). The dot operator between the vectors symbolizes the dot or scalar product of the two vectors. The two equations are equivalent. We will use the second form in practice because it is easier to define a vector of variables using TensorFlow than to define each variable one by one.

Similarly, for *w1*, *w2*, *w3*, and *w4*, the bias *b* is a variable, meaning that its value can change during the learning process.

With this constant factor built into each neuron, the neural network model becomes more flexible from the purpose of fitting a specific training dataset better.

> **Note**
>
> It may happen that the product **p = x1*w1 + x2*w2 + x3*w3 + x4*w4** is negative due to the presence of a few negative weights. We may still want to give the model the flexibility to fire a neuron with values above a given negative number. Therefore, adding a constant bias b = 5, for instance, can ensure that the neuron fires for values between -5 and 0 as well.

Use Cases for Artificial Neural Networks

Artificial neural networks have their place among supervised learning techniques. They can model both classification and regression problems. A classifier neural network seeks a relationship between features and labels. The features are the input variables, while each class the classifier can choose as a return value is a separate output. In the case of regression, the input variables are the features, while there is one single output: the predicted value. While traditional classification and regression techniques have their use cases in artificial intelligence, artificial neural networks are generally better at finding complex relationships between the inputs and the outputs.

Activation Functions

Different activation functions are used in neural networks. Without these functions, the neural network would be a linear model that could be easily described using matrix multiplication.

Activation functions of the neural network provide non-linearity. The most common activation functions are **sigmoid** and **tanh** (the hyperbolic tangent function).

The formula of **sigmoid** is as follows:

```python
import numpy as np
def sigmoid(x):
    return 1 / (1 + np.e ** (-x))
```

Let's plot this function using **pyplot**:

```python
import matplotlib.pylab as plt
x = np.arange(-10, 10, 0.1)
plt.plot(x, sigmoid(x))
plt.show()
```

The output is as follows:

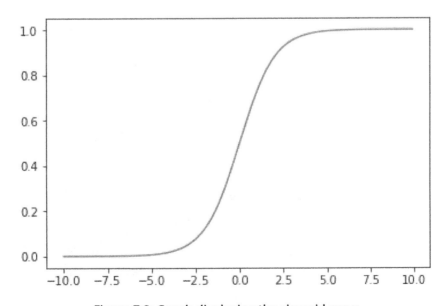

Figure 7.8: Graph displaying the sigmoid curve

There are a few problems with the sigmoid function.

First, it may disproportionally amplify or dampen weights.

Second, **sigmoid(0)** is not zero. This makes the learning process harder.

The formula of the hyperbolic tangent is as follows:

```
def tanh(x):
    return 2 / (1 + np.e ** (-2*x)) - 1
```

We can also plot this function like so:

```
x = np.arange(-10, 10, 0.1)
plt.plot(x, tanh(x))
plt.show()
```

The output is as follows:

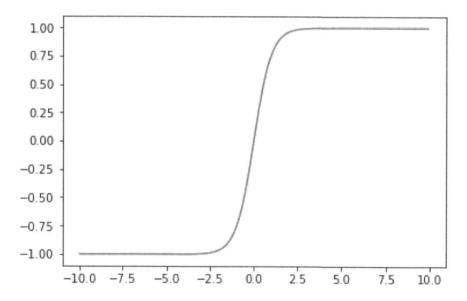

Figure 7.9: Graph after plotting hyperbolic tangent

Both functions add a little non-linearity to the values emitted by a neuron. The sigmoid function looks a bit smoother, while the tanh function gives slightly more edgy results.

Another activation function has become popular lately: **ReLU**. **ReLU** stands for Rectified Linear Unit:

```
def relu(x):
    return 0 if x < 0 else x
```

Making the neural network model non-linear makes it easier for the model to approximate non-linear functions. Without these non-linear functions, regardless of the number of layers of the network, we would only be able to approximate linear problems:

```
def reluArr(arr):
    return [relu(x) for x in arr]
x = np.arange(-10, 10, 0.1)
plt.plot(x, reluArr(x))
plt.show()
```

The output is as follows:

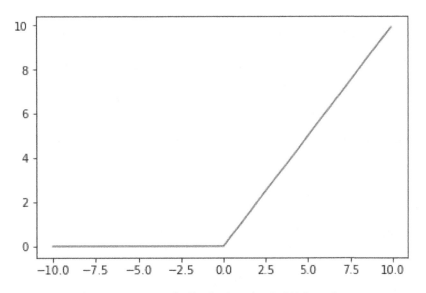

Figure 7.10: Graph displaying the ReLU function

The **ReLU** activation function behaves surprisingly well from the perspective of quickly converging to the final values of the weights and biases of the neural network.

We will use one more function in this chapter: **softmax**.

The **softmax** function shrinks the values of a list between 0 and 1 so that the sum of the elements of the list becomes 1. The definition of the **softmax** function is as follows:

```
def softmax(list):
    return np.exp(list) / np.sum(np.exp(list))
```

Here is an example:

```
softmax([1,2,1])
```

The output is as follows:

```
array([0.21194156, 0.57611688, 0.21194156])
```

The **softmax** function can be used whenever we filter a list, not a single value. Each element of the list will be transformed.

Let's experiment with different activator functions. Observe how these functions dampen the weighted inputs by solving the following exercise.

Exercise 23: Activation Functions

Consider the following neural network:

$y = f(2 * x1 + 0.5 * x2 + 1.5 * x3 - 3)$.

Assuming $x1$ is 1 and $x2$ is 2, calculate the value of y for the following x values: -1, 0, 1, 2, when:

- f is the **sigmoid** function
- f is the **tanh** function
- f is the **ReLU** function

Perform the following steps:

1. Substitute the known coefficients:

   ```
   def get_y( f, x3 ):
       return f(2*1+0.5*2+1.5*x3)
   ```

2. Use the following three activator functions:

   ```
   import numpy as np
   def sigmoid(x):
       return 1 / (1 + np.e ** (-x))
   def tanh(x):
       return 2 / (1 + np.e ** (-2*x)) - 1
   def relu(x):
       return 0 if x < 0 else x
   ```

3. Calculate the sigmoid values, using the following commands:

```
get_y( sigmoid, -2 )
```

The output is **0.5**

```
get_y(sigmoid, -1)
```

The output is **0.8175744761936437**

```
get_y(sigmoid, 0)
```

The output is **0.9525741268224331**

```
get_y(sigmoid, 1)
```

The output is **0.9890130573694068**

```
get_y(sigmoid, 2)
```

The output is **0.9975273768433653**

4. As you can see, the changes are dampened quickly as the sum of the expression inside the **sigmoid** function increases. We expect the **tanh** function to have an even bigger dampening effect:

```
get_y(tanh, -2)
```

The output is **0.0**

```
get_y(tanh, -1)
```

The output is **0.9051482536448663**

```
get_y(tanh, 0)
```

The output is **0.9950547536867307**

```
get_y(tanh, 1)
```

The output is **0.9997532108480274**

get_y(tanh, 2)

The output is **0.9999877116507956**

5. Based on the characteristics of the **tanh** function, the output approaches the 1 asymptote faster than the sigmoid function. For $x3 = -2$, we calculate **f(0)**. While **sigmoid(0)** is 0.5, **tanh(0)** is 0. As opposed to the other two functions, the **ReLu** function does not dampen positive values:

```
get_y(relu,-2)
```

The output is **0.0**

```
get_y(relu,-1)
```

The output is **1.5**

```
get_y(relu,0)
```

The output is **3.0**

```
get_y(relu,1)
```

The output is **4.5**

```
get_y(relu,2)
```

The output is **6.0**

Another advantage of the **ReLU** function is that its calculation is the easiest out of all of the activator functions.

Forward and Backward Propagation

As artificial neural networks provide a supervised-learning technique, we have to train our model using training data. Training the network is the process of finding the weights belonging to each variable-input pair. The process of weight optimization consists of the repeated execution of two steps: forward propagation and backward propagation.

The names forward and backward propagation imply how these techniques work. We start by initializing the weights on the arrows of the neural network. Then, we apply forward propagation, followed by backward propagation.

Forward propagation calculates output values based on input values. **Backward propagation** adjusts the weights and biases based on the margin of error measured between the label values created by the model and the actual label values in the training data. The rate of adjustment of the weights depend on the learning rate of the neural network. The higher the learning rate, the more the weights and biases are adjusted during the backward propagation. The momentum of the neural network determines how past results influence the upcoming values of weights and biases.

Configuring a Neural Network

The following parameters are commonly used to create a neural network:

- Number of hidden layers
- Number of nodes per hidden layer
- Activation function
- Learning rate
- Momentum
- Number of iterations for forward and backward propagation
- Tolerance for error

There are a few rules of thumb that can be used to determine the number of nodes per hidden layer. If your hidden layer contains more nodes than the size of your input, you risk overfitting the model. Often, a node count somewhere between the number of inputs and the number of outputs is reasonable.

Importing the TensorFlow Digit Dataset

Recognition of hand-written digits seems to be a simple task at first glance. However, this task is a simple classification problem with ten possible label values. TensorFlow provides an example dataset for the recognition of digits.

> **Note**
>
> You can read about this dataset on TensorFlow's website here: https://www.tensorflow.org/tutorials/.

We will use **keras** to load the dataset. You can install it in the Anaconda Prompt by using the following command:

```
pip install keras
```

Remember, we will perform supervised learning on these datasets, so we will need training and testing data:

```
import tensorflow.keras.datasets.mnist as mnist

(features_train, label_train),(features_test, label_test) =

mnist.load_ data()
```

The features are arrays containing the pixel values of a 28x28 image. The labels are one-digit integers between 0 and 9. Let's see the features and the label of the fifth element. We will use the same image library that we used in the previous section:

```
from PIL import Image

Image.fromarray(features_train[5])
```

Fig 7.11: Image for training

```
label_train[5]
```

```
2
```

In the activity at the end of this chapter, your task will be to create a neural network to classify these handwritten digits based on their values.

Modeling Features and Labels

We will go through the example of modeling features and labels for recognizing written numbers in the TensorFlow digit dataset.

We have a 28x28 pixel image as our input. The value of each image is either black or white. The feature set therefore consists of a vector of 28 * 28 = 784 pixels.

The images are grayscale and consist of images with colors ranging from 0 to 255. To process them, we need to scale the data. By dividing the training and testing features by 255.0, we ensure that our features are scaled between 0 and 1:

```
features_train = features_train / 255.0

features_test = features_test / 255.0
```

Notice that we could have a 28x28 square matrix to describe the features, but we would rather flatten the matrix and simply use a vector. This is because the neural network model normally handles one-dimensional data.

Regarding the modeling of labels, many people think that it makes the most sense to model this problem with just one label: an integer value ranging from 0 to 9. This approach is problematic, because small errors in the calculation may result in completely different digits. We can imagine that a 5 is similar to a 6, so the adjacent values work really well here. However, in the case of 1 and 7, a small error may make the neural network realize a 1 as a 2, or a 7 as a 6. This is highly confusing, and it may take a lot more time to train the neural network to make less errors with adjacent values.

More importantly, when our neural network classifier comes back with a result of 4.2, we may have as much trouble interpreting the answer as the hero in *The Hitchhiker's Guide to the Galaxy*. 4.2 is most likely a 4. But if not, maybe it is a 5, or a 3, or a 6. This is not how digit detection works.

Therefore, it makes more sense to model this task using a vector of ten labels. When using TensorFlow for classification, it makes perfect sense to create one label for each possible class, with values ranging between 0 and 1. These numbers describe probabilities that the read digit is classified as a member of the class the label represents.

For instance, the value `[0, 0.1, 0, 0, 0.9, 0, 0, 0, 0, 0]` indicates that our digit has a 90% of being a 4, and a 10% chance of it being a 2.

In case of classification problems, we always use one output value per class.

Let's continue with the weights and biases. To connect 28*28 = 784 features and 10 labels, we need a 784 x 10 matrix of weights that has 784 rows and 10 columns.

Therefore, the equation becomes `y = f( x   W + b )`, where x is a vector in a 784-dimensional space, W is a 784 x 10 matrix, and b is a vector of biases in ten dimensions. The y vector also contains ten coordinates. The f function is defined on vectors with ten coordinates, and it is applied on each coordinate.

> **Note**
>
> To transform a two-dimensional 28x28 matrix of data points to a one-dimensional vector of 28x28 elements, we need to flatten the matrix. As opposed to many other languages and libraries, Python does not have a flatten method.

Since flattening is an easy task, let's construct a flatten method:

```
def flatten(matrix):
    return [elem for row in matrix for elem in row]
```

```
flatten([[1,2],[3,4]])
```

The output is as follows:

```
[1, 2, 3, 4]
```

Let's flatten the features from a 28*28 matrix to a vector of a 784-dimensional space:

```
features_train_vector = [
    flatten(image) for image in features_train
]
features_test_vector = [
    flatten(image) for image in features_test
]
```

To transfer the labels to a vector form, we need to perform normalization:

```
import numpy as np
label_train_vector = np.zeros((label_train.size, 10))
for i, label in enumerate(label_train_vector):
    label[label_train[i]] = 1
label_test_vector = np.zeros((label_test.size, 10))
for i, label in enumerate(label_test_vector):
    label[label_test[i]] = 1
```

TensorFlow Modeling for Multiple Labels

We will now model the following equation in TensorFlow: $y = f(x \quad W + b)$

After importing TensorFlow, we will define the features, labels, and weights:

```
import tensorflow as tf
f = tf.nn.sigmoid
x = tf.placeholder(tf.float32, [None, 28 * 28])
W = tf.Variable(tf.random_normal([784, 10]))
b = tf.Variable(tf.random_normal([10]))
```

We can simply write the equation $y = f(x \quad W + b)$ if we know how to perform dot product multiplication using TensorFlow.

If we treat x as a 1x84 matrix, we can multiply it with the 784x10 W matrix using the **tf.matmul** function.

Therefore, our equation becomes the following: **y = f(tf.add(tf.matmul(x, W), b)
)**

You might have noticed that x contains placeholders, while W and b are variables. This
is because the values of x are given. We just need to substitute them in the equation.
The task of TensorFlow is to optimize the values of W and b so that we maximize the
probability that we read the right digits.

Let's express the calculation of y in a function form:

```
def classify(x):
    return f(tf.add(tf.matmul(x, W), b))
```

> **Note**
>
> This is the place where we can define the activator function. In the activity at the
> end of this chapter, you are better off using the softmax activator function. This
> implies that you will have to replace sigmoid with softmax in the code:
>
> **f = tf.nn.softmax**

Optimizing the Variables

Placeholders symbolize the input. The task of TensorFlow is to optimize the variables.

To perform optimization, we need to use a cost function: cross-entropy. Cross-entropy
has the following properties:

- Its value is zero if the predicted output matches the real output
- Its value is strictly positive afterward

Our task is to minimize cross-entropy:

```
y = classify(x)
y_true = tf.placeholder(tf.float32, [None, 10])
cross_entropy = tf.nn.sigmoid_cross_entropy_with_logits(
    logits=y,
    labels=y_true
)
```

Although the function computing y is called classify, we do not perform the actual classification here. Remember, we are using placeholders in the place of x, and the actual values are substituted while running the TensorFlow session.

The **sigmoid_cross_entropy_with_logits** function takes two arguments to compare their values. The first argument is the label value, while the second argument is the result of the prediction.

To calculate the cost, we have to call the **reduce_mean** method of TensorFlow:

```
cost = tf.reduce_mean(cross_entropy)
```

Minimization of the cost goes through an optimizer. We will use the **GradientDescentOptimizer** with a learning rate. The learning rate is a parameter of the Neural Network that influences how fast the model adjusts:

```
optimizer = tf.train.GradientDescentOptimizer(learning_rate = 0.5).
minimize(cost)
```

Optimization is not performed at this stage, as we are not running TensorFlow yet. We will perform optimization in the main loop.

If you are using a different activator function such as softmax, you will have to replace it in the source code. Instead of the following statement:

```
cross_entropy = tf.nn.sigmoid_cross_entropy_with_logits(
    logits=y,
    labels=y_true
)
```

Use the following:

```
cross_entropy = tf.nn.softmax_cross_entropy_with_logits_v2(
    logits=y,
    labels=y_true
)
```

> **Note**
>
> The _v2 suffix in the method name. This is because the original **tf.nn.softmax_cross_entropy_with_logits** method is deprecated.

Training the TensorFlow Model

We need to create a TensorFlow session and run the model:

```
session = tf.Session()
```

First, we initialize the variables using **tf.global_variables_initializer()**:

```
session.run(tf.global_variables_initializer())
```

Then comes the optimization loop. We will determine the number of iterations and a batch size. In each iteration, we will randomly select a number of feature-label pairs equal to the batch size.

For demonstration purposes, instead of creating random batches, we will simply feed the upcoming hundred images each time a new iteration is started.

As we have 60,000 images in total, we could have up to 300 iterations and 200 images per iteration. In reality, we will only run a few iterations, which means that we will only use a fraction of the available training data:

```
iterations = 300
batch_size = 200
for i in range(iterations):
    min = i * batch_size
    max = (i+1) * batch_size
    dictionary = {
        x: features_train_vector[min:max],
        y_true: label_train_vector[min:max]
    }
    session.run(optimizer, feed_dict=dictionary)
    print('iteration: ', i)
```

Using the Model for Prediction

We can now use the trained model to perform prediction. The syntax is straightforward: we feed the test features to the dictionary of the session, and request the **classify(x)** value:

```
session.run(classify(x), feed_dict={
    x: features_test_vector[:10]
} )
```

Testing the Model

Now that our model has been trained and we can use it for prediction, it is time to test its performance:

```
label_predicted = session.run(classify(x), feed_dict={
    x: features_test_vector
})
```

We have to transfer the **labelsPredicted** values back to integers ranging from 0 to 9 by taking the index of the largest value from each result. We will use a NumPy function to perform this transformation.

The **argmax** function returns the index of its list or array argument that has the maximum value. The following is an example of this:

```
np.argmax([0.1, 0.3, 0.5, 0.2, 0, 0, 0, 0.2, 0, 0 ])
```

The output is **2**.

Here is the second example with **argmax** functions

```
np.argmax([1, 0, 1])
```

The output is **0**.

Let's perform the transformation:

```
label_predicted = [
    np.argmax(label) for label in label_predicted
]
```

We can use the metrics that we learned about in the previous chapters using scikit-learn. Let's calculate the confusion matrix first:

```
from sklearn.metrics import confusion_matrix, accuracy_score, precision_score, recall_score, f1_score

confusion_matrix(label_test, label_predicted)

accuracy_score(label_test, label_predicted)

precision_score( label_test, label_predicted, average='weighted' )

recall_score( label_test, label_predicted, average='weighted' )

f1_score( label_test, label_predicted, average='weighted' )
```

Randomizing the Sample Size

Recall the training function of the neural network:

```
iterations = 300
batch_size = 200
for i in range(iterations):
    min = i * batch_size
    max = (i+1) * batch_size
    dictionary = {
        x: features_train_vector[min:max],
        y_true: label_train_vector[min:max]
    }
    session.run(optimizer, feed_dict=dictionary)
```

The problem is that out of 60,000 numbers, we can only take 5 iterations. If we want to go beyond this threshold, we would run the risk of repeating these input sequences.

We can maximize the effectiveness of using the training data by randomly selecting the values out of the training data.

We can use the **random.sample** method for this purpose:

```
iterations = 6000
batch_size = 100
sample_size = len(features_train_vector)
for _ in range(iterations):
    indices = random.sample(range(sample_size), batchSize)
    batch_features = [
        features_train_vector[i] for i in indices
    ]
    batch_labels = [
        label_train_vector[i] for i in indices
    ]
    min = i * batch_size
    max = (i+1) * batch_size
    dictionary = {
```

```
        x: batch_features,

        y_true: batch_labels

    }

    session.run(optimizer, feed_dict=dictionary)
```

> **Note**
>
> The random sample method randomly selects a given number of elements out of a list. For instance, in Hungary, the main national lottery works based on selecting 5 numbers out of a pool of 90. We can simulate a lottery round using the following expression:

```
import random

random.sample(range(1,91), 5)
```

The output is as follows:

```
[63, 58, 25, 41, 60]
```

Activity 14: Written Digit Detection

In this section, we will discuss how to provide more security for cryptocurrency traders via the detection of hand-written digits. We will be using assuming that you are a software developer at a new cryptocurrency trader platform. The latest security measure you are implementing requires the recognition of hand-written digits. Use the MNIST library to train a neural network to recognize digits. You can read more about this dataset at https://www.tensorflow.org/tutorials/.

Improve the accuracy of the model as much as possible by performing the following steps:

1. Load the dataset and format the input.

2. Set up the TensorFlow graph. Instead of the sigmoid function, we will now use the **ReLU** function.

3. Train the model.

4. Test the model and calculate the accuracy score.

5. By re-running the code segment that's responsible for training the dataset, we can improve its accuracy. Run the code 50 times.

6. Print the confusion matrix.

At the end of the fiftieth run, the confusion matrix has improved.

Not a bad result. More than 8 out of 10 digits were accurately recognized.

> **Note**
>
> The solution for this activity can be found on page 298.

As you can see, neural networks do not improve linearly. It may appear that training the network brings little to no incremental improvement in accuracy for a while. Yet, after a certain threshold, a breakthrough happens, and the accuracy greatly increases.

This behavior is analogous with studying for humans. You might also have trouble with neural networks right now. However, after getting deeply immersed in the material and trying a few exercises out, you will reach breakthrough after breakthrough, and your progress will speed up.

Deep Learning

In this topic, we will increase the number of layers of the neural network. You may remember that we can add hidden layers to our graph. We will target improving the accuracy of our model by experimenting with hidden layers.

Adding Layers

Recall the diagram of neural networks with two hidden layers:

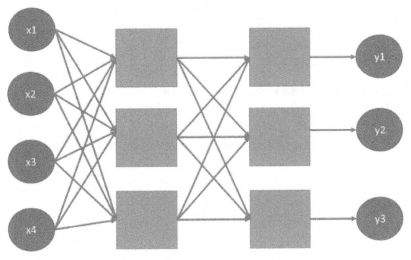

Figure 7.12: Diagram showing two hidden layers in a neural network

We can add a second layer to the equation by duplicating the weights and biases and making sure that the dimensions of the TensorFlow variables match. Note that in the first model, we transformed 784 features into 10 labels.

In this model, we will transform 784 features into a specified number of outputs. We will then take these outputs and transform them into 10 labels.

Determining the node count of the added hidden layer is not exactly science. We will use a count of 200 in this example, as it is somewhere between the feature and label dimensions.

As we have two layers, we will define two matrices (**W1**, **W2**) and vectors (**b1**, **b2**) for the weights and biases, respectively.

First, we reduce the 784 input dots using **W1** and **b1**, and create 200 variable values. We feed these values as the input of the second layer and use **W2** and **b2** to create 10 label values:

```
x = tf.placeholder(tf.float32, [None, 28 * 28 ])

f = tf.nn.softmax

W1 = tf.Variable(tf.random_normal([784, 200]))

b1 = tf.Variable(tf.random_normal([200]))

layer1_out = f(tf.add( tf.matmul(x, W1), b1))

W2 = tf.Variable(tf.random_normal([200, 10]))

b2 = tf.Variable(tf.random_normal([10]))

y = f(tf.add(tf.matmul(layer1_out, W2), b2))
```

We can increase the number of layers if needed in this way. The output of layer n must be the input of layer n+1. The rest of the code remains as it is.

Convolutional Neural Networks

Convolutional Neural Networks (**CNNs**) are artificial neural networks that are optimized for pattern recognition. CNNs are based on convolutional layers that are among the hidden layers of the deep neural network. A convolutional layer consists of neurons that transform their inputs using a convolution operation.

When using a convolution layer, we detect patterns in the image with an m*n matrix, where m and n are less than the width and the height of the image, respectively. When performing the convolution operation, we slide this m*n matrix over the image, matching every possibility. We calculate the scalar product of the m*n convolution filter and the pixel values of the 3x3 segment of the image our convolution filter is currently on. The convolution operation creates a new image from the original one, where the important aspects of our image are highlighted, and the less-important ones are blurred.

The convolution operation summarizes information on the window it is looking at. Therefore, it is an ideal operator for recognizing shapes in an image. Shapes can be anywhere on the image, and the convolution operator recognizes similar image information regardless of its exact position and orientation. Convolutional neural networks are outside the scope of this book, because it is a more advanced topic.

Activity 15: Written Digit Detection with Deep Learning

In this section, we will discuss how deep learning improves the performance of your model. We will be assuming that your boss is not satisfied with the results you presented in Activity 14 and has asked you to consider adding two hidden layers to your original model to determine whether new layers improve the accuracy of the model. To ensure that you are able to complete this activity correctly, you will need to be knowledgeable of deep learning:

1. Execute the steps from the previous activity and measure the accuracy of the model.

2. Change the neural network by adding new layers. We will combine the **ReLU** and **softmax** activator functions.

3. Retrain the model.

4. Evaluate the model. Find the accuracy score.

5. Run the code 50 times.

6. Print the confusion matrix.

This deep neural network behaves even more chaotically than the single layer one. It took 600 iterations of 200 samples to get from an accuracy of 0.572 to 0.5723. Not long after this iteration, we jumped from 0.6076 to 0.6834 in the same number of iterations.

Due to the flexibility of the deep neural network, we expect to reach an accuracy ceiling later than in the case of the simple model. Due to the complexity of a deep neural network, it is also more likely that it gets stuck at a local maximum for a long time.

> **Note**
>
> The solution for this activity can be found on page 302.

Summary

In this book, we have learned about the fundamentals of AI and applications of AI in chapter on principles of AI, then we wrote a Python code to model a Tic-Tac-Toe game.

In the chapter AI with Search Techniques and Games, we solved the Tic-Tac-Toe game with game AI tools and search techniques. We learned about the search algorithms of Breadth First Search and Depth First Search. The A* algorithm helped students model a pathfinding problem. The chapter was concluded with modeling multiplayer games.

In the next couple of chapters, we learned about supervised learning using regression and classification. These chapters included data preprocessing, train-test splitting, and models that were used in several real-life scenarios. Linear regression, polynomial regression, and Support Vector Machines all came in handy when it came to predicting stock data. Classification was performed using the k-nearest neighbor and Support Vector classifiers. Several activities helped students apply the basics of classification an interesting real-life use case: credit scoring.

In *Chapter 5, Using Trees for Predictive Analysis*, we were introduced to decision trees, random forests, and extremely randomized trees. This chapter introduced different means to evaluating the utility of models. We learned how to calculate the accuracy, precision, recall, and F1 Score of models. We also learned how to create the confusion matrix of a model. The models of this chapter were put into practice through the evaluation of car data.

Unsupervised learning was introduced in *Chapter 6, Clustering*, along with the k-means and mean shift clustering algorithms. One interesting aspect of these algorithms is that the labels are not given in advance, but they are detected during the clustering process.

This book was concluded with Chapter 7, *Deep Learning with Neural Networks*, where neural networks and deep learning using TensorFlow was presented. We used these techniques on a real-life example: the detection of written digits.

Appendix

About

This section is included to assist the students to perform the activities in the book. It includes detailed steps that are to be performed by the students to achieve the objectives of the activities.

Chapter 1: Principles of AI

In the code, backslash (\) indicates a line break, where the code does not fit a line. A backslash at the end of the line escapes the newline character. This means that the content in the line following the backslash should be read as if it started where the backslash character is.

Activity 1: Generating All Possible Sequences of Steps in the tic-tac-toe Game

This section will explore the combinatoric explosion possible when two players play randomly. We will be using a program, building on the previous results that generate all possible sequences of moves between a computer player and a human player. Determine the number of different wins, losses, and draws in terms of action sequences. Assume that the human player may make any possible move. In this example, given that the computer player is playing randomly, we will examine the wins, losses, and draws belonging to two randomly playing players:

1. Create a function that maps the **all_moves_from_board** function on each element of a list of boards. This way, we will have all of the nodes of a decision tree in each depth:

```
def all_moves_from_board(board, sign):
    move_list = []
    for i, v in enumerate(board):
        if v == EMPTY_SIGN:
            move_list.append(board[:i] + sign + board[i+1:])
    return move_list
```

2. The decision tree starts with **[EMPTY_SIGN * 9]**, and expands after each move:

```
all_moves_from_board_list( [ EMPTY_SIGN * 9 ], AI_SIGN )
```

3. The output is as follows:

```
['X........',
 '.X.......',
 '..X......',
 '...X.....',
 '....X....',
 '.....X...',
 '......X..',
 '.......X.',
 '........X']
['XO.......',
 'X.O......',
 'X..O.....',
```

```
        'X...O....',
        'X....O...',
        'X.....O..',
        'X......O.',



        '......OX.',
        '.......XO',
        'O.......X',
        '.O......X',
        '..O.....X',
        '...O....X',
        '....O...X',
        '.....O..X',
        '......O.X',
        '.......OX']
```

4. Let's create a **filter_wins** function that takes the ended games out from the list of moves and appends them in an array containing the board states won by the AI player and the opponent player:

```python
def filter_wins(move_list, ai_wins, opponent_wins):
    for board in move_list:
        won_by = game_won_by(board)
        if won_by == AI_SIGN:
            ai_wins.append(board)
            move_list.remove(board)
        elif won_by == OPPONENT_SIGN:
            opponent_wins.append(board)
            move_list.remove(board)
```

5. In this function, the three lists can be considered as reference types. This means that the function does not return a value, instead but it manipulating these three lists without returning them.

6. Let's finish this section. Then with a **count_possibilities** function that prints the number of decision tree leaves that ended with a draw, won by the first player, and won by the second player:

```python
def count_possibilities():
    board = EMPTY_SIGN * 9
    move_list = [board]
    ai_wins = []
    opponent_wins = []
    for i in range(9):
        print('step ' + str(i) + '. Moves: ' + \
        str(len(move_list)))
        sign = AI_SIGN if i % 2 == 0 else OPPONENT_SIGN
        move_list = all_moves_from_board_list(move_list, sign)
        filter_wins(move_list, ai_wins, opponent_wins)
    print('First player wins: ' + str(len(ai_wins)))
    print('Second player wins: ' + str(len(opponent_wins)))
    print('Draw', str(len(move_list)))
    print('Total', str(len(ai_wins) + len(opponent_wins) + \
    len(move_list)))
```

7. We have up to 9 steps in each state. In the 0th, 2nd, 4th, 6th, and 8th iteration, the AI player moves. In all other iterations, the opponent moves. We create all possible moves in all steps and take out the ended games from the move list.

8. Then execute the number of possibilities to experience the combinatoric explosion.

```python
count_possibilities()
```

9. The output is as follows:

```
step 0. Moves: 1
step 1. Moves: 9
step 2. Moves: 72
step 3. Moves: 504
step 4. Moves: 3024
step 5. Moves: 13680
step 6. Moves: 49402
step 7. Moves: 111109
step 8. Moves: 156775
First player wins: 106279
Second player wins: 68644
Draw 91150
Total 266073
```

As you can see, the tree of board states consists of 266,073 leaves. The **count_possibilities** function essentially implements a breadth first search algorithm to traverse all the possible states of the game. Notice that we do count these states multiple times, because placing an X on the top-right corner on step 1 and placing an X on the top-left corner on step 3 leads to similar possible states as starting with the top-left corner and then placing an X on the top-right corner. If we implemented a detection of duplicate states, we would have to check less nodes. However, at this stage, due to the limited depth of the game, we omit this step.

Chapter 2: AI with Search Techniques and Games

Activity 2: Teach the agent realize situations when it defends against losses

Follow these steps to complete the activity:

1. Create a function **player_can_win** such that it takes all moves from the board using the **all_moves_from_board** function and iterates over it using a variable **next_move**. On each iteration, it checks if the game can be won by the sign, then it return true else false.

```python
def player_can_win(board, sign):
    next_moves = all_moves_from_board(board, sign)
    for next_move in next_moves:
        if game_won_by(next_move) == sign:
            return True
    return False
```

2. We will extend the AI move such that it prefers making safe moves. A move is safe if the opponent cannot win the game in the next step.

```python
def ai_move(board):
    new_boards = all_moves_from_board(board, AI_SIGN)
    for new_board in new_boards:
        if game_won_by(new_board) == AI_SIGN:
            return new_board
    safe_moves = []
    for new_board in new_boards:
        if not player_can_win(new_board, OPPONENT_SIGN):
            safe_moves.append(new_board)
    return choice(safe_moves) if len(safe_moves) > 0 else \
        new_boards[0]
```

3. You can test our new application. You will find the AI has made the correct move.

4. We will now place this logic in the state space generator and check how well the computer player is doing by generating all the possible games.

```python
def all_moves_from_board( board, sign ):
```

5. We will now place this logic in the state space generator and check how well the computer player is doing by generating all the possible games.

```python
def all_moves_from_board(board, sign):
    move_list = []
    for i, v in enumerate(board):
        if v == EMPTY_SIGN:
            new_board = board[:i] + sign + board[i+1:]
            move_list.append(new_board)
            if game_won_by(new_board) == AI_SIGN:
                return [new_board]
    if sign == AI_SIGN:
        safe_moves = []
        for move in move_list:
            if not player_can_win(move, OPPONENT_SIGN):
                safe_moves.append(move)
        return safe_moves if len(safe_moves) > 0 else \
            move_list[0:1]
    else:
        return move_list
```

6. Count the possibilities that as possible.

```python
count_possibilities()
```

7. The output is as follows:

```
step 0. Moves: 1
step 1. Moves: 9
step 2. Moves: 72
step 3. Moves: 504
step 4. Moves: 3024
step 5. Moves: 5197
step 6. Moves: 18606
step 7. Moves: 19592
step 8. Moves: 30936
```

```
First player wins: 20843
Second player wins: 962
Draw 20243
Total 42048
```

We are doing better than before. We not only got rid of almost 2/3 of possible games again, but most of the time, the AI player either wins or settles for a draw. Despite our effort to make the AI better, it can still lose in 962 ways. We will eliminate all these losses in the next activity.

Activity 3: Fix the first and second moves of the AI to make it invincible

Follow these steps to complete the activity:

1. We will count the number of empty fields in the board and make a hard-coded move in case there are 9 or 7 empty fields. You can experiment with different hard coded moves. We found that occupying any corner, then occupying the opposite corner leads to no losses. If the opponent occupied the opposite corner, making a move in the middle results in no losses.

```python
def all_moves_from_board(board, sign):
    if sign == AI_SIGN:
        empty_field_count = board.count(EMPTY_SIGN)
        if empty_field_count == 9:
            return [sign + EMPTY_SIGN * 8]
        elif empty_field_count == 7:
            return [
                board[:8] + sign if board[8] == \
                    EMPTY_SIGN else
                board[:4] + sign + board[5:]
            ]
    move_list = []
    for i, v in enumerate(board):
        if v == EMPTY_SIGN:
            new_board = board[:i] + sign + board[i+1:]
            move_list.append(new_board)
            if game_won_by(new_board) == AI_SIGN:
                return [new_board]
    if sign == AI_SIGN:
```

```
            safe_moves = []
            for move in move_list:
                if not player_can_win(move, OPPONENT_SIGN):
                    safe_moves.append(move)
            return safe_moves if len(safe_moves) > 0 else \
                move_list[0:1]
        else:
            return move_list
```

2. Let's verify the state space

   ```
   countPossibilities()
   ```

3. The output is as follows:

   ```
   step 0. Moves: 1
   step 1. Moves: 1
   step 2. Moves: 8
   step 3. Moves: 8
   step 4. Moves: 48
   step 5. Moves: 38
   step 6. Moves: 108
   step 7. Moves: 76
   step 8. Moves: 90
   First player wins: 128
   Second player wins: 0
   Draw 60
   ```

4. After fixing the first two steps, we only need to deal with 8 possibilities instead of 504. We also guided the AI into a state, where the hard-coded rules were sufficient for never losing a game.

5. Fixing the steps is not important because we would give the AI hard coded steps to start with, but it is important, because it is a tool to evaluate and compare each step.

6. After fixing the first two steps, we only need to deal with 8 possibilities instead of 504. We also guided the AI into a state, where the hard-coded rules were sufficient for never losing a game.

Activity 4: Connect Four

This section will practice using the **EasyAI** library and develop a heuristic. We will be using connect four game. The game board is seven cells wide and cells high. When you make a move, you can only select the column in which you drop your token. Then gravity pulls the token down to the lowest possible empty cell. Your objective is to connect four of your own tokens horizontally, vertically, or diagonally, before your opponent does this, or you run out of empty spaces. The rules of the game can be found at: https://en.wikipedia.org/wiki/Connect_Four

1. Let's set up the TwoPlayersGame framework:

```
from easyAI import TwoPlayersGame
from easyAI.Player import Human_Player
class ConnectFour(TwoPlayersGame):
    def __init__(self, players):
        self.players = players
    def possible_moves(self):
        return []
    def make_move(self, move):
        return
    def unmake_move(self, move):
# optional method (speeds up the AI)
        return
    def lose(self):
        return False
    def is_over(self):
        return (self.possible_moves() == []) or self.lose()
    def show(self):
        print ('board')
    def scoring(self):
        return -100 if self.lose() else 0

if __name__ == "__main__":
    from easyAI import AI_Player, Negamax
    ai_algo = Negamax(6)
```

2. We can leave a few functions from the definition intact. We have to implement the following methods:

```
__init__
possible_moves
make_move
unmake_move (optional)
lose
show
```

3. We will reuse the basic scoring function from tic-tac-toe. Once you test out the game, you will see that the game is not unbeatable, but plays surprisingly well, even though we are only using basic heuristics.

4. Let's write the init method. We will define the board as a one-dimensional list, similar to the tic-tac-toe example. We could use a two-dimensional list too, but modeling will not get much easier or harder. Beyond making initializations like we did in the tic-tac-toe game, we will work a bit ahead. We will generate all of the possible winning combinations in the game and save them for future use:

```python
def __init__(self, players):
    self.players = players
    #  0  1  2  3  4  5  6
    #  7  8  9 10 11 12 13
    # ...
    # 35 36 37 38 39 40 41
    self.board = [0 for i in range(42)]
    self.nplayer = 1  # player 1 starts.
    def generate_winning_tuples():
        tuples = []
        # horizontal
        tuples += [
            list(range(row*7+column, row*7+column+4, 1))
            for row in range(6)
            for column in range(4)]
        # vertical
        tuples += [
            list(range(row*7+column, row*7+column+28, 7))
            for row in range(3)
            for column in range(7)
        ]
```

```
# diagonal forward
tuples += [
    list(range(row*7+column, row*7+column+32, 8))
    for row in range(3)
    for column in range(4)
]

# diagonal backward

tuples += [

    list(range(row*7+column, row*7+column+24, 6))
    for row in range(3)
    for column in range(3, 7, 1)
]
return tuples

self.tuples=generate_winning_tuples()
```

5. Let's handle the moves. The possible moves function is a simple enumeration. Notice we are using column indices from 1 to 7 in the move names, because it is more convenient to start column indexing with 1 in the human player interface than with zero. For each column, we check if there is an unoccupied field. If there is one, we will make the column a possible move.

```
def possible_moves(self):
    return [column+1
            for column in range(7)
            if any([
                self.board[column+row*7] == 0
                for row in range(6)
            ])
            ]
```

6. Making a move is similar to the possible moves function. We check the column of the move, and find the first empty cell starting from the bottom. Once we find it, we occupy it. You can also read the implementation of the dual of the make_move function: unmake_move. In the unmake_move function, we check the column from top to down, and we remove the move at the first non-empty cell. Notice we rely on the internal representation of easyAi so that it does not undo moves that it had not made. Otherwise, this function would remove a token of the other player without checking whose token got removed.

```
def make_move(self, move):
        column = int(move) - 1
        for row in range(5, -1, -1):
            index = column + row*7
            if self.board[index] == 0:
                self.board[index] = self.nplayer
                return


    def unmake_move(self, move):
# optional method (speeds up the AI)
        column = int(move) - 1
        for row in range(6):
            index = column + row*7
            if self.board[index] != 0:
                self.board[index] = 0
                return
```

7. As we already have the tuples that we have to check, we can mostly reuse the lose function from the tic-tac-toe example.

```
def lose(self):
        return any([all([(self.board[c] == self.nopponent)
                        for c in line])
                    for line in self.tuples])

    def is_over(self):
        return (self.possible_moves() == []) or self.lose()
```

8. Our last task is the show method that prints the board. We will reuse the tic-tac-toe implementation, and just change the variables.

```
def show(self):
        print('\n'+'\n'.join([
            ' '.join([['.', 'O', 'X'][self.board[7*row+column]]
                    for column in range(7)]
                )
            for row in range(6)])
    )
```

Now that all functions are complete, you can try out the example. Feel free to play a round or two against the opponent. You can see that the opponent is not perfect, but it plays reasonably well. If you have a strong computer, you can increase the parameter of the Negamax algorithm. I encourage you to come up with a better heuristic.

Chapter 3: Regression

Activity 5: Predicting Population

You are working at the government office of Metropolis, trying to forecast the need for elementary school capacity. Your task is to figure out a 2025 and 2030 prediction for the number of children starting elementary school. Past data are as follows:

Year	No of Students	Year	No of Students
2001	147026	2010	139452
2002	144272	2011	139722
2003	140020	2012	135300
2004	143801	2013	137289
2005	146233	2014	136511
2006	144539	2015	132884
2007	141273	2016	125683
2008	135389	2017	127255
2009	142500	2018	124275

Figure 3.21 Data of Elementary School

Plot tendencies on a two-dimensional chart. Use linear regression.

Our features are the years ranging from 2001 to 2018. For simplicity, we can indicate 2001 as year 1, and 2018 as year 18.

```
x = np.array(range(1, 19))
y = np.array([
    147026,
    144272,
    140020,
    143801,
    146233,
    144539,
    141273,
    135389,
    142500,
    139452,
    139722,
    135300,
    137289,
    136511,
    132884,
    125683,
    127255,
    124275
])
```

Use np.polyfit to determine the coefficients of the regression line.

```
[a, b] = np.polyfit(x, y, 1)
[-1142.0557275541753, 148817.5294117646]
```

Plot the results using matplotlib.pyplot to determine future tendencies.

```
import matplotlib.pyplot as plot
plot.scatter( x, y )
plot.plot( [0, 30], [b, 30*a+b] )
plot.show()
```

Activity 6: Stock Price Prediction with Quadratic and Cubic Linear Polynomial Regression with Multiple Variables

This section will discuss how to perform linear, polynomial, and support vector regression with scikit-learn. We will also learn to predict the best fit model for a given task. We will be assuming that you are a software engineer at a financial institution and your employer wants to know whether linear regression, or support vector regression is a better fit for predicting stock prices. You will have to load all data of the S&P 500 from a data source. Then build a regressor using linear regression, cubic polynomial linear regression, and a support vector regression with a polynomial kernel of degree 3. Then separate training and test data. Plot the test labels and the prediction results and compare them with the **y=x** line. And finally, compare how well the three models score.

Let's load the S&P 500 index data using **Quandl**, then prepare the data for prediction. You can read the process in the Predicting the Future section of the topic Linear Regression with Multiple Variables.

```
import quandl
import numpy as np
from sklearn import preprocessing
from sklearn import model_selection
from sklearn import linear_model
from sklearn.preprocessing import PolynomialFeatures
from matplotlib import pyplot as plot
from sklearn import svm
data_frame = quandl.get("YALE/SPCOMP")
data_frame[['Long Interest Rate', 'Real Price',
            'Real Dividend', 'Cyclically Adjusted PE Ratio']]
data_frame.fillna(-100, inplace=True)

# We shift the price data to be predicted 20 years forward
data_frame['Real Price Label'] = data_frame['RealPrice'].shift(-240)

# Then exclude the label column from the features
features = np.array(data_frame.drop('Real Price Label', 1))

# We scale before dropping the last 240 rows from the features
```

```python
scaled_features = preprocessing.scale(features)
# Save the last 240 rows before dropping them
scaled_features_latest240 = scaled_features[-240:]


# Exclude the last 240 rows from the data used for #
# modelbuilding
scaled_features = scaled_features[:-240]


# Now we can drop the last 240 rows from the data frame
data_frame.dropna(inplace=True)


# Then build the labels from the remaining data
label = np.array(data_frame['Real Price Label'])


# The rest of the model building stays
(features_train,
    features_test,
    label_train,
    label_test
) = model_selection.train_test_split(
    scaled_features,
    label,
    test_size=0.1
)
```

Let's first use a polynomial of degree 1 for the evaluation of the model and for the prediction. We are still recreating the main example from the second topic.

```
model = linear_model.LinearRegression()
model.fit(features_train, label_train)
model.score(features_test, label_test)
```

1. The output is as follows:

    ```
    0.8978136465083912
    ```

2. The output always depends on the test data, so the values may differ after each run.

    ```
    label_predicted = model.predict(features_test)
    plot.plot(
        label_test, label_predicted, 'o',
        [0, 3000], [0, 3000]
    )
    ```

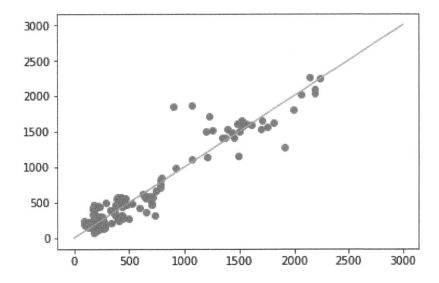

Fig 3.22: Graph showing the output

The closer the dots are to the y=x line, the less error the model works with.

It is now time to perform a linear multiple regression with quadratic polynomials. The only change is in the Linear Regression model

```
poly_regressor = PolynomialFeatures(degree=3)
poly_scaled_features = poly_regressor.fit_transform(scaled_features)
(poly_features_train,
 poly_features_test,
 poly_label_train,
 poly_label_test) = model_selection.train_test_split(
    poly_scaled_features,
    label,
    test_size=0.1)
model = linear_model.LinearRegression()
model.fit(poly_features_train, poly_label_train)
print('Polynomial model score: ', model.score(
    poly_features_test, poly_label_test))
print('\n')
poly_label_predicted = model.predict(poly_features_test)
plot.plot(
    poly_label_test, poly_label_predicted, 'o',
    [0, 3000], [0, 3000]
)
```

The model is performing surprisingly well on test data. Therefore, we can already suspect our polynomials are overfitting for scenarios used in training and testing.

We will now perform a Support Vector regression with a polynomial kernel of degree 3.

```
model = svm.SVR(kernel='poly')
model.fit(features_train, label_train)
label_predicted = model.predict(features_test)
plot.plot(
    label_test, label_predicted, 'o',
    [0,3000], [0,3000]
)
```

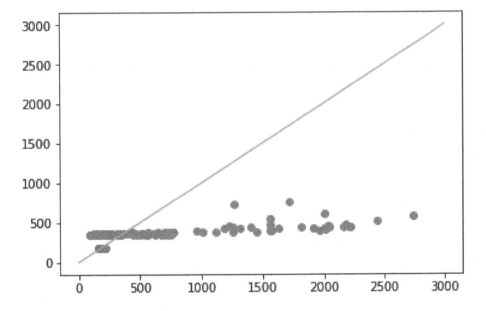

Fig 3.23: Graph showing the output

```
model.score(features_test, label_test)
```

The output will be **0.06388628722032952**.

We will now perform a Support Vector regression with a polynomial kernel of degree 3.

Chapter 4: Classification

Activity 7: Preparing Credit Data for Classification

This section will discuss how to prepare data for a classifier. We will be using german. data from https://archive.ics.uci.edu/ml/machine-learning-databases/statlog/german/, as an example and prepare the data for training and testing a classifier. Make sure all your labels are numeric, and the values are prepared for classification. Use 80% of the data points as training data.

1. Save german.data from https://archive.ics.uci.edu/ml/machine-learning-data-bases/statlog/german/, and open it in a text editor like Sublime Text or Atom. Add the following first row to it:

   ```
   CheckingAccountStatus DurationMonths CreditHistory CreditPurpose
   CreditAmount SavingsAccount EmploymentSince DisposableIncomePercent
   PersonalStatusSex OtherDebtors PresentResidenceMonths Property Age
   OtherInstallmentPlans Housing NumberOfExistingCreditsInBank Job
   LiabilityNumberOfPeople Phone ForeignWorker CreditScore
   ```

2. Import the data file using pandas and replace NA values with an outlier value:

   ```
   import pandas
   data_frame = pandas.read_csv('german.data', sep=' ')
   data_frame.replace('NA', -1000000, inplace=True)
   ```

3. Perform label encoding. We need to transform all labels in the data frame to integers. We could create all labels in a one dimensional array. However, this would be highly ineffective, because each label occurs in exactly one column. It makes a lot more sense to group our labels per column:

   ```
   labels = {
     'CheckingAccountStatus': ['A11', 'A12', 'A13', 'A14'],
     'CreditHistory': ['A30', 'A31', 'A32', 'A33', 'A34'],
     'CreditPurpose': ['A40', 'A41', 'A42', 'A43', 'A44', 'A45', 'A46', 'A47',
   'A48', 'A49', 'A410'],
     'SavingsAccount': ['A61', 'A62', 'A63', 'A64', 'A65'],
     'EmploymentSince': ['A71', 'A72', 'A73', 'A74', 'A75'],
     'PersonalStatusSex': ['A91', 'A92', 'A93', 'A94', 'A95'],
     'OtherDebtors': ['A101', 'A102', 'A103'],
     'Property': ['A121', 'A122', 'A123', 'A124'],
     'OtherInstallmentPlans': ['A141', 'A142', 'A143'],
     'Housing': ['A151', 'A152', 'A153'],
     'Job': ['A171', 'A172', 'A173', 'A174'],
     'Phone': ['A191', 'A192'],
   ```

```
    'ForeignWorker': ['A201', 'A202']
}
```

4. Let's create a label encoder for each column and encode the values:

```
from sklearn import preprocessing
label_encoders = {}
data_frame_encoded = pandas.DataFrame()
for column in data_frame:
    if column in labels:
        label_encoders[column] = preprocessing.LabelEncoder()
        label_encoders[column].fit(labels[column])
        data_frame_encoded[column] = label_encoders[
            column].transform(data_frame[column])
    else:
        data_frame_encoded[column] = data_frame[column]
```

Let's verify that we did everything correctly:

```
data_frame_encoded.head()
```

	CheckingAccountStatus	DurationMonths	CreditHistory	CreditPurpose	\
0	0	6	4	4	
1	1	48	2	4	
2	3	12	4	7	
3	0	42	2	3	
4	0	24	3	0	

	CreditAmount	SavingsAccount	EmploymentSince	DisposableIncomePercent	\
0	1169	4	4	4	
1	5951	0	2	2	
2	2096	0	3	2	
3	7882	0	3	2	
4	4870	0	2	3	

```
       PersonalStatusSex   OtherDebtors      ...      Property   Age  \
0                    2               0       ...             0   67
1                    1               0       ...             0   22
2                    2               0       ...             0   49
3                    2               2       ...             1   45
4                    2               0       ...             3   53
       OtherInstallmentPlans   Housing   NumberOfExistingCreditsInBank   Job  \
0                         2         1                               2     2
1                         2         1                               1     2
2                         2         1                               1     1
3                         2         2                               1     2
4                         2         2                               2     2

       LiabilityNumberOfPeople   Phone   ForeignWorker   CreditScore
0                            1       1               0             1
1                            1       0               0             2
2                            2       0               0             1
3                            2       0               0             1
4                            2       0               0             2


[5 rows x 21 columns]


label_encoders
{'CheckingAccountStatus': LabelEncoder(),
 'CreditHistory': LabelEncoder(),
 'CreditPurpose': LabelEncoder(),
 'EmploymentSince': LabelEncoder(),
 'ForeignWorker': LabelEncoder(),
 'Housing': LabelEncoder(),
 'Job': LabelEncoder(),
 'OtherDebtors': LabelEncoder(),
 'OtherInstallmentPlans': LabelEncoder(),
```

```
'PersonalStatusSex': LabelEncoder(),
'Phone': LabelEncoder(),
'Property': LabelEncoder(),
'SavingsAccount': LabelEncoder()}
```

All the 21 columns are available, and the label encoders have been saved in an object too. Our data are now pre-processed.

> You don't need to save these label encoders if you don't wish to decode the encoded values. We just saved them for the sake of completeness.

1. It is time to separate features from labels. We can apply the same method as the one we saw in the theory section:

```
import numpy as np
features = np.array(
    data_frame_encoded.drop(['CreditScore'], 1)
)
label = np.array(data_frame_encoded['CreditScore'])
```

Our features are not yet scaled. This is a problem, because the credit amount distances can be significantly higher than the differences in age for instance.

We must perform scaling of the training and testing data together, therefore, the latest step when we can still perform scaling is before we split training data from testing data.

2. Let's use a Min-Max scaler from scikit's Preprocessing library:

```
scaled_features = preprocessing.MinMaxScaler(
feature_range=(0,1)).fit_transform(features)
```

3. The final step is cross-validation. We will shuffle our data, and use 80% of all data for training, 20% for testing.

```
from sklearn import model_selection
features_train, features_test, label_train,
label_test = model_selection.train_test_split(
    scaled_features,
    label,
    test_size = 0.2
)
```

Activity 8: Increase the accuracy of credit scoring

This section will learn how the parametrization of the k-nearest neighbor classifier affects the end result. The accuracy of credit scoring is currently quite low: 66.5%. Find a way to increase it by a few percentage points. And to ensure that it happens correctly, you will need to do the previous exercises.

There are many ways to accomplish this exercise. In this solution, I will show you one way to increase the credit score by changing the parametrization.

You must have completed Exercise 13, to be able to complete this activity.

1. Increase the K-value of the k-nearest neighbor classifier from the default 5 to 10, 15, 25, and 50. Evaluate the results:

    ```
    You must have completed Exercise 13, to be able to complete this activity
    classifier = neighbors.KNeighborsClassifier(n_neighbors=10)
    classifier.fit(
        features_train,label_train
        )
    classifier.score(features_test, label_test)
    ```

2. After running these lines for all four **n_neighbors** values, I got the following results:

    ```
    K=10: accuracy is 71.5%
    K=15: accuracy is 70.5%
    K=25: accuracy is 72%
    K=50: accuracy is 74%
    ```

3. Higher K values do not necessarily mean better score. In this example though, **K=50** yielded a better result than **K=5**.

Activity 9: Support Vector Machine Optimization in scikit-learn

This section will discuss how to use the different parameters of a Support Vector Machine classifier. We will be using comparing and contrasting the different support vector regression classifier parameters you learned and find a set of parameters resulting in the highest classification data on the training and testing data loaded and prepared in previous activity. And to ensure that it happens correctly, you will need to have completed the previous activities and exercises.

We will try out a few combinations. You may choose different parameters, that

1. Linear kernel

```
classifier = svm.SVC(kernel="linear")
classifier.fit(features_train, label_train)
classifier.score(features_test, label_test)
```

2. Polynomial kernel of degree 4, C=2, gamma=0.05

```
classifier = svm.SVC(kernel="poly", C=2, degree=4, gamma=0.05)
classifier.fit(features_train, label_train)
classifier.score(features_test, label_test)
```

The output is as follows: 0.705.

3. Polynomial kernel of degree 4, C=2, gamma=0.25

```
classifier = svm.SVC(kernel="poly", C=2, degree=4, gamma=0.25)
classifier.fit(features_train, label_train)
classifier.score(features_test, label_test)
```

The output is as follows: 0.76.

4. Polynomial kernel of degree 4, C=2, gamma=0.5

```
classifier = svm.SVC(kernel="poly", C=2, degree=4, gamma=0.5)
classifier.fit(features_train, label_train)
classifier.score(features_test, label_test)
```

The output is as follows: 0.72.

5. Sigmoid kernel

```
classifier = svm.SVC(kernel="sigmoid")
classifier.fit(features_train, label_train)
classifier.score(features_test, label_test)
```

The output is as follows: 0.71.

6. Default kernel with a gamma of 0.15

```
classifier = svm.SVC(kernel="rbf", gamma=0.15)
classifier.fit(features_train, label_train)
classifier.score(features_test, label_test)
```

The output is as follows: 0.76.

Chapter 5: Using Trees for Predictive Analysis

Activity 10: Car Data Classification

This section will discuss how to build a reliable decision tree model capable of aiding your company in finding cars clients are likely to buy. We will be assuming that you are employed by a car rental agency focusing on building a lasting relationship with its clients. Your task is to build a decision tree model classifying cars into one of four categories: unacceptable, acceptable, good, very good.

The data set can be accessed here: https://archive.ics.uci.edu/ml/datasets/Car+Evaluation. Click the Data Folder link to download the data set. Click the Data Set Description link to access the description of the attributes.

Evaluate the utility of your decision tree model.

1. Download the car data file from here: https://archive.ics.uci.edu/ml/machine-learning-databases/car/car.data. Add a header line to the front of the CSV file to reference it in Python more easily:

    Buying,Maintenance,Doors,Persons,LuggageBoot,Safety,Class

    We simply call the label Class. We named the six features after their descriptions in https://archive.ics.uci.edu/ml/machine-learning-databases/car/car.names.

2. Load the data set into Python

    ```
    import pandas
    data_frame = pandas.read_csv('car.data')
    ```

    Let's check if the data got loaded correctly:

    ```
    data_frame.head()
      Buying Maintenance Doors Persons LuggageBoot Safety  Class
    0  vhigh       vhigh     2       2       small    low  unacc
    1  vhigh       vhigh     2       2       small    med  unacc
    2  vhigh       vhigh     2       2       small   high  unacc
    3  vhigh       vhigh     2       2         med    low  unacc
    4  vhigh       vhigh     2       2         med    med  unacc
    ```

3. As classification works with numeric data, we have to perform label encoding as seen in previous chapter.

```
labels = {
    'Buying': ['vhigh', 'high', 'med', 'low'],
    'Maintenance': ['vhigh', 'high', 'med', 'low'],
    'Doors': ['2', '3', '4', '5more'],
    'Persons': ['2', '4', 'more'],
    'LuggageBoot': ['small', 'med', 'big'],
    'Safety': ['low', 'med', 'high'],
    'Class': ['unacc', 'acc', 'good', 'vgood']
}
from sklearn import preprocessing
label_encoders = {}
data_frame_encoded = pandas.DataFrame()
for column in data_frame:
    if column in labels:
        label_encoders[column] = preprocessing.LabelEncoder()
        label_encoders[column].fit(labels[column])
        data_frame_encoded[column] = label_encoders[column].
transform(data_frame[column])
    else:
data_frame_encoded[column] = data_frame[column]
```

4. Let's separate features from labels:

```
import numpy as np
features = np.array(data_frame_encoded.drop(['Class'], 1))
label = np.array( data_frame_encoded['Class'] )
```

5. It is time to separate training and testing data with the cross-validation (in newer versions model-selection) featue of scikit-learn. We will use 10% test data:

```
from sklearn import model_selection
features_train, features_test, label_train, label_test = model_selection.
train_test_split(
    features,
    label,
    test_size=0.1
)
```

Note that the train_test_split method will be available in model_selection module, not in the cross_validation module starting in scikit-learn 0.20. In previous versions, model_selection already contains the train_test_split method.

6. We have everything to build the decision tree classifier:

```
from sklearn.tree import DecisionTreeClassifier
decision_tree = DecisionTreeClassifier()
decision_tree.fit(features_train, label_train)
```

The output of the fit method is as follows:

```
DecisionTreeClassifier(
    class_weight=None,
    criterion='gini',
    max_depth=None,
    max_features=None,
    max_leaf_nodes=None,
    min_impurity_decrease=0.0,
    min_impurity_split=None,
    min_samples_leaf=1,
    min_samples_split=2,
    min_weight_fraction_leaf=0.0,
    presort=False,
    random_state=None,
    splitter='best'
)
```

You can see the parametrization of the decision tree classifier. There are quite a few options we could set to tweak the performance of the classifier model.

7. Let's score our model based on the test data:

```
decision_tree.score( features_test, label_test )
```

The output is as follows:

```
0.9884393063583815
```

8. This is the point where your knowledge up until chapter 4 would take you on model evaluation. We will now go a bit further and create a deeper evaluation of the model based on the classification_report feature we learned in this topic:

```
from sklearn.metrics import classification_report
print(
    classification_report(
        label_test,
        decision_tree.predict(features_test)
    )
)
```

The output is as follows:

	precision	recall	f1-score	support
0	0.97	0.97	0.97	36
1	1.00	1.00	1.00	5
2	1.00	0.99	1.00	127
3	0.83	1.00	0.91	5
avg / total	0.99	0.99	0.99	173

The model has been proven to be quite accurate. In case of such a high accuracy score, suspect the possibility of overfitting.

Activity 11: Random Forest Classification for your Car Rental Company

1. This section will optimize your classifier to satisfy your clients better when selecting future cars for your car fleet. We will be performing random forest and extreme random forest classification on your car dealership data set you worked on in Activity 1 of this chapter. Suggest further improvements to the model to improve the performance of the classifier.

    We can reuse Steps 1 – 5 of Activity 1. The end of Step 5 looks as follows:

```
from sklearn import model_selection
features_train, features_test, label_train, label_test = model_selection.
train_test_split(
    features,
    label,
    test_size=0.1
)
```

If you are using IPython, your variables may already be accessible in your console.

2. Let's create a Random Forest and an Extremely Randomized Trees classifier and train the models.

```
from sklearn.ensemble import RandomForestClassifier,ExtraTreesClassifier

random_forest_classifier = RandomForestClassifier(n_estimators=100, max_
depth=6)
random_forest_classifier.fit(features_train, label_train)
extra_trees_classifier =ExtraTreesClassifier(
    n_estimators=100, max_depth=6
)
extra_trees_classifier.fit(features_train, label_train)
```

3. Let's estimate how well the two models perform on the test data:

```
from sklearn.metrics import classification_report
print(
    classification_report(
        label_test,
        random_forest_classifier.predict(features_test)
    )
)
```

The output for model 1 is as follows:

	precision	recall	f1-score	support
0	0.78	0.78	0.78	36
1	0.00	0.00	0.00	5
2	0.94	0.98	0.96	127
3	0.75	0.60	0.67	5
avg / total	0.87	0.90	0.89	173

The output for model 1 is as follows:

```
print(
    classification_report(
        label_test,
        extra_trees_classifier.predict(features_test)
    )
)
```

	precision	recall	f1-score	support
0	0.72	0.72	0.72	36
1	0.00	0.00	0.00	5
2	0.93	1.00	0.96	127
3	0.00	0.00	0.00	5
avg / total	0.83	0.88	0.86	173

4. We can also calculate the accuracy scores:

    ```
    random_forest_classifier.score(features_test, label_test)
    ```

    The output is as follows:

    ```
    0.9017341040462428
    ```

    The output for **extraTreesClassifier** is as follows:

    ```
    extra_trees_classifier.score(features_test, label_test)
    ```

    The output is as follows:

    ```
    0.884393063583815
    ```

    We can see that the random forest classifier is performing slightly better than the extra trees classifier.

5. As a first optimization technique, let's see which features are more important and which features are less important. Due to randomization, removing the least important features may reduce the random noise in the model.

    ```
    random_forest_classifier.feature_importances_
    ```

    The output is as follows:

    ```
    array([0.12656512, 0.09934031, 0.02073233, 0.35550329, 0.05411809,
    0.34374086])
    ```

    The output for **extra_trees_classifier** is as follows:

    ```
    extra_trees_classifier.feature_importances_
    ```

    The output is as follows:

    ```
    array([0.08699494, 0.07557066, 0.01221275, 0.38035005, 0.05879822,
    0.38607338])
    ```

Both classifiers treats the third and the fifth attributes quite unimportant. We may not be sure about the fifth attribute, as the importance score is more than 5% in both models. However, we are quite certain that the third attribute is the least significant attribute in the decision. Let's see the feature names once again.

```
data_frame_encoded.head()
```

The output is as follows:

Buying	Maintenance	Doors	Persons	LuggageBoot	Safety	Class
0	3	3	0	0	2	1
1	3	3	0	0	2	2
2	3	3	0	0	2	0
3	3	3	0	0	1	1
4	3	3	0	0	1	2

The least important feature is Doors. It is quite evident in hindsight: the number of doors doesn't have as big of an influence in the car's rating than the safety rating for instance.

6. Remove the third feature from the model and retrain the classifier.

```
features2 = np.array(data_frame_encoded.drop(['Class', 'Doors'], 1))
label2 = np.array(data_frame_encoded['Class'])
features_train2,
features_test2,
label_train2,
label_test2 = model_selection.train_test_split(
    features2,
    label2,
    test_size=0.1
)
random_forest_classifier2 = RandomForestClassifier(
    n_estimators=100, max_depth=6
)
random_forest_classifier2.fit(features_train2, label_train2)
extra_trees_classifier2 = ExtraTreesClassifier(
    n_estimators=100, max_depth=6
)
extra_trees_classifier2.fit(features_train2, label_train2)
```

7. Let's compare how well the new models fare compared to the original ones:

```
print(
    classification_report(
        label_test2,
        random_forest_classifier2.predict(features_test2)
    )
)
```

The output is as follows:

	precision	recall	f1-score	support
0	0.89	0.85	0.87	40
1	0.00	0.00	0.00	3
2	0.95	0.98	0.96	125
3	1.00	1.00	1.00	5
avg / total	0.92	0.93	0.93	173

8. Second Model:

```
print(
    classification_report(
        label_test2,
        extra_trees_classifier2.predict(features_test2)
    )
)
```

The output is as follows:

	precision	recall	f1-score	support
0	0.78	0.78	0.78	40
1	0.00	0.00	0.00	3
2	0.93	0.98	0.95	125
3	1.00	0.40	0.57	5
avg / total	0.88	0.90	0.88	173

Although we did improve a few percentage points, note that a direct comparison is not possible, because of following reasons. First, the train-test split selects different data for training and testing. A few badly selected data points may easily cause a few percentage point increase or decrease in the scores. Second, the way how we train the classifiers also has random elements. This randomization may also shift the performance of the classifiers a bit. Always use best judgement when interpreting results and measure your results multiple times on different train-test splits if needed.

9. Let's tweak the parametrization of the classifiers a bit more. The following set of parameters increase the F1 Score of the Random Forest Classifier to 97%:

```
random_forest_classifier2 = RandomForestClassifier(
    n_estimators=150,
    max_ depth=8,
    criterion='entropy',
    max_features=5
)
random_forest_classifier2.fit(features_train2, label_train2)
print(
    classification_report(
        label_test2,
        random_forest_classifier2.predict(features_test2)
    )
)
```

The output is as follows:

	precision	recall	f1-score	support
0	0.95	0.95	0.95	40
1	0.50	1.00	0.67	3
2	1.00	0.97	0.98	125
3	0.83	1.00	0.91	5
avg / total	0.97	0.97	0.97	173

10. Using the same parameters on the Extra Trees Classifier, we also get surprisingly good results:

```
extra_trees_classifier2 = ExtraTreesClassifier(
    n_estimators=150,
    max_depth=8,
    criterion='entropy',
    max_features=5
)
extra_trees_classifier2.fit(features_train2, label_train2)
print(
    classification_report(
        label_test2,
        extra_trees_classifier2.predict(features_test2)
    )
)
```

The output is as follows:

```
             precision    recall  f1-score   support
          0       0.92      0.88      0.90        40
          1       0.40      0.67      0.50         3
          2       0.98      0.97      0.97       125
          3       0.83      1.00      0.91         5
avg / total       0.95      0.94      0.94       173
```

Chapter 6: Clustering

Activity 12: k-means Clustering of Sales Data

This section will detect product sales that perform similarly in nature to recognize trends in product sales.

We will be using the Sales Transactions Weekly Dataset from this URL:

https://archive.ics.uci.edu/ml/datasets/Sales_Transactions_Dataset_Weekly Perform clustering on the dataset using the k-means Algorithm. Make sure you prepare your data for clustering based on what you have learned in the previous chapters.

Use the default settings for the k-means algorithm.

1. Load the dataset using pandas.

```
import pandas
pandas.read_csv('Sales_Transactions_Dataset_Weekly.csv')
```

2. If you examine the data in the CSV file, you can realize that the first column contains product id strings. These values just add noise to the clustering process. Also notice that for weeks 0 to 51, there is a W-prefixed label and a Normalized label. Using the normalized label makes more sense, so we can drop the regular weekly labels from the data set.

```
import numpy as np
drop_columns = ['Product_Code']
for w in range(0, 52):
    drop_columns.append('W' + str(w))
features = data_frame.drop(dropColumns, 1)
```

3. Our data points are normalized except for the min and max

```
from sklearn.preprocessing import MinMaxScaler
scaler = MinMaxScaler()
scaled_features = scaler.fit_transform(features)
```

4. Create a k-means clustering model and fit the data points into 8 clusters.

```
from sklearn.cluster import KMeans
k_means_model = KMeans()
k_means_model.fit(scaled_features)
```

5. The labels belonging to each data point can be retrieved using the labels_ property. These labels determine the clustering of the rows of the original data frame.

```
k_means_model.labels_
```

6. Retrieve the center points and the labels from the clustering algorithm:

```
k_means_model.cluster_centers_
```

The output will be as follows:

```
array([5, 5, 4, 5, 5, 3, 4, 5, 5, 5, 5, 5, 4, 5, 0, 0, 0, 0, 0, 4, 4, 4,
       4, 0, 0, 5, 0, 0, 5, 0, 4, 4, 5, 0, 0, 0, 0, 0, 0, 0, 0, 0, 0, 0,
       0, 0, 0, 0, 0, 5, 0, 0, 5, 0, 0, 0, 0, 0, 4, 0, 0, 5, 0, 0, 5, 0,
       ...
       1, 7, 3, 2, 6, 7, 6, 2, 2, 6, 2, 7, 2, 7, 2, 6, 1, 3, 2, 2, 6, 6,
       7, 7, 7, 1, 1, 2, 1, 2, 7, 7, 6, 2, 7, 6, 6, 6, 1, 6, 1, 6, 7, 7,
       1, 1, 3, 5, 3, 3, 3, 5, 7, 2, 2, 2, 3, 2, 2, 7, 7, 3, 3, 3, 3, 2,
       2, 6, 3, 3, 5, 3, 2, 2, 6, 7, 5, 2, 2, 2, 6, 2, 7, 6, 1])
```

How are these labels beneficial?

Suppose that in the original data frame, the product names are given. You can easily recognize that similar types of products sell similarly. There are also products that fluctuate a lot, and products that are seasonal in nature. For instance, if some products promoted fat loss and getting into shape, they tend to sell during the first half of the year, before the beach season.

Activity 13: Shape Recognition with the Mean Shift algorithm

This section will learn how images can be clustered. We will be assuming that you are working for a company detecting human emotions from photos. Your task is to extract pixels making up a face in an avatar photo.

Create a clustering algorithm with Mean Shift to cluster pixels of images. Examine the results of the Mean Shift algorithm and check if any of the clusters contains a face when used on avatar images.

Then apply the k-means algorithm with a fixed default number of clusters: 8. Compare your results with the Mean Shift clustering algorithm.

1. Select an image you would like to cluster and load the image.

2. We chose this image from the Author's Youtube channel:

Fig 7.13: An image with the Author's picture

3. The image size has been significantly reduced so that our algorithm would terminate more quickly.

```
image = Image.open('destructuring.jpg')
pixels = image.load()
```

4. Transform the pixels into a data frame to perform clustering

```
import pandas
data_frame = pandas.DataFrame(
    [[x,y,pixels[x,y][0], pixels[x,y][1], pixels[x,y][2]]
        for x in range(image.size[0])
        for y in range(image.size[1])
    ],
    columns=['x', 'y', 'r', 'g', 'b']
)
```

5. Perform Mean Shift clustering on the image using scikit-learn. Note that this time we will skip normalization of the features, because proximity of the pixels and proximity of color components are represented in close to equal weight. The largest difference in pixels distance is 750, while the largest difference in a color component is 256.

```
from sklearn.cluster import MeanShift

mean_shift_model = MeanShift()
mean_shift_model.fit(data_frame)
for i in range(len(mean_shift_model.cluster_centers_)):
    image = Image.open('destructuring.jpg')
    pixels = image.load()
    for j in range(len(data_frame)):
        if (mean_shift_model.labels_[j] != i ):
            pixels[ int(data_frame['x'][j]),
        int(data_frame['y'][j]) ] = (255, 255, 255)
    image.save( 'cluster' + str(i) + '.jpg' )
```

6. The algorithm found the following two clusters:

Fig 7.14: Images after performing k-means Clustering

7. The Mean Shift algorithm treated my skin and the yellow JavaScript and Destructuring text close enough to each other to form the same cluster.

8. Let's use the k-means algorithm to formulate eight clusters on the same data.

```
k_means_model = KMeans(n_clusters=8)
k_means_model.fit(data_frame)
for i in range(len(k_means_model.cluster_centers_)):
    image = Image.open('destructuring.jpg')
    pixels = image.load()
    for j in range(len(data_frame)):
        if (k_means_model.labels_[j] != i):
            pixels[int(data_frame['x'][j]), int(data_frame['y'][j])] =
(255, 255, 255)
    image.save('kmeanscluster' + str(i) + '.jpg')
```

9. The 8 clusters are the following:

    The output for the first is as follows:

Fig 7.15: Images after performing k-means Clustering

The output for the second is as follows:

Fig 7.16: Images after performing k-means Clustering

The output for the third is as follows:

Fig 7.17: Images after performing k-means Clustering

The output for the fourth is as follows:

Fig 7.18: Images after performing k-means Clustering

The output for the fifth is as follows:

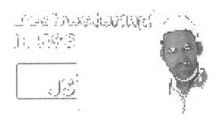

Fig 7.19: Images after performing k-means Clustering

The output for the sixth is as follows:

Fig 7.20: Images after performing k-means Clustering

The output for the seventh is as follows:

Fig 7.21: Images after performing k-means Clustering

The output for the eighth is as follows:

Fig 7.22: Images after performing k-means Clustering

As you can see, the fifth cluster recognized my face quite well. The clustering algorithm indeed located data points that are close and contain similar colors.

Chapter 7: Deep Learning with Neural Networks

Activity 14: Written digit detection

1. This section will discuss how to provide more security for the cryptocurrency traders via the detection of hand-written digits. We will be using assuming that you are a software developer at a new Cryptocurrency trader platform. The latest security measure you are implementing requires the recognition of hand-written digits. Use the MNIST library to train a neural network to recognize digits. You can read more about this dataset on https://www.tensorflow.org/tutorials/.

2. Improve the accuracy of the model as much as possible. And to ensure that it happens correctly, you will need to complete the previous topic.

3. Load the dataset and format the input

```
import tensorflow.keras.datasets.mnist as mnist
(features_train, label_train),
(features_test, label_test) = mnist.load_data()

features_train = features_train / 255.0
features_test = features_test / 255.0

def flatten(matrix):
    return [elem for row in matrix for elem in row]

features_train_vector = [
    flatten(image) for image in features_train
]
```

```
features_test_vector = [
    flatten(image) for image in features_test
]

import numpy as np
label_train_vector = np.zeros((label_train.size, 10))
for i, label in enumerate(label_train_vector):
    label[label_train[i]] = 1
label_test_vector = np.zeros((label_test.size, 10))
for i, label in enumerate(label_test_vector):
    label[label_test[i]] = 1
```

4. Set up the Tensorflow graph. Instead of the **sigmoid** function, we will now use the **relu** function.

```
import tensorflow as tf


f = tf.nn.softmax
x = tf.placeholder(tf.float32, [None, 28 * 28 ])
W = tf.Variable( tf.random_normal([784, 10]))
b = tf.Variable( tf.random_normal([10]))
y = f(tf.add(tf.matmul( x, W ), b ))
```

5. Train the model.

```
import random

y_true = tf.placeholder(tf.float32, [None, 10])
cross_entropy = tf.nn.softmax_cross_entropy_with_logits_v2(
    logits=y,
    labels=y_true
)

cost = tf.reduce_mean(cross_entropy)
optimizer = tf.train.GradientDescentOptimizer(
    learning_rate = 0.5
).minimize(cost)

session = tf.Session()
session.run(tf.global_variables_initializer())

iterations = 600
batch_size = 200
sample_size = len(features_train_vector)
```

```
for _ in range(iterations):
    indices = random.sample(range(sample_size), batchSize)
    batch_features = [
        features_train_vector[i] for i in indices
    ]
    batch_labels = [
        label_train_vector[i] for i in indices
    ]
    min = i * batch_size
    max = (i+1) * batch_size
    dictionary = {
        x: batch_features,
        y_true: batch_labels
    }
    session.run(optimizer, feed_dict=dictionary)
```

6. Test the model

```
label_predicted = session.run(classify( x ), feed_dict={
    x: features_test_vector
})
label_predicted = [
    np.argmax(label) for label in label_predicted
]
confusion_matrix(label_test, label_predicted)
```

The output is as follows:

```
array([[  0,   0, 223,  80,  29, 275, 372,   0,   0,   1],
       [  0, 915,   4,  10,   1,  13, 192,   0,   0,   0],
       [  0,  39, 789,  75,  63,  30,  35,   0,   1,   0],
       [  0,   6,  82, 750,  13, 128,  29,   0,   0,   2],
       [  0,  43,  16,  16, 793,  63,  49,   0,   2,   0],
       [  0,  22,  34, 121,  40, 593,  76,   5,   0,   1],
       [  0,  29,  34,   6,  44,  56, 788,   0,   0,   1],
       [  1,  54,  44, 123, 715,  66,  24,   1,   0,   0],
       [  0,  99, 167, 143,  80, 419,  61,   0,   4,   1],
       [  0,  30,  13,  29, 637, 238,  58,   3,   1,   0]], dtype=int64)
```

7. Calculate the accuracy score:

```
accuracy_score(label_test, label_predicted)
```

The output is as follows:

```
0.4633
```

8. By re-running the code segment responsible for training the data set, we can improve the accuracy:

```
for _ in range(iterations):
    indices = random.sample(range(sample_size), batch_size)
    batch_features = [
        features_train_vector[i] for i in indices
    ]
    batch_labels = [
        label_train_vector[i] for i in indices
    ]
    min = i * batch_size
    max = (i+1) * batch_size
    dictionary = {
        x: batch_features,
        y_true: batch_labels
    }
    session.run(optimizer, feed_dict=dictionary)
```

Second run: 0.5107

Third run: 0.5276

Fourth run: 0.5683

Fifth run: 0.6002

Sixth run: 0.6803

Seventh run: 0.6989

Eighth run: 0.7074

Ninth run: 0.713

Tenth run: 0.7163

Twentieth run: 0.7308

Thirtieth run: 0.8188

Fortieth run: 0.8256

Fiftieth run: 0.8273

At the end of the fiftieth run, the improved confusion matrix looks as follows:

```
array([
  [946,    0,    6,    3,    0,    1,   15,    2,    7,    0],
  [   0,1097,    3,    7,    1,    0,    4,    0,   23,    0],
  [  11,    3,  918,   11,   18,    0,   13,    8,   50,    0],
  [   3,    0,   23,  925,    2,   10,    4,    9,   34,    0],
  [   2,    2,    6,    1,  929,    0,   14,    2,   26,    0],
  [  16,    4,    7,   62,    8,  673,   22,    3,   97,    0],
  [   8,    2,    4,    3,    8,    8,  912,    2,   11,    0],
  [   5,    9,   33,    6,    9,    1,    0,  949,   16,    0],
  [   3,    4,    5,   12,    7,    4,   12,    3,  924,    0],
  [   8,    5,    7,   40,  470,   11,    5,  212,  251,    0]
  ],
        dtype=int64)
```

Not a bad result. More than 8 out of 10 digits are accurately recognized.

Activity 15 : Written Digit Detection with Deep Learning

This section will discuss how deep learning improves the performance of your model. We will be assuming that your boss is not satisfied with the results you presented in previous activity and asks you to consider adding two hidden layers to your original model and determine whether new layers improve the accuracy of the model. And to ensure that it happens correctly, you will need to have knowledge of Deep Learning.

1. Execute the code of previous Activity and measure the accuracy of the model.

2. Change the neural network by adding new layers. We will combine the **relu** and **softmax** activator functions:

```
x = tf.placeholder(tf.float32, [None, 28 * 28 ])
f1 = tf.nn.relu
W1 = tf.Variable(tf.random_normal([784, 200]))
b1 = tf.Variable(tf.random_normal([200]))
layer1_out = f1(tf.add(tf.matmul(x, W1), b1))
f2 = tf.nn.softmax
W2 = tf.Variable(tf.random_normal([200, 100]))
b2 = tf.Variable(tf.random_normal([100]))
layer2_out = f2(tf.add(tf.matmul(layer1_out, W2), b2))
f3 = tf.nn.softmax
W3 = tf.Variable(tf.random_normal([100, 10]))
b3 = tf.Variable( tf.random_normal([10]))
y = f3(tf.add(tf.matmul(layer2_out, W3), b3))
```

3. Retrain the model

```
y_true = tf.placeholder(tf.float32, [None, 10])
cross_entropy = tf.nn.softmax_cross_entropy_with_logits_v2(
    logits=y,
    labels=y_true
)

cost = tf.reduce_mean(cross_entropy)
optimizer = tf.train.GradientDescentOptimizer(
learning_rate=0.5).minimize(cost)

session = tf.Session()
session.run(tf.global_variables_initializer())

iterations = 600
batch_size = 200
sample_size = len(features_train_vector)
for _ in range(iterations):
    indices = random.sample(range(sample_size), batchSize)
    batch_features = [
        features_train_vector[i] for i in indices
    ]
    batch_labels = [
        label_train_vector[i] for i in indices
    ]
    min = i * batch_size
    max = (i+1) * batch_size
    dictionary = {
        x: batch_features,
        y_true: batch_labels
    }
    session.run(optimizer, feed_dict=dictionary)
```

4. Evaluate the model

```
label_predicted = session.run(y, feed_dict={
    x: features_test_vector
})
label_predicted = [
    np.argmax(label) for label in label_predicted
]
confusion_matrix(label_test, label_predicted)
```

The output is as follows:

```
array([[ 801,   11,    0,   14,    0,    0,   56,    0,   61,   37],
       [   2, 1069,    0,   22,    0,    0,   18,    0,    9,   15],
       [ 276,  138,    0,  225,    0,    2,  233,    0,  105,   53],
       [  32,   32,    0,  794,    0,    0,   57,    0,   28,   67],
       [  52,   31,    0,   24,    0,    3,  301,    0,   90,  481],
       [  82,   50,    0,  228,    0,    3,  165,    0,  179,  185],
       [  71,   23,    0,   14,    0,    0,  712,    0,   67,   71],
       [  43,   85,    0,   32,    0,    3,   31,    0,  432,  402],
       [  48,   59,    0,  192,    0,    2,   45,    0,  425,  203],
       [  45,   15,    0,   34,    0,    2,   39,    0,  162,  712]],
      dtype=int64)
```

5. Calculating the accuracy score.

```
accuracy_score(label_test, label_predicted)
```

The output is **0.4516**.

The accuracy did not improve.

Let's see if further runs improve the accuracy of the model.

Second run: 0.5216

Third run: 0.5418

Fourth run: 0.5567

Fifth run: 0.564

Sixth run: 0.572

Seventh run: 0.5723

Eighth run: 0.6001

Ninth run: 0.6076

Tenth run: 0.6834

Twentieth run: 0.7439

Thirtieth run: 0.7496

Fortieth run: 0.7518

Fiftieth run: 0.7536

Afterwards, we got the following results: 0.755, 0.7605, 0.7598, 0.7653

The final confusion matrix:

```
array([[ 954,    0,    2,    1,    0,    6,    8,    0,    5,    4],
       [   0, 1092,    5,    3,    0,    0,    6,    0,   27,    2],
       [   8,    3,  941,   16,    0,    2,   13,    0,   35,   14],
       [   1,    1,   15,  953,    0,   14,    2,    0,   13,   11],
       [   4,    3,    8,    0,    0,    1,   52,    0,   28,  886],
       [   8,    1,    5,   36,    0,  777,   16,    0,   31,   18],
       [   8,    1,    6,    1,    0,    6,  924,    0,    9,    3],
       [   3,   10,  126,   80,    0,    4,    0,    0,   35,  770],
       [   4,    0,    6,   10,    0,    6,    4,    0,  926,   18],
       [   4,    5,    1,    8,    0,    2,    2,    0,   18,  969]],
      dtype=int64)
```

This deep neural network behaves even more chaotically than the single layer one. It took 600 iterations of 200 samples to get from an accuracy of 0.572 to 0.5723. Not long after this iteration, we jumped from 0.6076 to 0.6834 in that number of iterations.

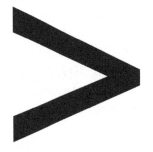

Index

About

All major keywords used in this book are captured alphabetically in this section. Each one is accompanied by the page number of where they appear.